DAVID GRIFFITHS

TOPICS IN
ADVANCED
SCIENTIFIC
COMPUTATION

RICHARD E. CRANDALL

Springer ⑨ TELOS® THE ELECTRONIC LIBRARY OF SCIENCE

Richard E. Crandall
Reed College
Portland, Oregon
USA

Publisher: Allan M. Wylde
Publishing Associate: Keisha Sherbecoe
Production Manager: Carol Wilson
Project Management: Jan Benes, Black Hole Publishing Service
  Copyeditor: John T. Selawsky
  Cover Designer: Irene Imfeld
Camera ready copy was prepared by the author on a NeXT computer.

Cataloging-in-Publication data is available from the Library of Congress

The use of general descriptive names, trademarks, etc., in this publication, even if the former are not
especially identified, is not to be taken as a sign that such names, as understood by the Trade Marks
and Merchandise Marks Act, may accordingly be used by anyone. Where those designations appear
in this book and Springer-Verlag was aware of a trademark claim, the designations follow the
capitalization style used by the manufacturer.
NEXTSTEP is a registered trademark of NeXT, Inc.
PostScript is a registered trademark of Adobe Systems, Inc.
Mathematica is a registered trademark of Wolfram Research, Inc.

Printed in the United States of America

9 8 7 6 5 4 3 2 1

ISBN 0-387-94473-7

TELOS, The Electronic Library of Science, is an imprint of Springer-Verlag New York with publishing facilities in Santa Clara, California. Its publishing program encompasses the natural and physical sciences, computer science, economics, mathematics, and engineering. All TELOS publications have a computational orientation to them, as TELOS' primary publishing strategy is to wed the traditional print medium with the emerging new electronic media in order to provide the reader with a truly interactive multimedia information environment. To achieve this, every TELOS publication delivered on paper has an associated electronic component. This can take the form of book/diskette combinations, book/CD-ROM packages, books delivered via networks, electronic journals, newsletters, plus a multitude of other exciting possibilities. Since TELOS is not committed to any one technology, any delivery medium can be considered.

The range of TELOS publications extends from research level reference works through textbook materials for the higher education audience, practical handbooks for working professionals, as well as more broadly accessible science, computer science, and high technology trade publications. Many TELOS publications are interdisciplinary in nature, and most are targeted for the individual buyer, which dictates that TELOS publications be priced accordingly.

Of the numerous definitions of the Greek word "telos," the one most representative of our publishing philosophy is "to turn," or "turning point." We perceive the establishment of the TELOS publishing program to be a significant step towards attaining a new plateau of high quality information packaging and dissemination in the interactive learning environment of the future. TELOS welcomes you to join us in the exploration and development of this frontier as a reader and user, an author, editor, consultant, strategic partner, or in whatever other capacity might be appropriate.

TELOS, The Electronic Library of Science
Springer-Verlag Publishers
3600 Pruneridge Avenue, Suite 200
Santa Clara, CA 95051

TELOS Diskettes

Unless otherwise designated, computer diskettes packaged with TELOS publications are 3.5" high-density DOS-formatted diskettes. They may be read by any IBM-compatible computer running DOS or Windows. They may also be read by computers running NEXTSTEP, by most UNIX machines, and by Macintosh computers using a file exchange utility.

In those cases where the diskettes require the availability of specific software programs in order to run them, or to take full advantage of their capabilities, then the specific requirements regarding these software packages will be indicated.

TELOS CD-ROM Discs

It is also clearly indicated to buyers of TELOS publications containing CD-ROM discs, or in cases where the publication is a standalone CD-ROM product, the exact platform, or platforms, on which the disc is designed to run. For example, Macintosh only; MPC only; Macintosh and Windows (cross-platform), etc.

TELOSpub.com (Online)

New product information, product updates, TELOS news and FTPing instructions can be accessed by sending a one-line message:

> **send info**

> to:

> **info@TELOSpub.com.**

The TELOS anonymous FTP site contains catalog product descriptions, testimonials and reviews regarding TELOS publications, data-files contained on diskettes accompanying the various TELOS titles, order forms and price lists.

Preface

Before this discovery [of the transcendency of certain numbers a^b] the problem of proving, for instance, the irrationality of $2^{\sqrt{2}}$ had been considered as extremely difficult, so that Hilbert liked to mention it as a problem whose solution lay still further in the future than the proof of Riemann's hypothesis or Fermat's conjecture. This shows that one cannot guess the real difficulties of a problem before having solved it.

[*Siegel* 1949]

For me, the writing of this book has been a distinct *treat* (there is no better English word) for the very reason that it stands as a kind of playground, a sequel to my more in-depth and detailed book, *Projects in Scientific Computation*, Springer-Verlag 1994. If the reader will allow, I think of the current presentation, *Topics*, as a kind of "dessert." It covers specific and, to me, intriguing problems that have come to my attention since the writing of *Projects*. While *Projects* attempts to stand fast on the educational imperative, with the exercises therein generally possessed of a "homework" or "introductory" flavor; the current *Topics* is a plunge into the world of specific, often difficult, research-oriented algorithms. There is no pretention whatsoever that I am covering herein any one subject to the epistemological depth it deserves. Indeed, because of my own limitations in this or that field, and given the occasionally extreme difficulty of a problem, I tend to convey that problem's essential flavor, together with references to the work of the *legitimate* experts.

One remarkable thing about our technological times is that so much of the technology has become, might I say, algorithm-heavy. We see algorithms used for the very design of new computer hardware that, in turn, will be used to harbor and execute yet more algorithms. We now have algorithms taught in schools. Algorithms are not even relegated merely to the professional or educational sectors: we see new imaging algorithms at work at the movies.

This book is a tour of modern algorithms–many of these new on the computational scene–with a view to scientific computation. In *Topics* I have endeavored to create a compendium of techniques for which engineers, mathematicians and scientists (and I hope that includes computer scientists) may find good use. Herein will be found a mix of applied and theoretical treatments. I have endeavored also to describe the state of the art, in certain domains such as factoring, signal analysis, complexity theory, and symbolic computation. It has been a pleasure to report some of the striking new achievements of investigators in these areas.

So this book is a sequel–both in content and in spirit–to my previous book, *Projects in Scientific Computation*. I should say that at many points herein I refer to the previous work with the notation [*Projects* 1994]. Almost all of the specific, and yes, hard problems herein arose through discourse with colleagues. I shall end this Preface with an all too brief statement of gratitude for the intelligence and productivity of those I continue to call the *legitimate* experts in their fields.

Support software

Various topics in this book are supported, and various algorithms exemplified, either by *Mathematica* or *C* source code, and sometimes by both. The *Mathematica* files should all run cleanly under *Mathematica* 2.0 and later versions. The *C* source is uniformly ANSI-*C* compliant and should be quite portable. The source code appearing either within chapters or in the final Appendix can be obtained via anonymous ftp to *ftp.telospub.com*, or by pointing a Web browser to *www.telospub.com*. Beyond the chapter and Appendix source code, there are longer sources, sound files, and so on too large for paper listing. Such larger files are also available at the aforementioned network sites.

Much of the code appearing here in *Topics* is of a specialized nature. The reader may like to know that a large number of more "fundamental" programs, still relevant to topics in the present book but designed along the traditional lines of numerical analysis, appeared previously in [*Projects* 1994]. That previous collection is where one should look for what might be called basic algorithms. The *Projects* code also is available at the aforementioned network sites.

Acknowledgments

From the industrial sector, especially from NeXT, Inc., I have received a great deal of support and ideas. I would like to thank S. Jobs, who more than any other living human believes in the notion that theory can lead the way to great practice; A. Tevanian, E. Videki, J. Seamons, P. Graffagnino, M. Paquette, T. Donahue, D. Clegg, C. Kleissner, B. Davirro, D. Wiebe, J. Coursey, E. Catmull, L. Hourvitz, B. Yamamoto, B. Serlet, J. M. Hullot, T. Matteson, K. Enderby, R. Zazula, J. Doenias, A. Bittner, and B. Fernandez.

As for the academic sector, I am indebted to T. Wieting, R. Mayer, D. Griffiths, J. Powell, N. Wheeler, J. Essick, S. Arch, M. McClellan, F. Gwilliam, B. McNamara, M. Beck, D. Perkinson and T. Dunne. R. Reynolds honored me with an incisive reading of the book manuscript. I am indebted to O. Vajk for uncovering mathematical mishaps in the text. I must acknowledge with emphasis the contributions of J. Buhler, who once again has been an invaluable and indefatigable theoretical colleague. I have benefitted greatly from the theoretical and computational insights of R. Brent, C. Pomerance, H. Lenstra, S. Wolfram, D. Bailey, and J. & P. Borwein. I thank P. Langston, I. Vardi, and S. Wagon for dialogue on specific topics herein. Some of the numerical work reported herein was only possible because of the tireless searching and testing of K. Dilcher and R. McIntosh.

For general help and inspiration in manuscript preparation, either theoretical or practical or literary or spiritual and sometimes fortuitous holistic combinations of these, I am obliged to J. Welch, S. Charles, P. Lupino, E.

Latincsics, and L. Martin, K. Logsdon, S. Gillespie. Special acknowledgment must be directed to A. Prinz and W. Langeveld for leading me through the maze of technical libraries at Stanford University. I remain grateful to M Matlack, G. Anderson, and J. Brasch of AFS, Inc. for their responsiveness during manuscript preparation (this whole book was set in *WriteUp*, a NEXTSTEP application product of AFS). I could not have completed the manuscript without the labors of L. Buhler, M. Huddleston, and J. Panzarella. I have drawn a great deal of my inspiration to write from the intellectual encouragement of L. Powell. Likewise, material and environmental support from B. and L. Barisich was critical to this work. Av. Barisich in particular has been a constant and unconditional inspiration for the scholarly labors represented herein.

I must once again offer undying thanks to P. Bragdon, who as a past President of Reed College was the first administrative leader of whom I am aware to take liberal arts academic computing so seriously as to allow scientists like myself to make real progress back in the 1980s. This book, though a decade in the making, would not have been possible were it not for his leadership. I am grateful also to N. Bragdon for her tireless moral support of my career changes and for her understanding of my penchant for scientific writing.

Much of this work occurred at the Center for Advanced Computation, situated on the green and glorious pasture of Reed College, which Center was founded by the uniquely enlightened and consummately intellectual college president, S. Koblik. I acknowledge also the fundamental academic support and lucrative decision-making of L. Mantel and L. Large. Center support of the most practical kind has come from E. McFarlane and T. Angell. Computer-technological expertise from H. Horde and N. Goetz has likewise been essential for the perpetuation of academic computation at the Center. G. Schlickeiser is to be thanked for his personal and professional support of academic computing, and perforce my own efforts, for over a decade. I am indebted to K. Creager and M. Colgrove for their expertise in administrative facets of liberal arts computing. M. Ringle, the Director of Computing and Information Services at Reed College, has been a crucial supporter of Center activity; without his support the Center and its productions–such as this book–would not have been possible. Many of the algorithms in this and past works have been strenuously tested by Reed College scientific computation students. I am compelled to say that such solid support from students is an indispensable resource to be encountered nowhere else in the cosmos.

I acknowledge also the virtually infinite faith shown by my publishers, A. Wylde, J. Benes, and P. Wellin at TELOS/Springer-Verlag. These men are the real power behind the pen; they are expert in the matter of applying just the right amount of positive pressure on an aspiring author.

My final acknowledgment must be set off from the rest. I have been fortunate during this work to joust with the unique mind of philosopher M. Levich, the Scholar in Residence at the Center for Advanced Computation. His expertise in regard to the highest intellectual aspects of modern computing is, well, a *caution*–I can think of no better English word. One benefits from such a genius perhaps once, or less than once, in a lifetime. On my request he was able to track down on the network obscure references and commentary, to point out references world-wide on advanced computation, and to settle various rumors pertinent to scientific computation; all of that rendering this book a better book. Then too our dialogues have served as a lucrative sanity check, keeping me from speculating too far. Sherlock Holmes once remarked: "Art in the blood is liable to take the strangest forms." Perhaps the same may be said about philosophy in the blood. I am thankful to have known a renowned and established philosopher who in the last decade has turned his unique powers onto modern computing, and in this way supported scientific computation as could nobody else. To him I owe my current perspective on the role of computation as an intellectual pursuit. At times even, I feel that I am exploring scientific computation in those little rooms on Baker Street, London, where it is still the year 1895.

Richard E. Crandall
Portland, Oregon
1995

Table of Contents

Initialize:

$$x \; := \; \frac{a}{2}$$

Then as we iterate:

$$x \; := \; x \; - \; \frac{\left(x^2 - a\right)\left(3x^2 + a\right)\left(3x^6 + 27\,a\,x^4 + 33\,a^2 x^2 + a^3\right)}{2x\left(x^4 + 10\,a\,x^2 + 5\,a^2\right)\left(5x^4 + 10\,a\,x^2 + a^2\right)}$$

we find that, *extremely* rapidly,

$$x \; \rightarrow \; \sqrt{a}$$

Iterative Gerlach scheme for square roots. The convergence is "decadic," meaning that the number of good digits expands tenfold on each iteration. One could in principle resolve $\sqrt{2}$ this way, say to a trillion digits, using about a dozen high-precision divides (in fact not every divide need be to full precision). The Gerlach method, one of many possible extensions to the celebrated Newton method, has origins dating back almost exactly 300 years, to the work of Halley.

1 — *Selected numerical algorithms*

In this chapter we explore some modern numerical algorithms, some of which were recently discovered. Many of the algorithms herein are applicable during the analyses found in future chapters. The first algorithm class we discuss is the Newton method (not the clever slide-rule system of the quote atop this page, but the celebrated iterative scheme for solving general equations).

1.1 *Variants of the Newton method*

Dynamic precision

The Newton method, in its simple, classical glory aims to solve an equation $f(x) = 0$. To simplify matters we shall assume x is a simple zero; *i.e.* that a graph of f actually cuts through the x axis. One chooses (adroitly) an initial guess x_0, then iterates:

$$x_{n+1} := x_n - \frac{f(x_n)}{f'(x_n)} \qquad (1.1.1)$$

for $n = 1, 2, \ldots$. For smooth enough functions f, it is well known that when an iterate x_m is sufficiently close to a solution; *i.e.*, $f(x_m)$ is sufficiently close to zero, the ensuing iterates provide quadratic convergence. This means that an ensuing iteration gives an error (a value of f) that declines, happily, as the *square* of the previous error.

Two common examples of the Newton method involve the computation of reciprocals and square roots, respectively. An iteration that yields $1/A$, for a given A, derived from the assignment $f(x) = 1/x - A$, is:

$$x_{n+1} := x_n + x_n(1 - Ax_n) \tag{1.1.2}$$

To find the square root of $1/A$, one may iterate:

$$x_{n+1} := x_n + \frac{x_n}{2}\left(1 - Ax_n^2\right) \tag{1.1.3}$$

These schemes are actually used in some modern computer hardware implementations of reciprocal and square root.

Our first mention of a new approach to this time-honored Newton scheme is as follows. An interesting new analysis of the required floating point precision at each step of a Newton iteration has been performed by [Karp and Markstein 1994]. They observe that, to perform a divide operation, say to obtain B/A at doubled precision, one may perform (1.1.2) up to some penultimate iterate x_n inclusive, at reduced precision most of the way, then compute two more steps:

$$y := Bx_n \tag{1.1.4}$$

$$Y := y + x_n(B - Ay)$$

at high precision, yielding Y as the approximant to B/A. The two final steps for the analogous square-root extraction are:

$$y := Ax_n \tag{1.1.5}$$

$$Y := y + \frac{x_n}{2}\left(A - y^2\right) \tag{1.1.6}$$

whence Y is the final approximant to $\sqrt{A}$. The Karp-Markstein approach is reported to be from two to ten times faster than an approach that uses high precision at each step.

An analogous dynamic-precision notion is relevant to the inversion of a series. During the Newton method for reciprocating a series, one may successively increase the precision at each step. Such ideas date back to the papers of [Sieveking 1972] and [Kung 1974]. The following *Mathematica* sequence shows how to invert the series: $1 + a_1 x + a_2 x^2 + ...$ through degree "deg:"

$$\tag{1.1.7}$$

```
(* Newton inversion of a polynomial. *)
          g = 1; prec = 1;
          While[prec < deg,
             prec *= 2;
             If[prec > deg, prec = deg];
             h = ptake[f, prec-1];
             g = g + g*(1- h*g);    (* Newton iteration. *)
             g = ptake[g, prec-1];
          ];
(* Now g is 1/f, through degree "deg." *)
```

Here, ptake[f, n] is a function that returns a polynomial f taken *through* degree n. Note that the precision effectively doubles each pass. For further remarks on this issue, see the comments following *Mathematica* example (1.5.10).

Problem 1.1.1: Implement polynomial inversion and apply same to a problem such as finding Bernoulli numbers (in connection with Fermat's "Last Theorem" [*Projects* 1994]), or the evaluation of the Riemann zeta function at integer arguments (as discussed in Chapter 2).

Higher-order variants

The previous remarks pertain to dynamic precision applied to the classical Newton iteration. A different Newton variant, this time a variant of the very form of the basic iteration, was outlined recently by [Gerlach 1994]. The scheme is a generalization of some formulae due to Halley, dating back to the 17th century. Say we are to solve $f(x) = 0$. Gerlach's theorem says that, if we can, for some m, establish a chain

$$f(a) = 0,\ f'(a) > 0,\ f''(a) = \dots = f^{(m-1)}(a) = 0;\ f^{(m)} \neq 0 \qquad (1.1.8)$$

then the function

$$F(x) \;=\; \frac{f(x)}{\sqrt[m]{f'(x)}} \qquad (1.1.9)$$

satisfies

$$F(a) = 0,\ \ F'(a) > 0,\ \ F''(a) = \dots = F^{(m)} = 0$$

Morevover, for $m \geq 3$,

$$F^{(m+1)}(a) \;=\; -\frac{1}{m}\frac{f^{(m+1)}(a)}{\sqrt[m]{f'(a)}}$$

Now the Newton iteration, this time to solve $F(x) = 0$, may be written on the basis of (1.1.9) like so:

$$x_{n+1} \;:=\; x_n - \frac{f(x_n)f'(x_n)}{f'(x_n)^2 - \frac{1}{m}f(x_n)f''(x_n)} \qquad (1.1.10)$$

Note that a solution to $F(x) = 0$ is also a solution to the original $f(x) = 0$. The steps of Gerlach's algorithm are, then, if a denotes the (exact, not numerical) solution to $f(x) = 0$:

1) If $f''(a) \neq 0$, set $m = 2$ (in which case the $f'(a) > 0$ part of the chain (1.1.8) is to be dropped); else identify the smallest $m > 2$ such that $f^{(m-1)}(a) = 0$ and $f^{(m)}(a) \neq 0$.

2) Now use the iteration (1.1.10) as the central Newton iteration.

Gerlach derives that (1.1.10) converges with order-$(m+1)$ speed, meaning that errors will decay as the $(m+1)$-th power. But one can go further, and repeat the derivation steps (1)-(2), using now the F implicit in step (1) as the new f in (1.1.10). In this way, for appropriate initial functions f, one may obtain arbitrarily fast convergence per Newton step, albeit at the expense of more and more complicated iteration formulae (1.1.10).

An example of Gerlach's algorithm runs as follows. We wish to obtain a numerical value for the cube root of 2. Thus $f(x) = x^3 - 2$, and from the theorem with $m = 2$, we obtain F via equation (1.1.9), as:

$$F(x) \;=\; \frac{x^3 - 2}{x\sqrt{3}} \tag{1.1.11}$$

One need not be alarmed by the appearance of $\sqrt{3}$, for this will symbolically cancel in the Newton iteration. In fact, we can either use F in the classical iteration, or use (1.1.10) to obtain the iteration:

$$x_{n+1} \;:=\; x_n - \frac{x_n\left(x_n^3 - 2\right)}{2x_n^3 + 2}$$

for the cube root of 2. This scheme will exhibit cubic convergence because $m + 1 = 3$. Now Gerlach's clever recursive step can be performed. We allow the F of (1.1.11) to pose as f in the theorem that started with (1.1.8), but now with $m = 3$. The new iteration, which can be obtained via (1.1.10) under the substitution $f \rightarrow F$, is:

$$x_{n+1} := x_n - \frac{3x_n\left(x_n^3 - 2\right)\left(x_n^3 + 1\right)}{2 + 16x_n^3 + 5x^6} \tag{1.1.12}$$

This iteration scheme exhibits quartic convergence. Starting with initial guess $x_0 = 2$, iteration (1.1.12) is correct to within $1, 7, 31, 125...$ good decimal digits of the cube root of 2. Indeed, the number of good digits does eventually quadruple every iteration.

To render the Gerlach iteration yet a little clearer, we give here a *Mathematica* example for a quintic-convergent iteration for the square root of two. The frontispiece of this chapter was done in precisely this way, except some by-hand simplifications were necessary to carry out the algebraic for more than quintic convergence.

(1.1.13)

```
(* Symbolic Gerlach iteration for square root,
   quintic convergence.
 *)
f[x_] := x^2-a;   (* We want the square root of a. *)
advance[g_, m_] := g[x]/D[g[x],x]^(1/m);
term[g_, m_] := g[x] D[g[x], x]/(D[g[x],x]^2 - 1/m g[x]
D[g[x],{x,2}]);
f2[x_] := Simplify[advance[f,2]]
f3[x_] := Simplify[advance[f2,3]]
Simplify[term[f3,4]]
```

Problem 1.1.2: Give the Gerlach iteration for some higher root. Try to take the convergence order yet higher, say as high as the "decadic" convergence of the frontispiece to this chapter. An interesting question is: when is a 2^k-convergent Gerlach scheme equivalent simply to the symbolic clumping together of every k consecutive standard Newton steps? Can the Gerlach scheme be applied effectively to anything beyond algebraic numbers (see next problem)?

Problem 1.1.3: Endeavor to work out a Gerlach scheme for evaluating π. For example, setting $x := 3$ and iterating:

$$x \ := \ x \ + \ \frac{6 \cos \frac{x}{2}}{2 + \sin \frac{x}{2}}$$

reveals, perhaps surprisingly, *quintic* convergence to π.

Problem 1.1.4: Does a higher-order Newton inverter for evaluation of $1/a$, such as the quartically convergent:

$$x_{n+1} \ := \ (2 - ax_n)\left(1 + (1 - ax_n)^2\right)x_n$$

also possess a Gerlach generalization to yet higher order?

1.2   *Fast divide and mod algorithms*

Divide vs. Mod

It is interesting that, even though the age of the notion of dividing two numbers can be measured in millenia, there have yet appeared modern ideas that render machine division progressively more efficient. We have discussed the Newton method for finding reciprocals $1/A$, or quotients B/A with enhanced efficiency. Such an approach is a good idea for, say, the division of very large numbers. One only need employ an arbitrary-precision integer multiply, and proceed with the Newton method. In practice, such a "Newton divide" usually takes some reasonable number of multiplications. For the division of numbers both, say, of million-bit size, a Newton divide can typically be effected in roughly 20 multiplies. (However, since a good number of these multiplies only need be done at reduced precision, the practical ratio of Newton divide time to one high-precision multiply time is more like 4:1).

Here we mention some new ideas that are applicable to numbers of all ranges, especially when the denominator has special properties, or is to be used continually for many divides. We note first that for a positive integer x, the number x (mod N) (which we sometimes call $x \% N$), meaning in the present context the reduced modulus lying in $[0, N-1]$, can be obtained via:

$$x \pmod{N} = x - N [x/N] \qquad (1.2.1)$$

where $[x/N]$ = Floor$[x/N]$ is the greatest integer function. Thus the mod operation is, up to a multiply, formally equivalent to a truncated division. But when N has special form, or is to be used repeatedly, important enhancements may be applied, for mod or divide or both. In some situations, as we shall see, a mod or divide can be brought down to the complexity of roughly one multiply.

An interesting approach to classical long division has been found by [Smith 1994], and uses a clever means of correcting quotient digits rapidly. As Smith points out, long division methods are still of interest for integers up to a few thousand decimal digits in size. Smith refers to a scheme due to R. Brent for enhancing classical multiplication in base b, in which overflows during the multiplication loop do not exceed $8b^2$, and proceeds to implement an analogous overflow scheme for division. The details are beyond the scope of this book, but the reader may be interested in the speed enhancement of factors of two or four over existing standard package division.

Problem 1.2.1: Implement a mod function, in *Mathematica* say, that computes x (mod y) but employs only If[ ] statements and adds (subtracts), but no explicit multiplies or divides. The idea is to use the detailed bit structure of each of x, y in a binary "long division" scheme. Can such a scheme be made practical? Can such a scheme be simply extended to some other base, such as base 3 or base 10?

Numbers of special form

When the denominator N is of special integer form, one may sometimes perform dramatically fast mod operations. For example, a situation important in number theoretical computations is that N be a number of the form $2^q \pm c$, where c is suitably small. Assume we want $x \pmod{N}$. Since $2^q = -(\pm c)$ $\pmod{N}$, all the bits of x from the q-th upward can be shifted over, multiplied by the small c, and added to the bits of x from the 0-th to the $(q-1)$-th. Explicitly, say we represent $x = a + b2^q$ with $a < 2^q$. Then

$$x \pmod{N} = a - b(\pm c) \pmod{N} \qquad (1.2.2)$$

$$= a - (x >> q)(\pm c) \pmod{N}$$

where $>>$ denotes right-binary-shift, with lower bits destroyed. If the result of (1.2.2) is still outside the reduced modulus range of $[0,1,...,N-1]$, one may apply (1.2.2) again. Particularly interesting cases are: N is a Mersenne number 2^q-1, or a Fermat number, 2^q+1. In these cases, the mod operation can be performed via nothing but shifts and adds/subtracts.

Problem 1.2.2: Implement functions that perform $x \pmod{2^q \pm 1}$ by virtue of shifting and adding (subtracting), but with no multiplies or divides.

Steady-state division

Now we turn to a scenario in which divides or mods are to be taken many times, but with respect to a *fixed* denominator N. This situation occurs often in number-theoretical work, such as in factoring problems for which N is usually the mystery number to be factored. We shall refer to this scheme as a "steady-state mod" scheme. A useful result is as follows. If we define a "reciprocal" R by:

$$R = [2^s / N] \qquad (1.2.3)$$

where s is chosen so that $2^s > N^2$, then for any $0 \le x < N^2$, we have:

$$[x/N] = ((Rx) >> s) + e \qquad (1.2.4)$$

where the error e is either 0 or 1. Thus, an algorithm for steady-state mod operations, meaning that the denominator N is fixed, reads like so:

$$(1.2.5)$$

Algorithm for steady-state divide (mod) by fixed denominator N:

1) Compute, just once, for example via Newton method, $R = [2^s/ N]$, where $s > 2 \log_2 N$.

2) For given x, with $0 \le x < N^2$, compute

$$m := x - ((Rx) >> s) N$$

3) If $m < 0$, set $x := m + N$; else set $x := m$. Now x has been reduced (mod N).

Clearly this mod algorithm requires, after the single divide of step (1), only two multiplications from step (2) to resolve x (mod N). It may further be observed that the right-shift by s bits in step (2) destroys some of the information residing in the product Rx. Thus a special multiply may be invoked for Rx, one that does not, say, perform all of the loops required for a normal multiplication. In this way it can be settled [Crandall *et. al.* 1995a] that a steady-state mod, after the initialization of step (1), can be performed in 3/2 of a multiply time.

Problem 1.2.3: Implement the steady-state divide/mod Algorithm (1.2.5). One way to proceed is to work with standard 32 bit integers, but another is to obtain "giants.[ch]" code from the network site(s) cited in the Preface, and use the large-integer routines for all three algorithm steps.

1.3   *Fast multiplication*

Grammar-school method

In spite of its extreme familiarity it is worthwhile to ponder momentarily the usual, elementary method of "grammar-school multiplication" (also called long multiplication).   One uses the digits of the two numbers x, y to be multiplied and develops a parallelogram full of digits; finally adding columnwise, with carry, to write down the product xy. Describing it this way, we see that the parallelogram area is $O(N^2)$, assuming each of x, y is possessed of N digits.   There are a few enhancements that apply in various circumstances. We study such enhancements in the following problems.

Problem 1.3.1: Assuming all digits to be in a base B of choice, write a grammar-school multiply function that uses look-up tables rapidly to repeat recurring rows of the parallelogram. In other words, if the n-th row arises from multiplication of x by a digit d of y, with of course $0 \le d < B$, store the whole row in a table, so the next occurrence of digit d merely copies the stored row.

Problem 1.3.2: By exploiting the fact that in (1.2.5), step (2) the product Rx is to have s bits shifted into oblivion, write an efficient steady-state divide routine. One intervenes into the usual grammar-school loop, avoiding much of the usual parallelogram. A good way to test such a routine is to choose a denominator N, and time say thousands of random, steady-state divisions.

Karatsuba method

For particular ranges on numbers x, y to be multiplied, the Karatsuba method is of interest. For N-digit multiplicands, the method requires $O(N^{\log 3 / \log 2})$ arithmetic operations. The idea is to invoke an identity by which one multiply is replaced with *three* multiplies of halved precision. Think of $x = a + bW$ and $y = c + dW$, where W is roughly the size of the square root of x. W then has about half as many digits as does x. Now

(1.3.1)

$$xy = (a + bW)(c + dW) = \frac{t+u}{2} - v + \frac{t-u}{2} W + vW^2$$

where

$$t = (a + b)(c + d)$$
$$u = (a - b)(c - d)$$
$$v = bd$$

It is convenient to make W a power of two, so that multiplication by W or W^2 is simply effected by shifting. In this way only three multiplies (to get t, u, v) are required, and as anticipated each of the three is on numbers having roughly half as many digits as does x. Thus, so far, the complexity of multiplication has been reduced by about 4/3. But one recurses, by observing that each of the multiplications to get t, u, v can likewise be reduced. One way to arrive at the overall complexity is to observe that the choice of a new W can be done about $\log_2 N$ times, so that the grammar-school complexity $O(N^2)$ can be reduced to:

$$O(N^2 \, (3/4)^{\log N / \log 2})$$

which boils down to $O(N^{\log 3 / \log 2})$. The following *Mathematica* function exemplifies the Karatsuba recursion:

(1.3.2)

```
(* Karatsuba recursion for multiplication. *)
karat[x_, y_] := Module[{e,w,a,b,c,d,u,v,t},
    e = Floor[Length[IntegerDigits[Max[x,y],2]]/2];
    If[e <= 8, Return[x * y]];
    w = 2^e;
    a = Mod[x, w]; b = Floor[x/w];
    c = Mod[y, w]; d = Floor[y/w];
    t = karat[a + b, c + d];
    u = karat[a - b, c - d];
```

```
    v = karat[b, d];
    Return[(t+u)/2 - v + (t-u)/2 w + v w^2];
];
```

One uses the function like so:

```
x = 746127364762847237218127;
y = 347839574823932472788778;
karat[x,y]
```

to print out an integer product *xy*.

Problem 1.3.3: By introducing a global counter, report for the Karatsuba algorithm as implemented above how many multiplies (caused by the statement "Return[x * y]") actually occur when karat[ ] is called. Show for example that if prior to multiplication the integers *x, y* are both squared, the global multiply count does indeed essentially triple.

Problem 1.3.4: Implement and compile a fast, practical Karatsuba multiplier for large integers. Compare the performance with grammar-school method, and if possible with FFT methods; noting in particular the various regions of magnitudes of the multiplicands where the respective schemes dominate.

Problem 1.3.5: With respect to example (1.3.2), work out a more compact Karatsuba recursion in *Mathematica*. For example, reduce the number of local variables from nine to a much smaller count. Another good exercise is to work out the optimal point at which recursion should "bottom out." In (1.3.2), the line:

```
          If[e <= 8, Return[x * y]];
```

is an arbitrary guess and may not be the optimal way to terminate the recursion. These issues carry over of course to any fast, compiled implementation.

FFT and related methods

Soon after the re-invention of the fast Fourier transform (FFT) within a signal processing context [Cooley and Tukey 1965] there appeared schemes for integer multiplication using the same algorithm [Schonhage and Strassen 1971]. (We say "re-invention" because it turns out the FFT algorithm was essentially known to Gauss.) It is known that two numbers of N digits each can be multiplied in $O(N \log N)$ arithmetic operations. (Alternatively, an FFT of signal length N requires $O(N \log N)$ operations.) But for integer multiplication the arithmetic operations require progressively deeper precision for larger N; that is, more bits are involved per operation for larger N. Thus the FFT multiply complexity is often stated this way: the *time* required to multiply (or, the "bit-complexity") is $O(N \log N \log \log N)$.

Because FFT multiply details and source code are presented in the companion reference [*Projects* 1994] we shall not go into depth here. We do mention, though, that there are some modern variants of the basic FFT idea. The reason the FFT works for multiplication is that it is being used to perform an acyclic convolution (equivalent to a multiply of two integers). The simplest method is to "zero-pad" the digits of each of x, y and use the FFT to perform the cyclic convolution of these padded signals. But in general one can use a discrete weighted transform (DWT) to reduce the signal length. Then there are other enhancements, such as "real-signal" FFTs which exploit the simple fact of all digits being real-valued, and so on [*Projects* 1994].

Yet other methods of approximately the same complexity include Nussbaumer convolution, where again cyclic (or what is called negacyclic) convolution is used to provide the desired acyclic convolution that is the equivalent of multiplication. There also exist some interesting new multiplication ideas in [Schonhage *et. al.* 1994]. Because these kinds of convolution schemes apply to much more than just integer multiplication, the details of Nussbaumer and other convolutions are discussed in Chapter 4.

Problem 1.3.6: Write an FFT multiply routine that uses a convenient digit base (2^{16} will work nicely on virtually any modern computer), zero pads the "signals" *x, y* to be multiplied, and proceeds to yield the digits of *xy*. A reference for the details is [*Projects* 1994].

Problem 1.3.7: Write a DWT multiply routine that applies to multiplication modulo Fermat numbers (and which therefore needs no zero-padding at all); or for multiplication modulo Mersenne numbers (which with care taken, also need not involve zero-padding). The latter circumstance is discussed in detail in Section 3.1, and a reference is [Crandall and Fagin 1994].

Problem 1.3.8: Write an integer multiplication function using some alternative convolution algorithm, such as number-theoretic transforms, Nussbaumer or Walsh-based schemes of Chapter 4.

Chinese remainder methods

The Chinese Remainder Theorem (CRT) tells us that if the remainders of a number *m* are known modulo each of a set of relatively prime bases q_i, then *m* modulo the product of all the q_i is uniquely determined. There exist fast algorithms for processing successive *m* given fixed bases q_i [Aho *et. al.* 1974]. As for multiplication, it is immediate that if, for each base q_i

$$x = r_i \,(\text{mod } q_i)$$

$$y = s_i \,(\text{mod } q_i)$$

then the product *xy* satisfies

$$xy = r_i \, s_i \,(\text{mod } q_i)$$

Thus in principle one can do multiplication of large integers via the CRT. Some interesting new methods have arisen recently that appear to apply to integers having hundreds of digits [Bernstein 1995].

Problem 1.3.9: Implement a CRT-based large-integer multiply. Note that fast "pre-conditioned" algorithms exist for reconstruction of a number from its residues [Aho *et. al.* 1974][Crandall 1991].

1.4   *Matrix algebra*

Matrix inversion

There have been some interesting new computational developments pertinent to certain aspects of matrix algebra. Consider the problem of matrix inversion, for example, in light of the Newton method for taking reciprocals via multiplications alone. Given an invertible matrix A, it turns out that for a sufficiently adroit initial matrix choice X_0 the iteration

$$X_{n+1} := 2X_n - X_n A X_n$$

which involves only matrix multiplication and addition, will converge to A^{-1}. The problem of initial choice is interesting. One effective choice of X_0 is a certain scaled version of A^T, the transpose of A, in a modified version of the Newton iteration [Jones and Mayer 1995]:

$$(1.4.1)$$

Algorithm for Newton inversion of a matrix

1) Given A to be inverted, define a new matrix

$$B := \frac{A}{s\sqrt{|A|_2}}$$

where the norm is defined

$$|A|_2 = \sum_{i,j} |A_{ij}|^2$$

and s is a scale factor greater than 1.

2) Set $X_0 := B^T$.

3) Iterate $X_{n+1} := 2X_n - X_n B X_n$.

4) Stopping at X_N now implies the approximation

$$A^{-1} \sim \frac{X_N}{s\sqrt{|A|_2}}$$

The following *Mathematica* example is a test of the method:

                                                                    (1.4.2)

```
(* Jones-Mayer matrix inversion algorithm. *)
Do[
    m = Table[Random[Real,1], {j,1,4},{k,1,4}];
    norm = Sqrt[Sum[m[[p,q]]^2,
            {p,1,Length[m[[1]]]},{q,1,Length[m]}]];
    (* Alternatively:
       norm = Sqrt[Flatten[m] . Flatten[m]];
     *)
    scale = 1.1;
    a = N[m/(scale*norm)];
    x = Transpose[a];
    Do[
    x = 2x - (x . a . x),
    {q,1,25}
    ];
    Print["Newton error: ",MatrixForm[N[x/(scale*norm) -
            Inverse[m]]]],
    {w,1,10}
]
```

The overall loop prints out ten instances of the element-by-element errors in random-element matrix inversion. Though we expect quadratic convergence as is characteristic of low order Newton methods, it typically takes on the order of twenty iterations to resolve each element to, say, 15-place accuracy. Thus a good rule of thumb is: the above matrix inversion algorithm will yield a good numerical inverse in a few dozen matrix multiplies.

Problem 1.4.1: Implement a fast, compiled program that carries out the Jones-Mayer algorithm for matrix inversion via Newton iteration. What turns out to be a good choice for the scale factor s?

Problem 1.4.2: Compare the speeds of various matrix inverters. The options abound. One has:

- The Jones-Mayer iterative inverter just discussed.
- Gauss-Jordan elimination inverters. A code implementation is given in [Press *et. al.* 1988] and a good discussion is in [Wong 1992].
- Recursive inverters, whereby a matrix is split into quadrants and inverted "piecewise." Such a scheme can be shown to be asymptotically only as expensive as a (typically small) constant times one matrix multiply [Aho *et. al.* 1974].
- Strassen inversion [*Projects* 1994].

In particular, compare speeds for relatively small (say 8-by-8) and separately for very large (say 1000-by-1000) matrix dimensions; and possibly even "moderate" dimensions.

Asymptotic complexity of matrix algebra

The theoretical complexity issues for the various inverter options of the last section are nontrivial ones. One good question is: in the face of the host of options, what good is the Newton inversion? Recall that a Newton scheme seems to require "dozens" of matrix multiplies for one inverse. Thus it can be expected to be slower than say Gauss-Jordan elimination, or recursive inversion, both of which requiring something like only a few matrix multiplies. Even if we invoke Strassen matrix multiplication, which for N-by-N matrices requires no more than $O(N^{\log 7 / \log 2})$ scalar multiplications rather than the classical $O(N^3)$, the Newton inversion might well beat the classical Gauss-Jordan for large N. But the recursive inversion scheme can also be "Strassen-ized," and thus there is no apparent dimension range in which the Newton inverter dominates. Nor does the story end here. A kind of resolution of all these notions seems to have appeared recently. The work of [Higham 1990] shows that, in a word, many fundamental matrix operations–not just multiplication and inversion–can be, if you will, "Strassen-ized," that is, endowed with fast recursive structure. This means complexity orders genuinely lower than $O(N^3)$ can be introduced into classical matrix algorithms. Thus, in spite of the elegance and theoretical attraction of the Newton inversion, there would seem to be only one good reason actually to adopt it in professional work: if you have so far implemented little else but a matrix multiply, the Newton scheme is certainly the easiest inverter to implement quickly.

Problem 1.4.3: Strassen multiplication is no longer a theoretical curiosity, but has in recent years enjoyed a certain practical vogue [Higham 1990]. Implement a Strassen matrix multiply [*Projects* 1994], and verify for sufficiently large N the expected time complexity. Answer, for your system: for what N-by-N matrices is the Strassen method faster than classical, $O(N^3)$ matrix multiplication? Incidentally [Bailey 1990] found a breakover value of $N \sim 128$ for Cray systems. Note that for some personal computers and workstations, the breakover N might be very small, on the order of 10 or 20.

Problem 1.4.4: Attempt a theoretical improvement, or a rigorous lower bound, on the $O(N^{\log 7 / \log 2}) \sim O(N^{2.781})$ Strassen matrix multiply complexity. [Coppersmith and Winograd 1987] were able to reduce the complexity exponent to 2.376. This appears to be an excellent problem for a clever human working with a modern symbolic processor.

Problem 1.4.5: Implement a parallel matrix multiplier (or inverter) that uses more than one networked computer to effect the required operations. One approach is found in [Koc and Gan 1992].

In every era of modern mathematics and computer science there have been fascinating theoretical algorithmic developments in the field of matrix algebra. Multiplication and inversion only scratch the surface. For example, recently surfaced is a method for solving linear algebraic equations without error, meaning that pure-integer arithmetic is used. One notes that ill-conditioned equations, though the relevant coefficient matrix is still technically non-singular, can give rise to unacceptable floating point roundoff errors during standard equation solving.

Another example of modern attention being paid to an aspect of matrix algebra is the problem of eigenvalues of random matrices. This statistical eigenvalue problem has been applied to fields as apparently diverse as field theories in physics and the theory of the Riemann zeta function.

Problem 1.4.6: Implement a Wang-Yu-Loh-Qin-Miller pure-integer equation solver [Wang J *et. al.* 1994]. Compare the performance (in this case meaning the handling of nearly singular situations) with some standard implementation such as an *LU*-decomposition or other solver. In the pure-integer scheme the authors give a good example of a nearly singular matrix, namely the Hilbert matrix:

$$A_{ij} = \frac{1}{i+j-1}$$

For example the 5-by-5 dimensional case has a nearly vanishing determinant:

$$\det A = \frac{1}{266716800000}$$

Problem 1.4.7: Perform experiments to verify Wigner's celebrated result that the eigenvalues of a random matrix (specifically: Gaussian normal distributed matrix elements, all with unit variance and mean zero) have a semicircular distribution [Wong 1992].

1.5   *Polynomial arithmetic*

Polynomial root finding

There is some interesting recent controversy over this seemingly ancient problem: how to find (numerically) all the roots of a polynomial. There are indeed efficient schemes for finding all roots *provided* said roots are all real-valued [*Projects* 1994]. The problem for general complex roots is more difficult. As stated in [Goedecker 1994], the problem of finding the roots of

$$p(x) = a_0 + a_1 x + \dots + a_n x^n \tag{1.5.1}$$

is equivalent to finding the eigenvalues of the *n*-by-*n* upper Hessenberg matrix

$$H = \begin{bmatrix} \frac{a_{n-1}}{-a_n} & \frac{a_{n-2}}{-a_n} & \frac{a_{n-3}}{-a_n} & \cdots & \frac{a_0}{-a_n} \\ 1 & 0 & 0 & \cdots & 0 \\ 0 & 1 & 0 & \cdots & 0 \\ & & & & 0 \\ \vdots & \vdots & \vdots & \cdots & \\ 0 & 0 & 0 & \cdots & 0 \end{bmatrix}$$

This elegant idea shows that, armed with enough matrix algebra software, one can find numerically all roots of a polynomial. Furthermore the Hessenberg matrix is sparse; in fact, about as sparse as can be. Here is a *Mathematica* example in which a polynomial's roots are found via the Eigenvalue[ ] function:

```
(* Hessenberg-eigenvalue root scheme for polynomials. *)
a = {1,1,1,1,1,-1};   (* Start with polynomial coefficients. *)
p = Sum[a[[i]] x^(i-1),{i,1,Length[a]}];
(* Alternative:
```

```
    p = a . (x^Range[0,Length[a]-1])
 *)
deg = Exponent[p,x];
h   = Table[If[i == 1, -a[[deg-j+1]]/a[[deg+1]],
               If[i == j+1, 1, 0]],
                 {i,1,deg},{j,1,deg}
       ];
roots = Eigenvalues[N[h]]   (* Report numerical roots. *)
```

Incidentally the polynomial being analyzed in this example is one of the "Fibonacci" class; that is, all the coefficients a_i = 1, except the leading coefficient is a_n = −1. For $n > 1$, each such polynomial has $n-1$ roots in the complex unit disk, and one root outside said disk. Such polynomials are good test cases because one can quickly check the positions of the final roots in the complex plane. As for custom implementations, it has been suggested that a QR-algorithm [Goedecker 1994][Wong 1992] is a good choice for the eigenvalue tracking. One should be cautious that a custom implementation does not simply find eigenvalues by way of the circular expedient of merely solving for polynomial roots!

The controversy to which we have alluded is this: whereas the elegant Hessenberg-eigenvalue scheme is claimed to be faster than standard schemes, yet one can find other publications that claim dominance over eigenvalue and in fact over other schemes. [Lang and Frenzel 1994] for example claim that a certain Newton variant–a combination of Newton and Muller methods–is faster than both an eigenvalue scheme and a Jenkins/Traub method. What makes the controversy harder to fathom is that it is not entirely clear which eigenvalue scheme is best to use with the Hessenberg matrix.

Problem 1.5.1: Implement a Hessenberg-eigenvalue polynomial root finder to find all roots of an input polynomial. Try to invoke an eigenvalue stage that exploits the sparseness of the relevant Hessenberg matrix.

Polynomial evaluation

An interesting problem whose solution can provide dramatic optimization of certain computations is that of evaluating a polynomial along arithmetic progression values. Say we are given a polynomial p defined as the n-th degree form (1.5.1), and we wish to evaluate that polynomial at the points $x = a, a+d, a+2d, ...a+(N-1)d$; i.e., along N points possessed of common difference d. Here is what might be called a "naive" algorithm: use Horner's rule, which evaluates a single $p(a+kd)$ using n multiplies and n adds; and do this for each of the N arithmetic progression terms. This algorithm thus expends $O(nN)$ multiplies and the same order of adds, to obtain all evaluations. But, when $N \gg n$, there is a way drastically to reduce the operation count for the (usually more costly) multiplications. As mentioned in [Knuth 1973, p. 469], the difference tableau of the first such $(n+1)$ evaluations completely determines the rest of the evaluations. An evaluation algorithm runs as follows:

$$(1.5.2)$$

Algorithm to obtain, for $p(x) = a_0 + a_1 x + ... + a_n x^n$ the N evaluations

$$p(a), p(a+d), p(a+2d), ..., p(a+(N-1)d)$$

where $N > n$. (The advantage over direct evaluation is most dramatic when $N \gg n$.)

1) Using some elementary method such as Horner's rule, compute the first $(n+1)$ evaluations $e_0, e_1, ..., e_n$, where

$$e_k = p(a+kd)$$

2) Form the difference tableau:

For $q = 1$ to n {
    For $k = n$ downto q
$$e_k := e_k - e_{k-1};$$

}

3) Find all N evaluations $E_k = p(a+kd)$ as follows. Set $E_0 := e_0$ then loop:

> For $q = 1$ to $N–1$ {
> $$E_q := E_{q-1} + e_1;$$
> For $k = 1$ to $n–1$
> $$e_k := e_k + e_{k+1};$$
> }

Via Horner's rule, step (1) will cost $O(n^2)$ multiplies and adds. Step (2) costs again $O(n^2)$ adds but no multiplies. Finally, step (3) carries a cost of $O(nN)$ adds. Thus Algorithm (1.5.2) involves:

$$O(n^2) \text{ multiplies}$$
$$O(n^2 + nN) \text{ adds}$$

which, as we have indicated, is quite favorable in multiply count, when $N \gg n$. This "arithmetic progression" scheme was used recently by [Crandall *et. al.* 1995a] to evaluate large factorials, in a search for Wilson primes, as discussed in Chapter 3. The factorial evaluation is a special case in which one may recurse on step (1) of the Algorithm (1.5.2), because in the factorial setting the *roots* of p lie also in arithmetic progression.

It is also possible to develop an algorithm that efficiently evaluates a polynomial p along a *geometric* progression; *e.g.* yields $p(g), p(g^2), p(g^3)$, and so on. Such an algorithm is discussed in Section 3.3.

It turns out that even the arithmetic progression scheme's speed is not asymptotically optimal, for there exists a way to find N *arbitrary* evaluations (*i.e.*, the evaluation points need not even lie in arithmetic progression) of the degree-n polynomial p in

$$O(N \log^2 \min(N,n)) \tag{1.5.3}$$

operations, which is asymptotically superior to any other known arbitrary evaluation scheme. The idea [Borwein and Borwein 1987][Montgomery 1992] is best expressed initially for the case $N = n = 2^k$, for the necessary recursion proceeds most smoothly when the degree is a power of two. So let the polynomial p be as in (1.5.2), and assume we wish to evaluate p at the points $y_0, y_1, ..., y_{n-1}$; remembering that these y_i are arbitrary. First define two new polynomials each of degree $n/2$:

$$q_0(x) = (x-y_0)(x-y_1) \ldots (x-y_{n/2-1})$$

$$q_1(x) = (x-y_{n/2})(x-y_{n/2+1}) \ldots (x-y_{n-1})$$

Now assume we possess means of polynomial remaindering, that is, we can obtain remainder polynomials r_0 and r_1 of degree less than $n/2$, such that for some quotient polynomials Q_k:

(1.5.4)

$$p(x) = Q_0(x) q_0(x) + r_0(x) = Q_1(x) q_1(x) + r_1(x)$$

or to say it more succinctly:

$$p(x) = r_k \pmod{q_k}$$

for $k = 0,1$. Notice now that from (1.5.3) that, because each q_k has been constructed to have $n/2$ zeros, the evaluation of p at a y_i becomes an evaluation at one of the reduced degree polynomials r_k. In fact,

$$p(a_i) = r_{[2i/n]}(y_i)$$

Thus, the problem of evaluating p (whose degree is n) at n points has become equivalent to that of evaluating *two* polynomials each of degree at most $n/2$, at $n/2$ points each; plus, of course, the remaindering operation used to get the r_k. By simply applying the same ideas to each of the reduced degree polynomials r_k one ignites a recursion that, because Newton iteration can be used to do remaindering (see next few sections), costs

$$O(n \log^2 n)$$

operations. Incidentally, as described in [Montgomery 1992] there are clever ways to handle N evaluation points, when $n \neq N$. For $\deg(p) = n > N$, we simply set

$$s(x) := p(x) \left(\mod \prod_{k=0}^{N-1} (x - y_k) \right) \tag{1.5.5}$$

and proceed to evaluate s at the N points $\{y_i\}$. This works because by construction, s has degree not exceeding N, yet s and p agree on each y_i. On the other hand, when $n < N$, we can simply find sets of n evaluations about N/n times. These considerations lead to the complexity estimate (1.5.3).

Here is a *Mathematica* example that creates a list of evaluations of a given polynomial. The example is most efficient when the length of the list of evaluation points, what we have called N, is divisible by many 2's:

$$\tag{1.5.6}$$

```
(* Function to evaluate, for polynomial p,
   evaluations over a List y:
   {p[y[[1]]], p[y[[2]]], ..., p[y[[Length[y]]]]}

 *)


eval[p_, y_] :=
   Module[{len = Length[y], yL, yR, qL, qR, rL, rR},
         If[OddQ[len],
            Return[Table[p /. (x->y[[m]]),{m,1,len}]]
         ];
         yL = Take[y,{1,len/2}];
         yR = Take[y,{len/2+1,len}];
         qL = Product[x-yL[[m]],{m,1,len/2}];
         qR = Product[x-yR[[m]],{m,1,len/2}];
         rL = PolynomialRemainder[p,qL,x];
         rR = PolynomialRemainder[p,qR,x];
         Join[eval[rL,yL], eval[rR,yR]]
   ];
```

```
p = Product[x+q,{q,0,6}];
y = Table[1 + 7 q,{q,0,11}];
Print[eval[p,y]];
```

Problem 1.5.2: Implement an arithmetic progression evaluator (*i.e.*, the points at which to evaluate a given polynomial are assumed to lie in arithmetic progression). Compare timing, and domains of dominance, with a "naive" evaluator that uses Horner's rule for every separate evaluation point. There is even a new scheme to add to one's battery of evaluators. The scheme, based on precomputation of Stirling numbers, has been introduced by [Veljan 1994]. The asymptotic complexity is similar to that of our arithmetic progression scheme, namely $O(n^2)$ multiplies and $O(nN + n^2)$ adds, where n is the polynomial degree and N is the number of arithmetic progression length. But due to the small differences the new scheme reportedly performs somewhat better in actual experiments. [Veljan 1994] found for example, for a degree n = 5 polynomial evaluated at N = 1000000 points, the new scheme required 5000015 adds and 15 multiplies; while our text scheme required 500040 adds and 25 multiplies. This seemingly slight advantage is non-trivial if, as sometimes happens, the multiplies (involving say gigantic integers) are extremely expensive.

Problem 1.5.3: Implement a recursive evaluator such as the *Mathematica* example, but consider improvements such as:

- Newton method for the polynomial remaindering (see Problem at end of this chapter).
- Handling of any polynomial degrees and evaluation point counts, regardless of how rich either is in 2's.

Problem 1.5.4: Use one or more of the previous evaluators to compute factorials. One idea is this: the evaluations of

$$(x+1)(x+2)(x+3)...(x+m)$$

at respective points $\{0, m, 2m, ..., (m-1)m\}$, when all multiplied together, yields $(m^2)!$. (See the discussion of Wilson primes in Chapter 3.)

The author feels that only in recent times have typical computers been capable of the memory and speed necessary to make good use of polynomial evaluation algorithms. It is thus no surprise that some recent applications of polynomial evaluation have surfaced. For example, polynomial evaluation and related FFT techniques can be used to factor large integers. Another example is the evaluation of large factorials, as in the previous Problem. These various applications are discussed in Chapter 3. For the moment, we turn to a completion of the ideas needed to make all stages of an evaluator run quickly.

Polynomial multiplication

A non-trivial operation that arises in the general evaluation setting is that of constructing a polynomial from its roots. That is, to create the explicit coefficients for $p(x)$, as appear in (1.5.2) starting from knowledge of all n roots of p. An efficient algorithm is needed in the product operation of (1.5.5), where many terms must be multiplied together. Thus the general problem is to expand:

$$p(x) \;=\; \prod_{k=0}^{n-1}(x - r_k)$$

where the r_i are known roots. One way to carry out such a product is to recurse as follows (assuming n is divisible by many 2's):

1) Multiply together every consecutive pair of factors, to get $n/2$ factors.
2) Multiply together every consecutive pair of factors, to get $n/4$ factors.
...etc.

In other words, one "anneals" the original chain of factors by fusing them together, pairs at a time, so that on each step of the recursion we halve the number of factors. The recursive chain is exemplified thus for degree $n = 8$:

$$(1.5.7)$$

$$(x–1)(x–3)\ (x–4)(x–7)\ (x–11)(x–13)\ (x–17)(x–5)$$

$$(x^2–4x+3)\ \ (x^2–11x+28)\ \ (x^2–24x+143)\ \ (x^2–22x+85)$$

$$(x^4–15x^3+75x^2–145x+84)\ \ \ (x^4–46x^3+756x^2–5186x+12155)$$

$$(x^8–61x^7+1521x^6–20121x^5+153399x^4–684759x^3+1727099x^2–2198099x+1021020)$$

Evidently the number of *polynomial* multiplications required, starting the count from the top of the recursion, and for n a power of two, is:

$$n/2\ +\ n/4\ +\ ...\ +\ 1\ =\ n-1$$

However, the polynomials get progressively more cumbersome as the chain proceeds. It is more realistic to count operations, because a polynomial multiply depends of course on the degrees. If we assume a polynomial multiplication of two polynomials each of degree d can be done FFT-style, in $O(d \log d)$ arithmetic operations, the total operation count for the multiply chain above is (this time we start counting from the *last* multiply, which involves degrees $n/2$):

$$O((n/2) \log (n/2)\ + 2(n/4) \log (n/4) + ...)$$

$$= O(n \log^2 n)$$

Evidently this operation complexity is the same as that of evaluating a degree n polynomial at n arbitrary points. This makes sense when one realizes that multiplication and remaindering can be done, up to an overall constant, in the same asymptotic time. (Recall from earlier in this chapter that ordinary multiplication and division are similarly related so there is no great surprise.)

Usual implementations of fast polynomial multiplication depend once again on the principle that an acyclic convolution can be embedded in a cyclic one (or a negacyclic one) via sufficient zero-padding. The following *Mathematica* example shows some non-trivial overhead, beyond the fast convolution that should ultimately be employed in a practical program for large-degree polynomials. Actual implementations of cyclic and negacyclic convolutions themselves are discussed in Chapter 4.

$$(1.5.8)$$

```
(* Structure of a fast polynomial multiply with
   the important monic cases properly handled.
   The literal, or "grammar-school" negacyclic or cyclic
   should be replaced ultimately with a fast negacyclic
   or cyclic.
 *)


(* First the literal negacyclic and cyclic convolutions,
   with explicit loops written out for clarity.
   Note that for each there is a more elegant rendition
   as shown in the code that follows this program.
 *)
neglit[x_, y_] := Table[
                Sum[x[[i+1]] y[[Mod[m-i,Length[x]]+1]] *
                    If[m < i, -1,1]
                  ,{i,0,Length[x]-1}
                 ],
                {m,0,Length[x]-1}
                 ];

cyclit[x_, y_] := Table[Sum[x[[i+1]] y[[Mod[m-i,Length[x]]+1]]
                  ,{i,0,Length[x]-1}]
                  ,{m,0,Length[x]-1}
            ];

pcoeff[p_, n_] := If[n==0, p /. x->0, Coefficient[p,x^n]];
pmul[p_, q_] := Module[{len, a, b, c, e, degp, degq},
      degp = Exponent[p, x]; degq = Exponent[q, x];
      len = 2^Ceiling[Log[2, degp + degq]];
      If[len < 2, Return[p * q]];
```

```
(* Next, zero-pad to get the acyclic convolution.
   After the padding one may use either cyclic
   or negacyclic convolution to yield the desired
   acyclic.  Yet another option is to perform
   an acyclic using no zeropadding; rather a cyclic
   and a negacyclic of reduced order.  See Chapter 4.
 *)
a = Table[If[e <= degp, pcoeff[p,e],0],{e,0,2*len-1}];
b = Table[If[e <= degq, pcoeff[q,e],0],{e,0,2*len-1}];
c = neglit[a, b];
                (* or cyclit[a,b], or a fast negacyclic
                   or cyclic;
                   see, e.g. Appendix "Nuss.ma." *)
If[degq + degp == 2*len,
    d = Sum[c[[e]] x^(e-1), {e,1,degp+degq}];
    err = pcoeff[p, degp] * pcoeff[q, degq] ;
    d += err * x^(degp + degq);
    d += err;
    Return[d]
];
    Return[Sum[c[[e]] x^(e-1), {e,1,degp+degq+1}]];
];


p = 1 + 2x + 3x^2 + 7x^3 + 8x^8;
q = 1 + 3x + 17x^5 - 3 x^7 + x^8;
Expand[p * q]
pmul[p,q]
```

The last two *Mathematica* lines serve to print out the correct expanded product, and the one obtained via pmul[ ] with its internal negacyclic convolution or cyclic. Section 4.4 and the Appendix code "Nuss.ma" show examples of literal and fast convolution. In Chapter 4 there is more discussion of how acyclic convolutions can be performed in various ways, using cyclic and negacyclic convolutions (and even a strange cousin we call "half-cyclic") as fundamental tools.

Incidentally a more streamlined rendition of literal negacyclic and cyclic convolutions in *Mathematica* is:

$$(1.5.9)$$

```
(* Streamlined literal convolutions. *)

cyclit[x_, y_] := Rest[NestList[RotateRight, Reverse[y],
        Length[x]]] . x;

neglit[x_, y_] := MapIndexed[If[Less @@ #2, -#1, #1]&,
        Rest[NestList[RotateRight, Reverse[y], Length[x]]],
            {2}] . x;

x = Array[a,4,0]; y = Array[b,4,0];
cyclit[x,y]
neglit[x,y]

{a[0] b[0] + a[3] b[1] + a[2] b[2] + a[1] b[3],
 a[1] b[0] + a[0] b[1] + a[3] b[2] + a[2] b[3],
 a[2] b[0] + a[1] b[1] + a[0] b[2] + a[3] b[3],
 a[3] b[0] + a[2] b[1] + a[1] b[2] + a[0] b[3]}

{a[0] b[0] - a[3] b[1] - a[2] b[2] - a[1] b[3],
 a[1] b[0] + a[0] b[1] - a[3] b[2] - a[2] b[3],
 a[2] b[0] + a[1] b[1] + a[0] b[2] - a[3] b[3],
 a[3] b[0] + a[2] b[1] + a[1] b[2] + a[0] b[3]}
```

Problem 1.5.5: Implement a function that multiplies two polynomials via a direct "grammar-school" method; but switches over to a Karatsuba and/or an FFT method for some optimized breakover degree(s). The FFT method would zero-pad each of two polynomials to an appropriate run length, then proceed as in integer multiplication. In fact the polynomial case is a little easier because there is no final "carry" of digits; rather, every coefficient absorbs a full convolution element without overflow. Note that signal lengths of the FFT problem should be carefully chosen. For example, if two polynomials to be multiplied are both monic, say each one starts out $x^{16} + ?x^{15} + ...$, then one's program should *not* sense that "there are 17 coefficients, so we need to zero-pad to length 64 to do acyclic multiplication via cyclic convolution." Instead, use the fact that if both m and k are powers of two, the cyclic convolution of

$$a = \{a_0, a_1, ..., a_{m-1}, 1, 0, 0, ..., 0\} \quad \text{and}$$

$$b = \{b_0, b_1, ..., b_{k-1}, 1, 0, 0, ..., 0\}$$

where there are just enough padded zeros so that each array length is $2^{ceiling(\log(m+k) / \log 2)}$, gives the acyclic convolution (of the non-zero-padded sequences that each end in 1), except for easily computed correction terms. This notion of handling the convolution "spill-over" for signal lengths just a little more than powers of two can be generalized into what is called "devil's convolution," as discussed in Chapter 4.

Problem 1.5.6: Using a polynomial multiplier such as that of the previous Problem, create an "annealing function" that starts with an array of n roots $\{r_i\}$ and creates a fully expanded polynomial from the product

$$\prod_{k=0}^{n-1} (x - r_k)$$

There are some interesting optimizations, especially as regards the use of memory. The test case (1.5.7) shows visually that at every stage *every polynomial is monic*. Thus, if one invokes some effective way of marking a polynomial type as "monic," then the annealing can occur *in-place*. For example, in the test case (1.5.7), it is obvious that at every recursive stage there are only eight relevant coefficients. Thus a good annealing function can operate on a single initial array of roots, eventually replacing them with the invariant number of relevant coefficients.

Polynomial division and remaindering

Armed with fast algorithms for polynomial multiplication, one still needs remaindering (*i.e.* division) to be fast in order to effect, say, complete and efficient polynomial evaluation programs. The basic idea for fast division is described in [Sieveking 1972][Kung 1974][Borwein and Borwein 1988][Montgomery 1992], and involves Newton division to find a "reciprocal" of the divisor polynomial. In fact, the problem comes down to applying the idea inherent in (1.1.7) to just the right precision level, which in turn depends on the degree of the polynomial being reciprocated. The following *Mathematica* functions implement fast polynomial reciprocation and remaindering. The main function polyrem[ ] can be checked against *Mathematica's* built-in PolynomialRemainder function, except that the new function below should be asymptotically as fast (up to a fixed proportionality constant) as the inherent polynomial multiplication:

$$(1.5.10)$$

```
(* Fast polynomial division functions. *)

reverse[f_, degf_] := Module[{u},
    Return[Expand[(u^degf (f /. x->1/u)) /. u->x]];
    ];
ptake[f_, deg_] := Normal[Series[f,{x,0,deg}]];
pcoeff[f_, n_] := If[n==0, f /. x->0, Coefficient[f,x^n]];
plow[f_, deg_] := Module [{d = deg},
        If[f == 0, Return[0]];
        While[pcoeff[f, d] == 0, ++d];
        d
        ];
precip[f_, deg_] := Module[{g, h, lim = deg+1, prec},
        g = 1; prec = 1;
        While[prec < lim,
          prec *= 2;
          If[prec > lim, prec = lim];
          h = ptake[f, prec-1];
          g = g + g*(1- h*g);
          g = ptake[g, prec-1];
          ];
```

```
        g
        ];
polyrem[p_, degp_, q_, degq_] := Module[{d, pr, qr, dr},
        If[degq == 0, Return[0]];
        d = degp - degq;
        If[d < 0, Return[p]];
        pr = reverse[p, degp];
        qr = reverse[q, degq];
        dr = precip[qr, d];
        dr = ptake[pr * dr, d];
        mod = Expand[pr - qr * dr];
        shift = plow[mod, d+1];
        mod = Expand[mod * x^-shift];
        reverse[mod, degp-shift]
        ];
```

Note an important fact about the reciprocation done in precip[ ]: in actual implementations, for example in *C* language programs, and especially when polynomials have huge degree, the precision for each loop pass of the Newton method should start small (*e.g.*, prec := 1) and be increased appropriately (*e.g.*, prec *= 2 on each pass). Furthermore, if one only needs to some degree *d* the product of two polynomials each of the same degree *d* not equal to a power of two, the half-cyclic convolution (Section 4.4) may be of interest.

Problem 1.5.7: Using the above remaindering scheme, and other relevant fast algorithms, implement a polynomial evaluator. Apply this to a problem such as factoring or factorial evaluation (such topics are discussed in Chapter 3).

Generic "rational-zeta" series:

$$\text{constant} = \sum_{n=2}^{\infty} (\zeta(n) - 1)(\text{rational}_n)$$

Unity:

$$1 = \sum_{k=1}^{\infty} (\zeta(2k) - 1) \frac{4}{3}$$

Euler constant γ:

$$1 - \gamma = \sum_{n=2}^{\infty} \frac{\zeta(n) - 1}{n}$$

Natural logarithm:

$$\log 2 = \sum_{k=1}^{\infty} \frac{\zeta(2k) - 1}{k}$$

Khintchine constant K_0 and Khintchine means K_p, $p = -1, -2, \dots$:

$$\log K_0 \ \log 2 = \sum_{k=1}^{\infty} (\zeta(2k) - 1) \left(1 - \frac{1}{2} + \frac{1}{3} - \dots + \frac{1}{2k-1} \right)$$

$$K_p^{\,p} \ \log 2 = \sum_{n=2}^{\infty} (\zeta(n-p) - 1) Q_{np}$$

And a host of oddities, such as:

$$\frac{7}{2\pi^2} \zeta(3) - \log \frac{512}{81} + \frac{3}{2} = \sum_{k=1}^{\infty} \frac{\zeta(2k) - 1}{4^k (k+1)}$$

Which fundamental constants can be cast conveniently in terms of an explicit "rational-zeta" series, the generic form atop this page? Evidently, a good many, of which the collection here is but a sampling.

2   *Evaluation of constants & functions*

[*Having used a certain arcsin series to calculate* π *to* 15 *digits*] *Newton was later to write "I am ashamed to tell you to how many figures I carried these computations, having no other business at the time."*

[*Borwein and Borwein 1987*]

Since Archimedes' revolutionary resolution of the number π to the equivalent of three decimals, the problem of finding successively more precise values of such celebrated constants has held the fascination of analysts over the centuries. In more modern times, specifically since the advent of Newtonian physics, the same can be said of the fascination with various evaluations of those elementary and special functions so ubiquitous in the sciences.

2.1   *Celebrated constants*

The number π

It is fair to say that historically, π has been the ultimate testing bed for numerical analysis. What is more, π has also been a testing ground for *theoretical* advances. Even the Archimedean triumph was essentially an iterative scheme (Archimedes had worked out the theoretical perimeter of a 96-sided regular polygon) that, in principle, can be pushed to arbitrary accuracy. Amongst modern schemes are rapidly convergent ones suitable for millions or billions of digits. We shall mention these later, but for the moment we shall consider an elementary, amusing algorithm called a "spigot" algorithm. This kind of algorithm generates digits of a number (in this case π) and emits said digits in serial fashion. [Rabinowitz and Wagon 1995] have developed such an algorithm, starting from a Wallis-class formula:

$$\pi = \sum_{n=0}^{\infty} \frac{(n!)^2 2^{n+1}}{(2n+1)!} \qquad (2.1.1)$$

A central and elegant theme of the Rabinowitz-Wagon algorithm is that *only integer arithmetic is used*. There is not a floating-point operation to be found. The following *Mathematica* program implements the algorithm:

$$(2.1.2)$$

```
(* Rabinowitz-Wagon
   "spigot" algorithm to generate serial digits of Pi. *)
digits = 40;
len = Floor[10 digits/3];
a = Table[2,{len}];
nines = predigit = 0;
Do[
    q = 0;
    Do[
      x = 10*a[[i]]+q*(i);
      a[[i]] = Mod[x, 2i-1];
      q = Floor[x/(2i-1)]
      ,{i,len,1,-1}
    ];
    a[[1]] = Mod[q, 10]; q = Floor[q/10];
    If[q ==9, ++nines,
          If[q ==10, Print[predigit+1];
                        Do[Print[0],{k,1,nines}];
                   predigit = nines = 0,
                   If[j > 0, Print[predigit]];
                   predigit = q;
                        Do[Print[9],{k,1,nines}];
                        nines = 0;
          ]
    ];
    ,{j,0,digits-1}
```

```
] ;
```

Note that the requested total number of output digits is specified in the first line of the above code example.

Problem 2.1.1: Show that the spigot algorithm realized in the above code does indeed generate correct digits of π. This can be proved in the style of the reference [Rabinowitz and Wagon 1995], but it is instructive to attempt a proof from scratch.

Problem 2.1.2: Work out a spigot algorithm for some other fundamental constant such as e.

Problem 2.1.3: The spigot idea is attractive, but it is difficult to generate, say, one million digits in this fashion. The main difficulty is not the high-precision required, for it is not that high; in fact the loop variable i only runs to about (10*$digits$/3), neither $a[[i]]$ nor q gets larger than about $2i$, and x does not exceed about 200 $digits^2$/9. The real problem is in the nested looping, whose required time is something like the square of $digits$. Thus we pose: Is there a way to generate say one million digits of π in "spigot" fashion? One would somehow handle the nested looping in such a way as to reduce the total time to something much less than $digits^2$. Another possibility pointed out in [Rabinowitz and Wagon 1995] is to exploit the parallelizability of the spigot.

For hundreds to thousands of digits of π, a reasonable option is to use one of the beautiful series of Ramanujan [Borwein and Borwein 1987]. These generally derive from the theory of modular equations and elliptic integrals. Two series examples are:

$$\frac{1}{\pi} = \sum_{n=0}^{\infty} \frac{(2n)!^3 (42n+5)}{n!^6 2^{12n+4}} \tag{2.1.3}$$

$$\frac{1}{\pi} = \frac{\sqrt{8}}{9801} \sum_{n=0}^{\infty} \frac{(4n)!\,(1103 + 26390n)}{n!^4\, 396^{4n}} \tag{2.1.4}$$

Problem 2.1.4: Describe the convergence rate (*e.g.*, in terms of good decimal digits per iteration) for each of the Ramanujan formulae (2.1.3), (2.1.4). Implement one of these formulae, and use the other to check the calculations.

Now, for thousands to millions (or billions) of digits, a reasonable choice is one of the highly convergent algorithms of modern vintage. These algorithms are not based on explicit series, rather on clever iterations that (like Newton method iterations we saw in Chapter 1) exhibit quadratic or higher convergence. Such algorithms, though anticipated by Gauss, did not appear until Brent and Salamin described explicit π algorithms in the 1970's [Brent 1976a, 1976b][Salamin 1976]. One such is the Borweins' quartic convergence algorithm that was used by [Bailey 1988] to resolve π to 29 million decimal places. This quartic algorithm runs as follows:

$$\tag{2.1.5}$$

$$a_0 := 6 - 4\sqrt{2}\ ; \qquad y_0 := \sqrt{2} - 1$$

$$y_{k+1} := \frac{1 - \left(1 - y_k^4\right)^{1/4}}{1 + \left(1 - y_k^4\right)^{1/4}}$$

$$a_{k+1} := a_k\left(1 + y_{k+1}\right)^4 - 2^{2k+3} y_{k+1}\left(1 + y_{k+1} + y_{k+1}^2\right)$$

whence the value a_k converges to $1/\pi$. Being a quartic algorithm, the number of decimal places roughly *quadruples* every iteration. Actually, Bailey used a quadratic alternative due to the Borweins to check the 29 million place final approximation. In more recent times, D. and G. Chudnovsky, and independently Y. Kanada, have reported computations to billions of digits.

Problem 2.1.5: Implement a rapidly convergent algorithm such as (2.1.5) and verify that the number of good decimal digits (doubles, trebles, quadruples, ...) according to the theoretical convergence rate (quadratic, cubic, quartic...) of the algorithm. There exist at least *quintic* formulae as well. One such is given in [Borwein *et. al.* 1989]. Here are some milestones along the quest for more and more decimal digits of π:

(We shall count strictly to the right of the decimal, so in 3.14159... the 4 is the "second" place)
1000-th digit of π: 9
10000000-th digit: 7
1000000000-th digit: 9 [Kanada 1995]
3000000000-th digit: 8 [Kanada 1995]

For some isolated digits in a different base, yet much further away from the decimal point, see Problem 2.1.6.

A very recent breakthrough in the problem of digit computation is due to Bailey, Borwein, and Plouffe [Bailey *et. al.* 1995b]. They have produced some remarkable formulae, such as:

$$\pi = \sum_{k=0}^{\infty} \frac{1}{16^k} \left(\frac{4}{8k+1} - \frac{2}{8k+4} - \frac{1}{8k+5} - \frac{1}{8k+6} \right)$$

with which to resolve isolated digit positions in base-16 (hexadecimal). One interesting facet of this "BBP" formalism is that one may achieve good results using a mere workstation. What is more, arbitrary-precision arithmetic is not required.

Problem 2.1.6: Implement the BBP formula immediately preceding, and give some isolated hexadecimal digits of π. For example, according to [Bailey *et.*

al. 1995b] some hexadecimal digit strings according to their starting positions are:

Position   Digit string starting at position

10^6 26C65E52CB4593...

10^8 ECB840E21926EC...

10^{10} 921C73C6838FB2...

It is remarkable that we now know the *ten billionth* hexadecimal digit, as a "9." However, note that the BBP calculations, unlike those of Kanada and the Chudnovskys, do not resolve *all* the digits from the decimal point to the given place.

Problem 2.1.7: Here are some identities as possible means for discovering yet more BBP-type formulae. One idea is to multisection the standard series for $\log(1-x)$. For given N and a in $[0, N-1]$, we have:

$$\frac{-1}{N} \sum_{k=0}^{N-1} \omega^{-ak} \log\left(1 - x\omega^k\right) = \sum_{\substack{k>0 \\ k = a(\mathrm{mod}\, N)}} \frac{x^k}{k}$$

where ω is a primitive N-th root of unity. Use this with $N = 8$ and $x = 1/\sqrt{2}$ to establish the BBP identity for hexadecimal base. Another potentially useful identity, valid for any real t in $(0, \pi)$, is:

$$\frac{\pi}{2} - t = \sum_{k=0}^{\infty} \frac{\cos^k t}{k} \sin k t$$

Setting $t := 2\pi/N$ for various power-of-two N yields BBP-like formulae. As of this writing, a spectacular open problem is: does a base-10 identity exist? That is, can one develop a BBP approach for finding isolated digits in standard decimal?

The Khintchine constant

The Khintchine constant arises in a beautiful and natural way in the measure theory of continued fractions. Every irrational x in (0,1) admits of a unique simple continued fraction:

$$x = \cfrac{1}{a_1 + \cfrac{1}{a_2 + \cfrac{1}{a_3 + ...}}}$$

where the elements a_i are all positive integers. We also denote this:

$$x = [a_1, a_2, a_3, ...]$$

It is a stunning theorem of Khintchine that for almost all x the limiting geometric mean

$$\lim_{n \to \infty} \sqrt[n]{a_1 a_2 \cdots a_n}$$

exists, and furthermore equals, for almost all x, the *same constant* [Khintchine 1964]. This universal limit is called the Khintchine constant, which we shall denote K_0. Khintchine derived his constant on the basis of the Gauss-Kuz'min density that gives the "probability" that a random element a_n is a given integer k:

(2.1.6)

$$Prob\{a_n = k\} = -\log_2\left(1 - \frac{1}{(k+1)^2}\right)$$

with this probability holding amongst the elements of a fixed x, for almost all x. Thus for example, for almost all x, the element "1" appears in the list of continued fraction elements of x a fraction of the time: $\log_2(4/3)$, and so on. The Khintchine constant then turns out to be:

$$K_0 = \prod_{j=1}^{\infty} \left(1 + \frac{1}{j(j+2)}\right)^{\log_2 j} \tag{2.1.7}$$

A numerical value is:

$K_0 \sim 2.685452001065306445309714835481795693820382293994 46...$

In addition, for non-zero real exponents $p < 1$, also with probability one, the elements of x have a Holder mean limit

$$\lim_{n \to \infty} \left(\frac{1}{n} \sum_{i=1}^{n} a_i^p\right)^{\frac{1}{p}}$$

existing and equal to a universal constant K_p, which in turn is given by

$$K_p = \left\{\sum_{j=1}^{\infty} \left(-j^p \log_2\left(1 - \frac{1}{(j+1)^2}\right)\right)\right\}^{\frac{1}{p}} \tag{2.1.8}$$

Note that K_1 does not exist; the sum (2.1.8) diverges. This means that almost nowhere do a number's fraction elements have a well-defined arithmetic mean (*i.e.*, average). But the *harmonic* mean ($p = -1$) exists with probability one, and furthermore with probability one has the value:

$K_{-1} \sim 1.745405662407346863494596309683661067294936618777 98...$

Problem 2.1.6: Give (at least an heuristic) argument that the Gauss-Kuz'min density should indeed lead to limiting geometric mean (2.1.7) and furthermore to limiting Holder mean (2.1.8) for p non zero and less than 1. Show that (2.18) yields K_0 in the limit $p \to 0$.

Problem 2.1.7: Perform statistical experiments in order to ascertain the Khintchine theorem, that with probability 1, the geometric mean of the elements of x has limiting value K_0. Extend this analysis to some of the Holder means K_p, with $p < 0$.

There have been some interesting old and new developments involving the Khintchine constant, to which developments we now turn. It is evident that the product definition (2.1.7) is poorly convergent. [Shanks and Wrench 1959] worked out a converging series for the constant, this series involving the Riemann zeta function. An interesting class of series was also worked out by [Vardi 1991], which series involve difficult-to-compute derivatives of the Riemann zeta function, but are otherwise much more efficient than (2.1.7). Such a series can be used to obtain hundreds or perhaps thousands of digits of K_0. Incidentally, since it is often asked of *any* massive decimal expansion, "What good is this much accuracy?," we have an excellent answer for K_0 in particular. Namely, look at Problem 2.1.9.

A certain series due to [Shanks and Wrench 1959] is both practical and elegant:

$$\log K_0 \log 2 \;=\; \sum_{s=1}^{\infty} \frac{\zeta(2s) - 1}{s}\left(1 - \frac{1}{2} + \frac{1}{3} - \ldots + \frac{1}{2s - 1}\right) \qquad (2.1.9)$$

and it is now known that for negative integers p, the order-p Khintchine mean can always be expanded in a form

$$K_p^p \log 2 = \sum_{n=2}^{\infty} (\zeta(n-p) - 1)\; Q_{np} \qquad (2.1.10)$$

where the Q coefficients are all rational [Bailey *et. al.* 1995a]. These formulae, particularly the class represented by (2.1.9) with its pure-even zeta arguments, allow the Khintchine constant to be resolved to thousands of digits (at the time of this writing K_0 is known [Bailey *et. al.* 1995a] to over 7000 decimal digits).

Problem 2.1.8: Use series (2.1.9) to obtain the Khintchine constant K_0 to 100 or more places. (Note that means for evaluating the Riemann zeta function are given in Section 2.2 next.) Note that the series can be accelerated as follows. "Peel off" a numerator term so that the fraction within the sum reads $(\zeta(2s)-1-1/2^{2s})/s$, and evaluate in closed form the correction due to the $1/2^{2s}$ perturbation. This yields a summand that decays like 9^{-s}, and of course this "peeling" method can be taken as far as is computationally efficient [Bailey *et. al.* 1995a].

Problem 2.1.9: Determine an empirical geometric mean for the elements of the continued fraction for K_0 itself, using the result of the previous Problem (or some other source of many digits of K_0). The issue of when to terminate a continued fraction expansion $x = [a_0, a_1, ...]$ for a given decimal value of x is an interesting one. Here is one simple criterion which should be explored theoretically: terminate the list of elements a_i when the current convergent p/q satisfies $|x - p/q| < 1/(2q^2)$. This tends to give almost the same number of elements as you have decimal digits.

It is fascinating that, in spite of Khintchine's theorem and the universality of K_0, not a single explicit x is known that has geometric mean K_0. Consider some celebrated continued fractions of history. The number e is determined by:

$$e - 1 \ = [1,1,2,1,1,4,1,1,6,1,1,8,1,1,10,...]$$

which element list is a meshing of two arithmetic progressions: one, $\{1,1,1...\}$ with null difference, and a second $\{2,4,6,8,10,...\}$ which diverges. It turns out that any continued fraction with elements in a *single* arithmetic progression is known in terms of special functions; *viz.*:

$$(2.1.11)$$

$$[a,\ a+d,\ a+2d,\ a+3d,\ ...]\ =\ \frac{I_{\frac{a}{d}-1}\left(\frac{2}{d}\right)}{I_{\frac{a}{d}}\left(\frac{2}{d}\right)}$$

where I_{ν} is the modified Bessel function of order ν [Abramowitz and Stegun 1965]. Then there is the classic theorem of Lagrange, that the elements of x are eventually periodic if and only if x is a quadratic irrational; *i.e.* x is of the form $A+\sqrt{B}$, where A, B are rational. For such a fraction it is clear that the p-th Holder mean is completely determined by one period, and furthermore must be algebraic for any non-negative integral p. It thus seems unlikely that any quadratic irrational has geometric mean (0-th Holder mean) equal to K_0 (unless of course you do not believe the Khintchine constant to be transcendental!).

Problem 2.1.10: Show that the harmonic mean (*i.e.* the Holder mean with power $p := -1$) for e is 3/2, which is certainly not the number K_{-1}. Show that the fraction $[a,\ a+d,\ a+2d,...]$ either has each constant K_p equal to a (when d is zero), or has each K_p divergent (when $d > 0$).

Problem 2.1.11: Imagine a real number whose fraction elements consist of only 2's and n's, for some fixed n, such that the limiting geometric mean is in fact K_0. What is the proportion of 2's in the fraction?

In spite of this theoretical impasse–that no explicit real numbers whose fractions enjoy geometric mean K_0 are known–it is possible to describe sets of fraction elements themselves, which sets have the mean K_0 [Bailey *et. al.,* 1995]. For instance, there is a number constructed in Monte Carlo fashion and now known to have the requisite geometric mean. The number is called Z_2 and was first defined by the present author after discussions with [Wieting 1995]. Denote by $d(n)$ the van der Corput discrepancy sequence [Niederreiter

1992], where for a non-negative integer n whose base expansion is $n = b_k b_{k-1} ... b_0$, we set $d(n) = 0.b_0 b_1 ... b_k$, where this $d(n)$ value is interpreted to be binary also. In other words, $d(n)$ lies in $[0,1)$ and is formed by reversing the bits of n and placing said reversal to the right of the point. It has been proved [Wieting 1995] that the elements defined for positive integers n by

$$a_n = \left[\frac{1}{2^{d(n)} - 1} \right]$$

define a real number Z_2 having geometric mean K_0. An experiment was recently performed [Plouffe 1995] in which over two million elements of Z_2 were generated. Plouffe's values for the geometric and harmonic means, up through the 5179392-th element, were:

$$2.685483280... \quad 1.745407463...$$

respectively. More recently, D. Moore has calculated the geometric mean through the 19990000-th element, obtaining:

$$2.685455304...$$

amounting to an error of about one part in 10^6. The present author conjectures that the approach to the K_0 constant should be rapid, in the sense that, if G_n denotes the geometric mean of a_1 through a_n, then the error decays *faster* than $1/\sqrt{n}$:

$$| G_n - K_0 | = o(1/\sqrt{n})$$

Problem 2.1.12: Study the recently introduced number Z_2. Do the first several hundred (or thousand?) elements of Z_2 appear to follow the Gauss-Kuz'min density? Does the geometric mean appear to be converging, and if so does the $o(1/\sqrt{n})$ conjecture look good? What about numbers defined Z_B, where base B = (one of 3,4,5,...) is used for the discrepancy sequence?

2.2　　*Riemann zeta function*

Zeta values in the complex plane

The Riemann zeta function $\zeta(s)$ is defined for $Re(s) > 1$ as a literal sum:

$$\zeta(s) = \sum_{n=1}^{\infty} \frac{1}{n^s} \qquad (2.2.1)$$

and defined for other s via analytic continuation. Since the pioneering work of Riemann, various profound conjectures and theorems have been cast in terms of the function's properties. The "most wanted" result is the Riemann hypothesis, a conjecture that all of the zeros of $\zeta(s)$ with $0 \le Re(s) \le 1$ happen to lie on the critical line: $Re(s) = 1/2$. It is now known that the first 1.5 *billion* zeros lie *exactly* on the critical line. It is fascinating that this has been shown rigorously, but using only moderate-precision values of the zeta function [Odlyzko 1995a]. Quite separate, in some sense, from investigations of this hypothesis, there are many questions concerning the properties of $\zeta(s)$ when s is a positive integer. For example, thanks to Apery it is now known that $\zeta(3)$ is irrational but the question of irrationality for $\zeta(5)$ remains open.

Some studies of the Riemann zeta function can make good use of precise numerical evaluations. There are four main modes of zeta evaluation:

1) Evaluate *many* values of $\zeta(s)$; for s complex, to *moderate* precision, to ascertain such as the celebrated Riemann conjecture up to some height on the critical line.

2) Evaluate *many* values of $\zeta(s)$; for s complex, to *high* precision, in order to assail other conjectures. (The Mertens conjecture was shown to be false [Odlyzko and te Riele 1985] via the computation of thousands of zeros of zeta, each to 100-decimal precision.)

3) Evaluate *one* value of $\zeta(s)$; for s integer, to *high* precision in order, for example, to resolve some other constant or ascertain some conjecture.

4) Evaluate *many* values, at positive integers s, to *high* precision , as in the circumstance that many zetas with integer argument are needed in a summation (see for example the formulae (2.1.9)-(2.1.10)).

As for evaluations of type (1), an old standard algorithm that remains quite useful is the Euler-Maclaurin summation technique. For many of the historical numerical explorations of the Riemann hypothesis, the Euler-Maclaurin method was the method of choice. More recently, there have appeared variants of the so-called Riemann-Siegel formula. It should be noted that Euler-Maclaurin is generic: many types of summations (and not just say (2.2.1)) can be handled; while Riemann-Siegel is customized for the zeta function and related Dirichlet series [Odlyzko 1995a]. The Euler-Maclaurin formula turns out to require $O(t)$ operations to resolve $\zeta(1/2 + it)$ to a given precision; whereas Riemann-Siegel methods only have complexity $O(t^{1/2})$. Thus the newer methods and variants are used more and more in the deeper studies, especially when the height (t value up the critical line) is large.

Zeta function evaluation via summation is one of the clearest examples of the use of Euler-Maclaurin methods. One may start with the formula for an infinite sum, where c (summation cutoff) and t (derivative cutoff) are ultimately to be chosen for efficiency:

$$(2.2.2)$$

$$\sum_{n=1}^{\infty} f(n) = \sum_{n=1}^{c-1} f(n) + \frac{1}{2} f(c) + \int_{c}^{\infty} f(x)\, dx -$$

$$\sum_{k=1}^{t} \frac{B_{2k}}{(2k)!} f^{(2k-1)}(c) + E(t,c)$$

assuming the relevant integral and derivatives exist. The total error E is bounded by:

$$|E(t,c)| \leq \left| \frac{cB_{2t+2}}{(2t+2)!} \sup_{x \geq c} \left| f^{(2t+2)}(x) \right| \right| \tag{2.2.3}$$

However, when f has certain monotonicity properties, the magnitude of E is bounded simply by the magnitude of the first missing term in the second line summation (the Bernoulli number summation) of (2.2.2). Indeed, when neither $f^{(2t+2)}$ nor $f^{(2t+4)}$ changes sign for x in $[c, \infty]$, the magnitude of E is simply so bounded.

For experimental purposes (or, indeed, to check other schemes!) here is a *Mathematica* example of generic Euler-Maclaurin summing machinery:

$$\tag{2.2.4}$$

```
(* Generic Euler-Maclaurin summing machine,
   to evaluate the sum of f[n], {n,1,Infinity}.
   The function gen returns a list of
   summation value and error bound.
 *)
t = 14;
s = 1/2 + I t;
f[x_] := 1/x^s;
term[k_, y_, end_] := BernoulliB[2k]/(2k)! *
               (D[f[x],{x,2k-1+end}] /. x->y);
gen[cut_, top_] := Module[{n, sum, x, k},
        sum = Sum[f[n],{n,1,cut-1}];
        sum += 1/2 f[cut];
        (* sum += Integrate[f[x],{x,cut,Infinity}]; *)
        sum += 1/(s-1) cut^(1-s);
        sum -= Sum[term[k, cut, 0],{k,1,top}];
        err = term[top+1, cut, 1];
        {sum, Abs[cut * err]}
    ];
N[gen[20,20],30]

{0.022241142609993589246213199 -
0.10325812326645005790236309560 I,
```

$$-29$$
$$1.88670421406519699390058375096 \ 10 \quad \}$$

This example is calculating $\zeta(1/2 + 14\ i)$, that is the value of the zeta function exactly 14 units up the critical line. Note that the generic Euler-Maclaurin function gen[ ] returns a list. The first list member is the approximation to the infinite sum on the left of (2.2.2), while the second member is the error bound (2.2.3). Note that for the special case of $f = \zeta$, the program uses the exact definite integral in the Euler-Maclaurin formalism.

Problem 2.2.1: Study the Euler-Maclaurin complexity of computing zeta values. In particular, for given complex s, optimize c and t theoretically to obtain an estimate for how many total summands are required on the right-hand side of (2.2.2) in order to resolve D good decimal digits in both the real and imaginary parts of $\zeta(s)$. Note that $Re(s)$ never need be taken less than 1/2 because the functional equation for ζ, namely

$$\zeta(s) \ = \ 2^s \pi^{s-1} \sin \frac{\pi s}{2} \ \Gamma(1-s)\ \zeta(1-s) \qquad\qquad (2.2.5)$$

allows one always to restrict s to be on or to the right of the critical line. Address the complexity issue also for the relatively more efficient Euler-Maclaurin method that obtains when s is real.

Problem 2.2.2: Use the generic Euler-Maclaurin summation machine (2.2.4), or some equivalent scheme in a language of choice, to find some zeros of Riemann zeta on the critical line. A certain milestone that one might attempt reenacting would be Titchmarsh *et. al.*'s establishment in 1936 that the lowest-lying 1041 zeros in the critical strip (*i.e.*, the first 1041 values scanning upward from the real axis) indeed lie on the critical line $Re(s) = 1/2$. A discussion of how to use a functional symmetry of the Riemann zeta function (relation (2.2.5) above) *rigorously* to isolate zeros, even when precision is limited, can be found in [Odlyzko 1995a].

Problem 2.2.3: For exclusively positive integer arguments, simplify the generic

Euler-Maclaurin summation machine (2.2.4) on the basis of the easier error criterion, to obtain a high-precision (say ≥ 100 decimal digits precise) value of $\zeta(3)$. How can the whole process, for given precision, be optimized? Is there a convenient rule-of-thumb for optimization of c and t?

Problem 2.2.4: Set up an Euler-Maclaurin scheme to evaluate the polylogarithm function:

$$Li_s(z) = \sum_{n=1}^{\infty} \frac{z^n}{n^s}$$

at, say, integer powers s. Verify numerically the exact relation

$$Li_2\left(\frac{1}{2}\right) = \frac{\pi^2}{12} - \frac{1}{2}\log^2 2$$

In spite of its utility and universality, the Euler-Maclaurin scheme has a defect: it does not yield an explicit infinite convergent series. Indeed, for a given summation cutoff c in (2.2.2), the Bernoulli sum cutoff must be deftly chosen. In fact, for fixed c the error estimate (2.2.3) generally diverges in t. Thus in general the Bernoulli summation index cannot be taken to infinity. Still, there are alternative series that do converge for certain ranges of complex s. One example known to Riemann was:

$$(2.2.6)$$

$$\zeta(s)\,\Gamma\left(\frac{s}{2}\right) = \frac{\pi^{s/2}}{s(s-1)} + \sum_{n=1}^{\infty}\left(\frac{\Gamma\left(\frac{s}{2}, \pi n^2\right)}{n^s} + \pi^{s-\frac{1}{2}}\frac{\Gamma\left(\frac{1-s}{2}, \pi n^2\right)}{n^{1-s}}\right)$$

valid for *all* complex $s \neq 1$. Here, $\Gamma(a, z)$ is the incomplete gamma function; the standard gamma function being $\Gamma(z) = \Gamma(0, z)$ [Abramowitz and Stegun 1965]. The good thing about this Riemann series is the rapid convergence, due to the favorable asymptotic behavior:

$$\Gamma(a, z) \sim z^{a-1} e^{-z} \tag{2.2.7}$$

Another series which is not generally as rapidly convergent as (2.2.6) but which enjoys other conveniences can be developed as follows. Starting with the integral representation:

$$\zeta(s) = \frac{1}{\Gamma(s)} \int_0^\infty \frac{x^{s-1} dx}{e^x - 1} \tag{2.2.8}$$

split the integral into $\int_0^\infty = \int_0^\lambda + \int_\lambda^\infty$ where λ is a free parameter, except that $|\lambda| < 2\pi$. Now for the integral over $(0, \lambda)$ use the expansion

$$\cot \pi z = -\frac{2}{\pi} \sum_{s=0}^\infty \zeta(2s) z^{2s-1} \tag{2.2.9}$$

which is equivalent to the classical Bernoulli expansion of $1/(e^{2\pi z}-1)$ and valid for $|z| < 1$ (see (2.2.15) and Section 3.2), while for the second integral simply expand $1/(e^x-1)$ in powers of e^{-x}. This splitting leads to the following series, valid for any complex $s \neq 1$, and any choice of free parameter λ whose magnitude is less than 2π:

$$\tag{2.2.10}$$

$$\Gamma(s) \zeta(s) = -\frac{\lambda^s}{2s} + \frac{\lambda^{s-1}}{s-1} + \sum_{n=0}^\infty \frac{\Gamma(s, \lambda n)}{n^s} - \frac{2}{\lambda^{1-s}} \sum_{n=1}^\infty \left(\frac{-\lambda^2}{4\pi^2} \right)^n \frac{\zeta(2n)}{2n+s-1}$$

One advantage of this series is the fact that for positive integer s, the incomplete gamma appearing is an elementary function. In fact, from the recurrence relation

$$\Gamma(a, z) = z^{a-1} e^{-z} + (a-1) \Gamma(a-1, z) \tag{2.2.11}$$

it is evident that $\Gamma(n, z)$ for positive integer n is e^{-z} times a polynomial in z; while for negative integer n, $\Gamma(n, z)$ can be written in terms of elementary functions and the "exponential integral" $\Gamma(0, z)$. We shall see later how these properties of incomplete gamma can be exploited in practical computations. Note also that (2.2.10) depends on $\zeta(2n)$ values, but as we shall see these are relatively easy to come by, being obtainable in a rapid, "parallel" fashion.

An intriguing recurrence relation which the present author feels has not been thoroughly studied as an evaluation mechanism is the following, communicated by [Keiper 1994] and similar to a formula in [Apostol 1976]. For positive integer N the relation reads:

$$(2.2.12)$$

$$\zeta(s, N) = \frac{1}{1-s} \sum_{k=1}^{\infty} \left[N - 1 + \frac{s+k}{1+k} \right] (-1)^k \binom{s+k-1}{k} \zeta(s+k, N)$$

where $\zeta(s, N)$ is the Hurwita zeta function:

$$\zeta(s, N) = \sum_{n=0}^{\infty} \frac{1}{(n+N)^s}$$

This function, for positive integer N, is simply a zeta function minus the first $(N–1)$ terms; that is, $\zeta(s, 1) = \zeta(s)$ and generally $\zeta(s, N) = \zeta(s) - 1/1^s - 1/2^s - 1/3^s - ... - 1/(N-1)^s$. One may contemplate code realizations of the natural recursion implicit in the Keiper relation (2.2.12), a *Mathematica* example being:

$$(2.2.13)$$

```
(* Keiper recursion for calculating Riemann zeta. *)
depth = 6; (* Recursion depth. *)
cutoff = 12; (* Summation cutoff. *)
k = 20;   (* Hurwitz offset parameter. *)
hzeta[s_, a_] :=   (* hzeta calls itself. *)
    If[s > depth, Zeta[s, a],
    -1/(s-1) Sum[(-1)^k (a-1+(s+k)/(k+1)) *
                Binomial[s+k-1,k] *
                hzeta[s + k, a], {k, 1, cutoff}
```

```
                   ]
      ];
kzeta[s_] := Simplify[hzeta[s, k] + Sum[ 1/j^s  ,{j,1,k-1}]];
N[kzeta[3] - Zeta[3], 30]
```

$$
-16
$$
$$
-3.04029216513225 \; 10
$$

The example above does resolve $\zeta(3)$ to about 15 good decimal digits. It is true that the built-in Hurwitz function Zeta[s, a] is called for s exceeding the depth parameter. But the whole idea is not fundamentally circular. In fact, Keiper's idea was, for large enough depth value, one should be able to estimate Zeta[s, a] easily and quickly, say with leading term $a^{1-s}/(s-1)$.

Reminiscent of the Keiper scheme, there is another interesting class of asymptotic evaluation formulae [P Borwein 1995]:

$$
\zeta(s) \underset{N\to\infty}{\widetilde{}} \frac{1}{2^{N-s+1}-2^N} \sum_{k=0}^{2N-1} \frac{(-1)^k}{(k+1)^s} \left(\sum_{m=0}^{k-N} \binom{N}{m} - 2^N \right) \qquad (2.2.14)
$$

It is interesting that in practice, for real values of s greater than 1, this relation for chosen parameter N yields roughly N good decimal digits of ζ.

Problem 2.2.5: As in Problem 2.2.1, but this time using the Riemann formula (2.2.6), determine theoretically the complexity of resolving $\zeta(s)$, s complex, to D good decimal digits in both real and imaginary parts. Note that issues of complexity for hypergeometric functions of which incomplete gamma is an example are discussed in [Borwein and Borwein 1987], and touched upon later in this chapter. Formulae for convenient computation of incomplete gamma are given in [*Projects* 1994] and later in this chapter.

Problem 2.2.6: Implement a zeta function calculating routine which uses (2.2.10) for arbitrary complex s. In particular, demonstrate the fact that as the parameter λ is varied within the allowed range $[0, 2\pi)$, one expects an invariant result. This invariance when realized is a strong indication of the correctness of a program. (Note also that the Riemann formula (2.2.6) also has a free-parameter generalization, which can be found in various texts [Henrici 1977].) As for the $\zeta(2n)$ values in the final sum of (2.2.10), one can simply use recurrences and relations at the beginning of the next section; or one may employ the powerful parallel scheme discussed later in the chapter.

Problem 2.2.7: Study the Keiper relation (2.2.12) in the context of asymptotic complexity. In terms of the *Mathematica* example (2.2.13), the task becomes that of optimizing the three parameters (depth, cutoff, k) to most efficiently resolve $\zeta(s)$ to D digits. This appears to be an open problem.

Problem 2.2.8: Implement the Borwein evaluation formula (2.2.14). Give the theoretical complexity of the scheme for positive real s, and also for arbitrary complex s. [Borwein P 1995] has derived rigorous error bounds for this scheme.

Problem 2.2.9: Use some method of computing zeta values to explore the statistical properties of zeta functions and related Dirichlet series. There is a connection with Guassian unitary matrix ensembles, as touched upon in Problem 1.4.7. These investigations have achieved a certain modern vogue, as exemplified in [Berry 1988][Bogomolny and Leboeuf 1994].

Zeta function at integer arguments

First we have the classic relations

$$(2.2.15)$$

$$\zeta(2n) = \frac{(-1)^{n-1}(2\pi)^{2n}}{2(2n)!} B_{2n} \quad ; \quad n = 0, 1, 2, 3, \ldots$$

$$\zeta(-2n+1) = -\frac{B_{2n}}{2n} \quad ; \quad n = 1, 2, 3, \ldots$$

$$\zeta(-2n) = 0 \quad ; \quad n = 1, 2, 3, \ldots$$

There exist further interrelations between the zetas of integer argument. For example, the identity

(2.2.16)

$$\sum_{k=0}^{m} \frac{(-1)^k \pi^{2k+1}}{(2k+1)!} \left(1 - 2^{2k-2m+1}\right) \zeta(2m-2k) = 0$$

valid for $m \geq 1$, is essentially a recurrence for Bernoulli numbers. Another recurrence, again being a disguised Bernoulli number relation but this time involving products of zeta functions at even arguments, is:

'(2.2.17)

$$\sum_{0 < j < k;\ j\,\text{even}} \zeta(j)\,\zeta(k-j) = \frac{k+1}{2}\,\zeta(k) \qquad ; (k \geq 4,\ \text{even})$$

It is a great deal harder to find relations amongst zeta functions of *odd* integer arguments. But we can at least find an "almost finite" relation, in the sense that $\zeta(\text{odd})$ values can be related with a finite sum, up to a rapidly converging series. One theorem that can be derived from the formula (2.2.10), in the case s is an odd integer, uses the parameter choice $\lambda = i\pi$. The resulting formula can be put in the following form. Let s be an odd integer ≥ 3. Then

(2.2.18)

$$\frac{2 - 2^{1-s}}{\pi^{s-1}} (-1)^{\frac{s+1}{2}} \zeta(s) = \sum_{k=1}^{\frac{s-3}{2}} \left(1 - \frac{1}{4^k}\right) \frac{(-1/\pi^2)^k}{(s-2k-1)!} \zeta(2k+1)$$

$$+ \frac{T_s}{(s-1)!}$$

where

$$T_s = \log 2 - \frac{1}{s-1} + \sum_{n=1}^{\infty} \frac{\zeta(2n)}{4^n \left(n + \frac{s-1}{2}\right)}$$

This relation between zetas at odd integer arguments is useful for calculating a few to a moderate number of such zeta values. For very large numbers of desired values, there is the option of doing the k-sum in (2.2.18) as a convolution. Note that for $s = 3$ the k-sum is in fact empty, and we have:

$$(2.2.19)$$

$$\zeta(3) = \frac{2\pi^2}{7}\left(\log 2 - \frac{1}{2} + \sum_{n=1}^{\infty} \frac{\zeta(2n)}{4^n(n+1)}\right)$$

As discussed in Problem 2.1.8, the notion of "peeling off" terms from the $\zeta(2n)$ numerator will acceleratre convergence. Thus for example a more rapidly converging relation for $\zeta(3)$ reads:

$$(2.2.20)$$

$$\frac{7}{2\pi^2}\zeta(3) = \log\frac{512}{81} - \frac{3}{2} + \sum_{n=1}^{\infty} \frac{\zeta(2n)-1}{4^n(n+1)}$$

Now the summands decay as 16^{-n}, so one resolves more than one decimal digit per iteration. One may attempt to carry this peeling practice somehow to its ultimate limit. Attempts to do so result in such oddities as:

$$(2.2.21)$$

$$\zeta(3) = \frac{5\pi^2}{36} - \frac{2\pi^2}{3}\sum_{n=1}^{\infty}\left\{-\frac{5}{12} - 2n^2 + \log\left[\frac{\left(1+\frac{1}{2n}\right)^{n(n+1)(2n+1)}}{\left(1-\frac{1}{2n}\right)^{n(n-1)(2n-1)}}\right]\right\}$$

which is evidently not too efficient. Evidently, as discussed in [Bailey *et. al.* 1995a] for computations relevant to the Khintchine constant, one should find the *optimal* number of terms to peel off the $\zeta(2n)$ numerator in these kinds of series. In the course of such study, the present author found a "peeled series" representation of the Catalan constant. The constant is defined as the Dirichlet series value:

$$C = \frac{1}{1^2} - \frac{1}{3^2} + \frac{1}{5^2} - \frac{1}{7^2} + \dots$$

$$\sim\ 0.9159655941772190150546035149323841077414937\dots$$

The new representation found is:

$$\frac{4}{\pi} C = -\frac{9}{4} + \frac{1}{2} \log \frac{123735750094056129455566640625}{193428131138340667955298816} +$$

$$\sum_{n=1}^{\infty} \frac{\zeta(2n) - 1}{n+1} \left(\frac{5}{2} \frac{1}{4^n} - \frac{1}{16^n} \right)$$

This means that the appropriate combination of C, π, and logarithm implicit in this last identity belongs to a class of zeta series with rational coefficients, to which class also belong the Khintchine means, as in (2.1.9), (2.1.10). Incidentally, beyond the Khintchine and Catalan constant, there is also a similar zeta-series formula for the Euler constant γ:

$$\gamma = 1 - \frac{1}{2} \log 2 - \sum_{k=3,\,\text{odd}}^{\infty} \frac{\zeta(k) - 1}{k} \qquad (2.2.22)$$

Yet another scheme for evaluation of $\zeta(\text{odd})$ is essentially due to Ramanujan and runs as follows [Bailey *et. al.* 1995a]:

$$(2.2.23)$$

$$\zeta(4N+1) = -\frac{2}{N} \sum_{k=1}^{\infty} \frac{(\pi k + N) e^{2\pi k} - N}{k^{4N+1} \left(e^{2\pi k} - 1 \right)^2} +$$

$$\frac{1}{2N\pi} \left\{ (2N+1)\zeta(4N+2) + \sum_{k=1}^{2N} (-1)^k 2k\zeta(2k)\zeta(4N+2-2k) \right\}$$

$$\zeta(4N+3) = -2 \sum_{k=1}^{\infty} \frac{1}{k^{4N+3} \left(e^{2\pi k} - 1 \right)} +$$

$$\frac{2}{\pi} \left\{ \frac{4N+7}{4} \zeta(4N+4) - \sum_{k=1}^{N} \zeta(4k)\zeta(4N+4-4k) \right\}$$

These formulae depend on knowledge of various values of $\zeta(\text{even})$. However, as seen in the next section, such values are not only easy to evaluate but can be done in a kind of parallel fashion.

Problem 2.2.10: Implement one or more schemes for evaluating $\zeta(3)$ to high precision. Compare the efficiencies of the schemes used. Besides Euler-Maclaurin there are the possible formulae (2.2.6), (2.2.10), (2.2.14), (2.2.18), and (2.2.20).

"Parallel" computation of zeta values

We have referred to "parallel" schemes for computation of zeta values. What is meant is, one can sometimes exploit information that exists in common across all zeta values in some class. In such circumstances, N separate zeta values can be computed in much less than N times the time to compute one isolated such value.

A primary example of this parallelism is embodied in the expansion (2.2.9), where the zeta values for non-negative *even* arguments appear. The notion of evaluating many $\zeta(\text{even})$ at once with this series has been exploited in studies relevant to Fermat's "Last Theorem," as discussed in Section 3.2; and in generating the requisite zeta values for such as the Khintchine constant representation (2.1.9) [Bailey *et. al.* 1995a] . Even the numbers $\zeta(3)$ as in (2.2.20) and the Catalan constant enjoy expansions that can be evaluated on the basis of large sets of $\zeta(\text{even})$ values. The following *Mathematica* example shows how very simple is the algorithm for generation of many $\zeta[\text{even}]$ values at once (Note: the functions ptake[ ] and precip[ ] are the fast polynomial functions in the code (1.5.9)) :

(2.2.23)

```
(* Algorithm for parallel generation of Zeta[even].
   Newton inversion of the Cot[] function's denominator
   polynomial is the key. *)
numzetas = 20;
prec = 40;
```

```
cos = Normal[Series[Cos[Pi x],{x,0,numzetas}]];
sin = Normal[Series[Sin[Pi x]/(Pi x),{x,0,numzetas}]];
Expand[N[-1/2 ptake[cos * precip[sin, numzetas],
        numzetas],prec]]
```

```
-0.5 + 1.6449340668482264364724151666466025189219 x²  +
   1.0823232337111381915160036965411167902775 x⁴  +
   1.0173430619844491397145179297909209020527902 x⁶  +
   1.0040773561979443393786852385086524652459 x⁸  +
   1.0009945751278180853371459589003190170 06 x¹⁰ +
   1.0002460865533080482986379980 4773967096  x¹² +
   1.0000612481350587048292585451051 35333747 x¹⁴
```

Note that each coefficient $\zeta(2)$ through $\zeta(14)$ is numerically correct and even the exact theoretical value $\zeta(0) = -1/2$ appears in the output.

In order to evaluate a great many ζ(even) values, the parallel scheme requires a correspondingly great deal of memory. This is because polynomials of large degree must be kept in storage. However, there is a technique known as "multisectioning" which decreases the memory requirement. Multisectioning is discussed in Section 3.2.

Problem 2.2.11: Implement a parallel scheme for numerical evaluations of ζ(even), in order to evaluate one or more of the following constants:

$$\zeta(3), \ C \text{ (Catalan constant)}, K_0 \text{ (Khintchine constant)}$$

or some other number of interest that enjoys a ζ(even) expansion. Note that the technique of multisectioning in Section 3.2 is recommended if, during massive parallel evaluation, one runs into memory limitations.

Problem 2.2.12: Implement a parallel scheme for numerical evaluations of ζ(even) to verify the identities:

$$\sum_{k=2,\text{ even}}^{\infty} (\zeta(k) - 1) = \frac{3}{4}$$

$$\sum_{k=2,\text{ even}}^{\infty} \frac{\zeta(k) - 1}{k} = \frac{1}{2}\log 2$$

Incidentally either of these relations (or both) can be put to good use in the numerical testing of a collection of many ζ(even).

Problem 2.2.13: Study the complexity of the parallel ζ(even) evaluation, that is, give the complexity of evaluating $\zeta(2)$ through $\zeta(2N)$, each of these to D decimal digits.

Problem 2.2.14: Investigate the computational complexity of the general Euler-Maclaurin algorithm which, by virtue of the appearance of Bernoulli numbers, can now, in principle, make use of the parallelization of zetas. Can such a combination of Euler-Maclaurin and parallel zeta values be competitive with the best known methods for evaluation of certain constants, such as the Euler constant γ [Borwein and Borwein 1987][Henrici 1977] ?

Problem 2.2.15: Show that, by peeling off the optimal number of successive terms from the $\zeta(2n)$ numerator in (2.2.20), and evaluating enough of the $\zeta(2n)$ in parallel, one can resolve $\zeta(3)$ to D good digits in

$$O(D \log D/\log \log D)$$

arithmetic operations. (One assumes here an arithmetic operation is a D-digit high-precision operation.) Determine whether the same complexity applies to *any* ζ(odd), or to the Khintchine or Catalan constants K_0 and C, respectively. The present author is unaware of any asymptotically faster scheme for a ζ(odd), or for K_0 or C.

As for parallel evaluation of ζ(odd), there are two basic approaches. One is to use recurrence relations for incomplete gamma, and the other is to endeavor to find a function that plays the role, for the ζ(odd), that the cotangent function did for the ζ(even). We shall discuss first the recurrence relation approach.

On the basis of the Riemann expansion (2.2.6) and the recurrence relation (2.2.11), it is evident that if we can evaluate *just once* the numbers

$$\Gamma(1/2, \pi n^2) \quad \text{(essentially the error function)}$$
$$\Gamma(0, \pi n^2) \quad \text{(the exponential integral)}$$

for a suitable range of n, then the only remaining work to resolve a large number of the ζ(odd) is to apply the recurrence within the summations. An explicit algorithm runs as follows:

$$(2.2.24)$$

Algorithm for parallel ζ(odd) evaluation:

Given: *lim*: meaning we shall calculate $\zeta(3), \zeta(5), \zeta(7), ..., \zeta(lim)$

   D: number of decimal digits required for each zeta value

1) Initialize three tables where each entry of each table is good to D digits:

$$\{\Gamma(1/2, \pi n^2), \{n, 1, [\sqrt{D}]\}\}$$
$$\{\Gamma(0, \pi n^2), \quad \{n, 1, [\sqrt{D}]\}\}$$
$$\{\theta(q) \,, \{q, -(lim-1)/2, (lim-3)/2\}\}$$

where we define

$$\theta(q) := \sum_{n=1}^{\left[\sqrt{D}\right]} \left(\pi n^2\right)^q e^{-\pi n^2}$$

2) Now execute the main loop:
   For $s = 3$ to *lim* step 2 {
      $t := s/2; \quad u := (1-s)/2;$

$$s_1 := \pi^t \sum_{n=1}^{-u} \theta(-n) \prod_{j=1}^{n}(t-j) + \prod_{j=1}^{[t]}(t-j) \sum_{n=1}^{[\sqrt{D}]} \frac{\Gamma(1/2, \pi n^2)}{n^s} ;$$

$$s_2 := -\pi^u \sum_{n=0}^{-1-u} \theta(n) \prod_{j=0}^{n} \frac{1}{u+j} + \frac{(-1)^u}{|u|!} \sum_{n=1}^{[\sqrt{D}]} \frac{\Gamma(0, \pi n^2)}{n^{1-s}} ;$$

$$\zeta(s) \sim \frac{\frac{\pi^t}{s(s-1)} + s_1 + \pi^{s-\frac{1}{2}} s_2}{\Gamma(\frac{s}{2})} ;$$

(* Record this zeta value, for each $s = 3, 5, 7, \ldots$ *)

}

It could be argued that the above algorithm suffers from the requirement of high-precision values for error function and exponential integral tables. Thus the algorithm is suitable only under both of the following conditions: some means are available for evaluating the special functions; and second, enough zeta values are desired that the time to evaluate those special functions is not too large a fraction of total time. The remarks in Section 2.4 later may be useful for the evaluation of the relevant special functions.

Now we turn to a second possible parallel approach for the $\zeta(\text{odd})$ values, which is to establish a generating function in the fashion of (2.2.9). It turns out that the standard psi function, which is the logarithmic derivative of the gamma function, can serve (at least theoretically) in this capacity. We have

$$\psi(z) = \frac{d \log \Gamma(z)}{dz} = \frac{\Gamma'(z)}{\Gamma(z)}$$

admitting of series expansion:

$$\psi(1-z) = -\gamma - \sum_{s=2}^{\infty} \zeta(s) z^{s-1} \qquad (2.2.25)$$

Unfortunately the psi function does not have any known elementary form. In fact, the $\zeta(\text{even})$ terms in the expansion (2.2.25) can be grouped into a cotangent term as we have previously, but that leaves a sum involving ζ(odd) that itself has no apparent elementary form. Still, the situation is not hopeless because one can use an approximation to the psi function, as follows. [Borwein and Borwein 1987] give an approximation to the gamma function, in the form:

(2.2.26)

$$\left| \Gamma(z) - N^z \sum_{k=0}^{6N} \frac{(-1)^k}{k!} \frac{N^k}{z+k} \right| \le 2Ne^{-N} \quad ; \ z \in [1,2]$$

where N is a positive integer. (The authors use this approximation to argue that the gamma function can be evaluated to D digits in $O(D^{1/2}\log^2 D)$ operations.) Now calculation of the derivative $\Gamma'(1-z)/\Gamma(1-z)$ from this approximation involves some convenient cancellation, and it suffices to evaluate numerically the logarithmic derivative of:

$$g_N(z) \ = \ \sum_{k=0}^{6N} \frac{(-1)^k}{k!} \frac{N^k}{k+1-z} \qquad\qquad (2.2.27)$$

as in the following *Mathematica* example, in which further enhancement appears (symbolic precomputation of series coefficients for the g_N function):

(2.2.28)

```
(* A semi-symbolic Newton method for zeta. *)
n = 30;
terms = 7;
prec = 20;
coe = Table[(-1)^(k-1) n^(k-1)/k!, {k,1,6n}];
c[m_] := Sum[N[coe[[k]]]/k^m, 2 prec], {k,1, 6n}];
den = N[Sum[c[k] z^k, {k,0,terms}], prec];
rat = D[den, z]/den;
ratse = N[Series[rat,{z,0,terms}], prec];
ratse - (ratse /. z->0)


1.644934066846875029 z + 1.20205690316179983 z^2  +
```

```
1.0823232337089505 z³  + 1.036927755144858 z⁴  +
1.01734306198371 z⁵  + 1.0083492773822 z⁶  -
228.2717112783364 z⁷  + O[z⁸]
```

The output reveals all values $\zeta(2)$, $\zeta(3)$, ..., $\zeta(7)$, with the value for $\zeta(8)$ having blown up, as will always happen on the highest term of the Newton inversion. The good zeta values are each correct to at least 11 digits, as expected for the choice of function g_{30} which should involve errors of order e^{-30}.

Problem 2.2.16: Implement a parallel scheme for numerical evaluations of $\zeta(\text{odd})$, and use this to evaluate a constant such as one of the Khintchine means K_p or the Euler constant γ.

Problem 2.2.17: Implement a parallel scheme for numerical evaluations of $\zeta(\text{odd})$, and use this to verify the relation

$$\sum_{k=3,\,\text{odd}}^{\infty} (\zeta(k) - 1) = \frac{1}{4}$$

Incidentally this is a good relation to use as a test of any parallel assessment of many $\zeta(\text{odd})$.

Problem 2.2.18: Is there an algorithm in the fashion of (2.2.24) that applies to *complex* values of s, for example complex values lying in an arbitrary arithmetic progression? For if such an algorithm can be effected, one could conceivably resolve a tightly meshed grid of values along Riemann's critical line.

Problem 2.2.19: Implement a psi function parallel scheme, with a goal to rendering the text methods much more efficient. In order for the algorithm embodied in (2.2.28) to be competitive with other schemes, the work must be reduced considerably.

2.3   *Multidimensional sums*

Euler sums

Beyond the Riemann zeta function, Euler also analyzed double sums of the form:

$$\zeta(r,s) = \sum_{n=2}^{\infty} \frac{1}{n^s} \sum_{m=1}^{n-1} \frac{1}{m^r} = \sum_{m<n} \frac{1}{n^s m^r} \qquad (2.3.1)$$

which enjoys a simple symmetry relation:

$$\zeta(r,s) + \zeta(s,r) = \zeta(r)\zeta(s) - \zeta(r+s) \qquad (2.3.2)$$

Beyond this, Euler himself knew that for *integers r, s* with $r + s$ odd,

$$(2.3.3)$$

$$\zeta(r,s) = -\frac{1}{2}\zeta(r+s) + \sum_{j=1,\,\text{odd}}^{r+s} \left\{ \binom{j-1}{s-1} + \binom{j-1}{r-1} \right\} \zeta(j)\,\zeta(r+s-j)$$

and further, that for s of any parity when $r = 1$,

$$\zeta(1,s) = \frac{s}{2}\zeta(s+1) - \frac{1}{2}\sum_{j=1}^{s-2}\zeta(j+1)\zeta(s-j) \qquad (2.3.4)$$

Few exact results are known beyond what one can glean from (2.3.2)-(2.3.4). There is a small set of interesting side relations, such as [D Borwein *et. al.* 1994]:

$$\zeta(2,4) = \zeta^2(3) - \frac{4}{3}\zeta(6)$$

yet, the sum $\zeta(6,2)$ and many others remain mysterious in the sense that finite evaluations in terms of fundamental numbers (such as Riemann zeta values) are unknown.

Recently, there have appeared converging series for general Euler sums, one such series being a generalization of the Euler formula (2.3.3), as follows [Crandall and Buhler 1995]:

$$(2.3.5)$$

$$\zeta(r,s) = -\frac{1}{2}\zeta(r+s) + \sum_{k=3,\text{ odd}}^{\infty} \Phi_k \sum_{j=0,\text{ even}}^{k-1} \binom{k}{j}\eta(r-j)\eta(s-k+j)$$

where η is the regular function:

$$\eta(s) = \left(1 - 2^{1-s}\right)\zeta(s)$$

and the coefficients Φ_k for $k \geq 3$ are defined:

$$\Phi_k = -\frac{2}{\pi}\sum_{d=1,\text{ odd}}^{k-2}(-1)^{(d-1)/2}\frac{\pi^d}{d!}\zeta(k-d+1)$$

The series (2.3.5) can be shown to agree with Euler (that is, terminate after a finite number of terms) when r, s are integers with $r+s$ odd. Unfortunately, when the series is infinite the convergence is slow. Happily, there exist series that converge more rapidly. An example is the following series with free parameter λ, $0 \leq |\lambda| < 2\pi$. When s is *not* an integer, we have:

$$(2.3.6)$$

$$\zeta(r,s) = \zeta(r)\zeta(s) - \frac{1}{\Gamma(r)}\sum_{m=1}^{\infty}\sum_{n=1}^{m}\frac{\Gamma(r,m\lambda)}{m^r n^s}$$

$$- \frac{1}{\Gamma(r)}\sum_{\mu=0}^{\infty}\frac{\zeta(s-\mu)(-1)^\mu}{\mu!}H_{\mu+r-1}(\lambda)$$

$$- \frac{\Gamma(1-s)}{\Gamma(r)}H_{r+s-2}(\lambda)$$

while for *s* integer, one avoids the singularity in the ζ summation above, and replaces the third line with the term:

$$\frac{(-1)^s}{\Gamma(r)\Gamma(s)}\left\{H_{s+r-2}(\lambda)\sum_{m=1}^{s-1}\frac{1}{m} - G_{s+r-2}(\lambda)\right\}$$

Here, the *H* and *G* functions are defined:

$$H_\nu(z) = \sum_{m=0}^{\infty}\frac{(-1)^m B_m z^{m+\nu}}{m!(m+\nu)} \quad ; \quad G_\nu(z) = \frac{d}{d\nu}H_\nu(z)$$

There is yet another approach, which involves trigonometric integral representations of the Euler sum, and which gives for the mysterious $\zeta(6,2)$ the following convergent series [Crandall and Buhler 1995]:

$$(2.3.7)$$

$$\zeta(6,2) = -\frac{1}{2}\zeta(8) - \frac{8\pi^6}{945}\sum_{j=1}^{7}\frac{a_j}{2^j}\left\{\sum_{n=0}^{\infty}\frac{\zeta(2n)}{4^n}\frac{1+(2n+j)(1-\log\pi)}{(2n+j)^2}\right.$$

$$\left. + \sum_{n=1}^{\infty}\frac{1}{4^n(2n+j)}\sum_{k=1}^{n}\frac{\zeta(2k)\zeta(2n-2k)}{k(2k+1)}\right\}$$

where the *a* sequence is $\{a_j\} = \{1, 0, -21, 0, 105, -126, 42\}$.

Problem 2.3.1: Calculate a high-precision value of the mystery sum $\zeta(2,6)$ using, say, convergent series (2.3.7). (Note that symmetry relation (2.3.2) makes this task essentially equivalent to calculating $\zeta(6,2)$.) Then use some other method, such as the free-parameter series (2.3.6), to obtain a numerical evaluation of $\zeta(3,5)$. Finally, test the following known theoretical relation to effect a strenuous check on all the calculations:

$$5\,\zeta(2,6) + 2\,\zeta(3,5) \;=\; 10\,\zeta(3)\zeta(5) - \frac{7\pi^8}{5400}$$

Problem 2.3.2: Verify numerically the following known theoretical relation:

$$\zeta(2,6) + \zeta(2,8) + \zeta(2,10) + \dots \;=\;$$
$$-\frac{1}{2} + \frac{\pi^2}{12} - \frac{\pi^4}{120} + \frac{4\pi^6}{2835} + \frac{1}{2}\zeta(3) - \zeta^2(3)$$

It is interesting that every term being summed on the left-hand side is an as-yet-unknown Euler sum.

Problem 2.3.3: The generalization (2.3.5) of the classical Euler identities suffers from slow convergence. A good open problem is: work out means, whether via some transformation or some convergence acceleration algorithm, by which the series can be rapidly summed.

Problem 2.3.4: Study the related sums [D Borwein *et. al.* 1994]:

$$\zeta^{\pm\pm}(r,s) \;=\; \sum_{n=2}^{\infty} \frac{(\pm 1)^n}{n^s} \sum_{m=1}^{n-1} \frac{(\pm 1)^{m-1}}{m^r}$$

for which Euler-like identities exist, and for which there are, as perhaps expected, "mysterious" cases, *i.e.* instances of *r, s* for which closed form evaluations are not known.

Problem 2.3.5: Consider the generalized multidimensional zeta sum:

$$\zeta(s_1, s_2, \ldots) \;=\; \sum_{0 < n_1 < n_2 < \ldots} \frac{1}{n_1^{\,s_1} n_2^{\,s_2} \cdots}$$

Establish rapidly convergent series for some dimension(s) higher than 2. Provide in this way numerical verification of interesting conjectures such as that of [Zagier 1994]:

$$\zeta(1, 3, 1, 3, \ldots, 1, 3) \;=\; \frac{2\pi^{4n}}{(4n+2)!}$$

where n is the total number of "1,3" pairs. One fascinating approach to these multidimensional sums is to invoke the formal identity:

$$\zeta(s_1, \ldots, s_m) \;=\; \frac{1}{\prod \Gamma(s_i)} \int_0^1 \cdots \int_0^1 \frac{dx_1 \ldots dx_m \left(\prod_{i=1}^{m-1} x_i^{\,m-i} \right) \prod_i \log^{s_i - 1} x_i}{(1 - x_1)(1 - x_1 x_2) \ldots (1 - \prod x_i)}$$

which follows upon substitution $u_i := \log x_i$ and elementary binomial expansion of the reciprocal of the integrand's denominator. There are then at least two interesting pathways down which to tread. One way is to use Monte Carlo integration, for example discrepancy integration [*Projects* 1994], to effect the m-dimensional integral. Note how convenient it is that the integral is over the positive unit m-cube. The second way is to attempt closed-form evaluation, perhaps using a symbolic processor. For example, the simplest case of the aforementioned Zagier conjecture, namely that of $\zeta(1,3)$, can be proved via:

$$\int_0^1 \int_0^1 \frac{a \log^2 a \, da \, db}{(1-a)(1-ab)} \;=\; \frac{\pi^4}{180}$$

This identity can be established by doing the b integral, then expressing the a integral as a mixed third derivative of a beta function.

For manipulation of three-dimensional zeta sums in particular, see [Markett 1994]. Incidentally, multidimensional sums have recently enjoyed application and relevance in theoretical physics; for example, in the connection between knot theory and quantum field theory. Along these lines [Broadhurst and Kreimer 1995] [Broadhurst 1992] find some interesting relations between multidimensional sums, all of this within the context of a ϕ^4 field theory.

The Madelung problem

The Madelung problem of chemistry and physics is to evaluate the electrostatic potential at the spatial origin, due to an infinite lattice of charges. Ignoring the self-potential of the origin charge in a perfect rock salt crystal (sodium chloride, or NaCl crystal) the Madelung constant M is the total electrostatic potential seen from the origin. This potential is, at least formally,

$$M = \sum_{x,y,z \in Z}{}' \frac{(-1)^{x+y+z}}{r} \tag{2.3.8}$$

where $r^2 = x^2 + y^2 + z^2$. The prime after the summation symbol means that the sum is to be carried out over all integer triples (x, y, z), these triples being the locations of + or − charges in the lattice, except that the singularity at the origin $(0,0,0)$ is to be avoided. It turns out that this sum only converges for certain summation strategies. For example, if you sum over ever-growing origin-centered cubes, the sum converges. But if you sum over ever-growing origin-centered spheres, the sum does *not* converge. It has become fashionable therefore to define M in a more uniform and rigorous fashion, in terms of a function of complex s:

$$M_3(s) = \sum_{x,y,z \in Z}{}' \frac{(-1)^{x+y+z}}{r^{2s}} \tag{2.3.9}$$

which is absolutely convergent for $Re(s) > 3/2$, analytically continued to the location $s = 1/2$. With this definition, $M_3(1/2)$ is the Madelung constant, and we may use the formidable apparatus of complex function theory to evaluate it. Although the constant is not yet known in closed form (as, say, a finite combination of more "fundamental" constants), it has been calculated to well over 1000 decimal places, starting out:

$$M_3(1/2) \quad \sim \quad -1.74756459463318219063621203554439740348516143666...$$

An important historical approach to the problem of evaluating M was to create a convergent series, in the spirit of (2.2.6), the latter as we have seen being one way to evaluate the Riemann zeta function. (After all, the definition (2.3.9) is a multidimensional zeta function, a particular instance of an Epstein zeta function.) To this end, we contemplate the introduction of an arbitrary integrable function and write the formal scaling relation:

$$M_3(s) \quad = \quad \frac{\int_0^\infty t^s \left\{ \sum_{x,y,z \in Z}{}' (-1)^{x+y+z} f(r^2 t) \right\} \frac{dt}{t}}{\int_0^\infty t^s f(t) \frac{dt}{t}} \tag{2.3.10}$$

The numerator and denominator are essentially Mellin transforms of index s of the function f. It is interesting that so much follows from the formal ratio (2.3.10), even though the derivation of (2.3.9) from the ratio is trivial: simply substitute variable $t \to u/r^2$ in the numerator integral; again, formally: because for rigor we require certain convergence properties of f and its Mellin transform. Now one choice of f is $f(x) = e^{-x}$. This causes the denominator of (2.3.10) to be $\Gamma(s)$, while the summation in the numerator is

$$\sum_{x,y,z \in Z}{}' (-1)^{x+y+z} e^{-\left(x^2+y^2+z^2\right)t} \quad = \quad \theta_4^3\left(e^{-t}\right) - 1$$

where we have introduced the Jacobi theta function

$$\theta_4(q) = \sum_{n \in Z} (-1)^n q^{n^2} \tag{2.3.11}$$

Now the Jacobi transformation:

$$\theta_4(e^{-t}) = \sqrt{\frac{\pi}{t}} \sum_{m \in O} e^{-\frac{\pi^2 m^2}{4t}} = \sqrt{\frac{\pi}{t}} \, \theta_2\left(e^{-\pi^2/t}\right) \tag{2.3.12}$$

where O denotes the set of (positive and negative) odd integers, can be applied in the numerator of (2.3.10) in the following way. In the spirit of Riemann, split the integral into one over $(0, \lambda)$ and another over (λ, ∞). The result of these machinations (the integral over $(0, \lambda)$ requires a change of variable $t \to 1/u$) is the following free-parameter form for the Madelung constant:

$$\tag{2.3.13}$$

$$\Gamma(s) \, M_3(s) = -\frac{\lambda^s}{s} + \sum_{x,y,z \in Z}{}' \frac{(-1)^{x+y+z}}{r^{2s}} \Gamma(s, \lambda r^2) +$$

$$\frac{\pi^{2s-3/2}}{2^{2s-3}} \sum_{x,y,z \in O} r^{2s-3} \Gamma\left(\frac{3}{2} - s, \frac{\pi^2 r^2}{4\lambda}\right)$$

which is essentially what is known historically as the Ewald expansion [Glasser and Zucker 1980]. For the physical Madelung case $s = 1/2$, the second sum has elementary summands, but the first sum involves $\Gamma(1/2, .)$ which is essentially an error function. This is not the first time we have encountered a need for evaluations of the error function, and we do finally turn to that subject later in this chapter.

In modern times, there have appeared elementary expansions for Madelung constants. It turns out to be possible to select f in (2.3.10) so that the resulting series, in the style of (2.3.13), involves only elementary evaluations (and not, for example, error functions or other special functions). One example starts from $f(x) = \operatorname{sech}^2 x$ as follows [Crandall and Buhler 1987]:

$$(2.3.14)$$

$$M_3\left(\frac{1}{2}\right) = -\lambda + \sum_{x,y,z \in Z} ' \frac{(-1)^{x+y+z}}{r}(1 - \tanh \lambda r) +$$

$$\frac{2\pi}{\lambda} \sum_{x,y,z \in O} \frac{1}{r} \operatorname{csch}\left(\frac{\pi^2 r}{2\lambda}\right)$$

where as usual, $r^2 = x^2 + y^2 + z^2$ and in this case, λ is any positive real parameter. It is interesting that such elementary function expansions can be derived for any periodic neutral charge structure. But for the case of NaCl and a few other special crystals, there exist even simpler expansions. In fact, the NaCl Madelung constant can be cast in terms of only two-dimensional summations, such as the following due to Hautot [Crandall and Buhler 1987]:

$$M_3\left(\frac{1}{2}\right) = -\frac{\pi}{2} + 3 \sum_{x,y \in Z} '(-1)^x \frac{\operatorname{csch} \pi r}{r} \qquad (2.3.15)$$

where $r^2 = x^2 + y^2$, or a fairly old and elegant expansion due to Sherman [Glasser and Zucker 1980]:

$$M_3\left(\frac{1}{2}\right) = -12\pi \sum_{x,y \in O^+} \operatorname{sech}^2\left(\frac{\pi}{2}r\right) \qquad (2.3.16)$$

where in this case the sum is carried out over all pairs of positive odd integers.

Certain evaluations for other dimensions than the third, as well as improvements in the physical third dimension case, can be obtained via more Jacobi theta function identities. For example,

$$\theta_4^{\,2}(q) = 1 + 4 \sum_{n=1}^{\infty} \frac{(-1)^n q^{2n-1}}{1 - q^{2n-1}} \qquad (2.3.17)$$

$$\theta_4{}^4(q) \;=\; 1 + 8 \sum_{\substack{m>0 \\ m\equiv 1,2,3 \,(\mathrm{mod}\,4)}} \frac{m(-q)^m}{1-(-q)^m} \tag{2.3.18}$$

are identities that can be applied to two- and four-dimensional Madelung problems respectively. Using further identities due to [Glasser and Zucker 1980] it has been shown for example that the NaCl Madelung constant can be written [Crandall and Buhler 1987]:

$$\tag{2.3.19}$$

$$M_3\!\left(\frac{1}{2}\right) \;=\; -2\pi + 2^{7/4}\left(\sum_{n\in Z} e^{\frac{-\pi}{\sqrt{2}}\left(n-\frac{1}{2}\right)^2} \right)^2 +$$

$$2\sum_{n=1}^{\infty}(-1)^n \frac{r_3(n)}{\sqrt{n}} \frac{1}{\left(e^{4\pi\sqrt{n}}+1\right)}$$

where $r_3(n)$ denotes the number of representations of n as a sum of three integral squares. This particular formula is close to the truth (gives the Madelung constant to five decimals) even if one neglects the final summation. Along these lines, it turns out that one could finally resolve the NaCl Madelung constant in closed form, if one knew a sharp enough asymptotic evaluation of the function:

$$S(t) \;=\; \sum_{x,y,z\in O} \frac{\mathrm{csch}\,\pi t r}{r} \tag{2.3.20}$$

for small t.

Problem 2.3.6: Perform a high-precision numerical evaluation of the NaCl Madelung constant, using one of the formulae (2.3.14), (2.3.15), (2.3.16) or (2.3.19). Which of these seems most efficient?

Problem 2.3.7: Denote the Madelung constant for a d-dimensional lattice of $\pm$ charges as $M_d(1/2)$. Using simple summation, or for $d > 1$ using Jacobi identities such as (2.3.17), (2.3.18) derive the exact evaluations:

$$M_1\left(\frac{1}{2}\right) = -2\log 2$$

$$M_2\left(\frac{1}{2}\right) = -4\zeta\left(\frac{1}{2}\right)\beta\left(\frac{1}{2}\right)\left(1 - \sqrt{2}\right)$$

$$M_4\left(\frac{1}{2}\right) = -8\zeta\left(\frac{1}{2}\right)\zeta\left(-\frac{1}{2}\right)\left(1 - \sqrt{2}\right)\left(1 - 2^{3/2}\right)$$

for 1-, 2- and 4-dimensional "salt crystals" respectively. Here, the β function is the analytic continuation of

$$\beta(s) = \sum_{n \in O^+} \frac{(-1)^{(n-1)/2}}{n^s}$$

(a sum over positive odd indices) whose value $\beta(2)$ we have already encountered as the Catalan constant.

Problem 2.3.8: Investigate the Delord conjecture, which says the following [Crandall and Buhler 1990]. Whereas the sum (2.3.8) is known *not* to converge if carried out over ever-growing origin-centered spheres, J. F. Delord conjectured that if we *subtract out the net electrostatic potential due to the charge error* at radius R, then the resulting sum with correction should converge. What the conjecture says, then, is:

$$\lim_{R \to \infty} \sum_{\substack{x,y,z \in Z \\ x^2+y^2+z^2 < R^2}}' \left(\frac{(-1)^{x+y+z}}{\sqrt{x^2 + y^2 + z^2}} - \frac{(-1)^{x+y+z}}{R} \right) = M_3\left(\frac{1}{2}\right)$$

The Delord conjecture is known to be true, but still the investigation of the convergence phenomena is instructive. Avenues of study include proving the conjecture in some new way (the extant proof uses properties of multidimensional zeta functions), or accumulating impressive numerical evidence that the limit is correct, and so on. Incidentally the conjecture has an elegant physical interpretation; namely, if one cut a sphere of radius R out of an NaCl crystal, then there would be in general a net charge to the ball, and nature would endeavor to neutralize that with the asymptotically precise surface charge to correct the Madelung potential at the origin. Nature's way of establishing the above limit formula and stabilizing a crystal!

Problem 2.3.9: The following problem was communicated to the author, on the idea that the plain volume of a unit d-dimensional sphere is *not* monotonic at d, rather peaks at $d \sim 5$ [Wheeler 1995]: "Are the Madelung constants $M_d(1/2)$ monotonic in d?" They certainly are for $d = 1,2,3,4$; but some kind of numerical analysis using a correct generalization of the various Madelung series is called for.

Problem 2.3.10: Here is the kind of tantalizing open problem that, in all probability, will either lead nowhere or give rise to a powerful line of analysis. It is evident (Problem (2.3.7), Jacobi identities (2.3.17), (2.3.18)) that the Madelung constants are evaluable in terms of fundamental numbers for 1, 2, and 4 dimensions. One explanation for the crisis in three dimensions is the lack of suitable Jacobi-like identities for the cube of the function θ_4. Yet, magically enough, there is a beautiful new identity developed by [Andrews 1986]:

$$\theta_4{}^3(q) = 1 + 4 \sum_{n=1}^{\infty} \frac{(-q)^n}{1+q^n} - 2 \sum_{\substack{n=1 \\ |k|<n}}^{\infty} q^{n^2-k^2} \frac{(1-q^n)(-1)^k}{1+q^n}$$

The open problem, then, is to apply this new identity in an effort to resolve the physical Madelung constant $M_3(1/2)$.

Integer relation algorithms

Recently there have appeared some strong algorithms for testing whether certain numerical values are in fact combinations of other values; especially: "Is such-and-such a number, given in decimal, a combination of fundamental constants?" As explained in [Bailey *et. al.* 1994], it was in 1993 that E. Au-Yeung, an undergraduate at the University of Waterloo, noticed the *merely numerical* coincidence:

$$\sum_{k=1}^{\infty} \frac{\left(1 + \frac{1}{2} + \dots + \frac{1}{k}\right)^2}{k^2} \sim 4.59987\dots \sim \frac{17}{4} \zeta(4) \qquad (2.3.21)$$

based on summation of 500000 terms. Surprisingly perhaps, the $17\zeta(4)/4$ approximation still held fast after computations to 100 decimals. The relation has by now been proved, and there is no question that, generally speaking, such research is aided by numerical coincidence. For one thing, upon seeing what the numerical value might be, one can usually focus, then, on a particular field of analysis in an effort to prove exact equality.

One aspect of integer relation theory starts with a vector $x = (x_1, x_2, \dots, x_n)$ of real numbers, and we ask whether there exists an integer vector $a = \{a_i\}$ whose dot product with x vanishes. An integer relation algorithm, then, is one which *exhaustively* rules out any such dot product relation up to some bound on the a_i. The history of this algorithm development is interesting. A typical result is as follows. While it is known that

$$\zeta(n) = Q_n \sum_{k=1}^{\infty} \frac{(-1)^{nk}}{k^n \binom{2k}{k}} \quad ; \quad n = 2, 3, 4 \qquad (2.3.22)$$

where each of $Q_{2,3,4}$ is a rational coefficient, the hypothesis that $\zeta(5)$ is of the same form seems to fail. It is now known on the basis of integer relation algorithms that, if Q_5 satisfies a polynomial of degree ≤ 25 with integral coefficients, then the Euclidean norm of said coefficients must exceed 2 x 10^{37} [Bailey *et. al.* 1994]. Such results can be derived on the basis of a modern variant called the "PSLQ" algorithm (for "Partial Sum of squares and LQ matrix factorization").

A *Mathematica* implementation of the PSLQ integer relation detection algorithm is listed in the Appendix as "PSLQ.ma." Details of theory and practice can be found in [Bailey *et. al.* 1994][Ferguson and Bailey 1994].

Problem 2.3.11: It is known that for any positive integer n the integral

$$I_n = \int_0^{1/2} x^n \cot \pi x \, dx$$

is a rational linear combination of numbers from the set $\{(\log 2)/\pi, \zeta(3)/\pi^3, \zeta(5)/\pi^5, \zeta(7)/\pi^7, ...\}$. For example,

$$I_5 = \frac{\log 2}{32\pi} - \frac{15}{32\pi^3} \zeta(3) + \frac{225}{64\pi^5} \zeta(5)$$

Using numerical integer relation methods, find some other I_n. There are no known relations for nonintegral n, but perhaps such can be found in this way. A good open question is: "What are the corresponding integrals for integer n but with upper integration limit 1/4." It is likely that the Catalan constant will figure strongly in such an investigation.

Problem 2.3.12: Use some flavor of integer relation software (such as the Appendix example "PSLQ.ma") to find (*i.e.* find "blindly" because the exact rationals are known in the literature) Q_2, Q_3, Q_4 for the zeta relations (2.3.22). A maximum Euclidean norm of 100 will do.

Problem 2.3.13: It is unknown whether the Euler constant γ be irrational. On the assumption that $\gamma = a/b$, for integers a and b, obtain a lower bound on b.

Problem 2.3.14: Find a quintic polynomial with (reasonably small) integer coefficients that possesses a root lying no more than 10^{-30} away from:

$$-1.277883036387392943188151033564172541018\overline{17}$$

Problem 2.3.15: Find a *numerical* representation (to 12 digits, say) of the integral

$$\int_0^1 \frac{dx}{1+x^3}$$

as a combination $(a \log 2 + b \ \pi/\sqrt{3})$, where a and b are rational. Indeed there exists such an exact representation of the integral and most modern *symbolic* processors should be able to find it.

2.4   *Examples of special function evaluation*

Gamma function

Recently there has appeared a very efficient algorithm for evaluation of the gamma function for arbitrary complex z. [Spouge 1994] has improved upon a classical Lanczos algorithm, by giving an especially simple correction to the celebrated Stirling formula. The Spouge theorem may be paraphrased as follows. For a real parameter $a \geq 3$, set an integer parameter $N = ceiling(a)$ -1. Then the approximation:

$$(2.4.1)$$

$$\Gamma(z) \ \sim \ \sqrt{2\pi} \ (z+a-1)^{z-1/2} \ e^{-z-a+1}\left(1 + \sum_{k=1}^{N} \frac{c_k}{z+k-1}\right)$$

where

$$c_k \ = \ \frac{1}{\sqrt{2\pi}} \ \frac{(-1)^{k-1}}{(k-1)!} \ (a-k)^{k-1/2} e^{a-k}$$

has *relative* error not exceeding

$$\frac{\sqrt{a}}{(2\pi)^{a+1/2}} \frac{1}{Re(z+a)}$$

This is, practically speaking, a very sharp error bound. In fact, for z positive real, the relative error is less than $(2\pi)^{-a}$. But even if z is not real, one can with impunity take its real part to be $\geq 1/2$, and establish a lower bound on parameter a to guarantee some relative accuracy of choice. Such a choice for a appears in the recursive program below. The series (2.4.1) is reminiscent certainly of the [Borwein and Borwein 1987] approximation (2.2.26). A *Mathematica* example of a recursive gamma function, which example allows restriction of the argument z always to $Re(z) \geq 1/2$, is as follows:

(2.4.2)

```
(* [Spouge 1994] algorithm for the gamma function. *)
digs = 20;
(* Next, guarantee digs correct digits by choice of a.
   The 5/4 factor is to guarantee precision over all
   complex arguments.  *)
a = Ceiling[N[5/4 digs/Log[10, 2Pi]]];
c[k_] := 1/Sqrt[2Pi] (-1)^(k-1)/(k-1)! *
                (-k+a)^(k-1/2) Exp[-k+a];
gam[z_] := If[Re[z] < 1/2, Pi Csc[Pi z]/gam[1-z],
              (z+a-1)^(z-1/2) Exp[-z-a+1] Sqrt[2Pi] *
              (1 + Sum[c[k]/(z+k-1) ,{k,1,Ceiling[a]-1}])
          ];

Abs[N[gam[1 + 7 I], 50]] - N[Sqrt[7 Pi/Sinh[7 Pi]], 50]

1. 10^-44
```

Note that about 40 digits of relative accuracy are achieved in this example, even though we asked for digs = 20 digits. The error bound specified by "digs" is therefore conservative. Note also that we have used a convenient checking relation for certain complex arguments to gamma, namely:

$$|\Gamma(1 + iy)| = \sqrt{\frac{\pi y}{\sinh \pi y}}$$

Problem 2.4.1: Implement a high-precision Spouge algorithm to evaluate the gamma function over the entire complex plane, where the only input parameter
is the number of good decimal digits for both real and imaginary parts. Note that in the *Mathematica* example (2.4.2), it is possible to change the *a* parameter definition to be argument-dependent, so that a more efficient program obtains for real arguments to gamma.

Problem 2.4.2: Attempt an implementation of the psi function, which is the logarithmic derivative of gamma, with the goal of generating values of $\zeta(\text{integer})$, in the style of (2.2.26)-(2.2.28).

Problem 2.4.3: Can the Spouge series be accelerated, in the sense of the general hypergeometric acceleration described in [Borwein and Borwein 1987], to yield D good digits for gamma in significantly less than $O(D)$ operations?

Problem 2.4.4: Can the Spouge algorithm be rendered significantly faster by "ratcheting up" the argument, as follows? One would be given the argument z, then compute $\Gamma(z + K)$ for a carefully chosen positive integer K, then divide by $(z+K-1)(z+K-2)...(z)$ to yield the desired $\Gamma(z)$. The point would be, that the larger real part of $z + K$ might allow sufficiently faster convergence, but one has to balance this with the cost of the ratcheting and product division.

Error function

We have encountered already at various junctures a need for high-precision evaluations of the error function. A multifaceted approach for *erfc*(*z*) uses:

• Ascending series, for small $|z|$;
• Asymptotic series, for large $|z|$;
• Perhaps, a continued fraction representation for intermediate $|z|$.

These methods are discussed in several references, *e.g.* [*Projects* 1994]. Yet, in the 1960's there was an interesting development that deserves attention. Using an adroit application of Plana's theorem and contour integration, [Chiarella and Reichel 1968] derived the following interesting formula:

(2.4.3)

$$erfc(z) = \frac{e^{-z^2}\varepsilon z}{\pi}\left(\frac{1}{z^2} + 2\sum_{m=1}^{\infty}\frac{e^{-m^2\varepsilon^2}}{m^2\varepsilon^2 + z^2}\right) + \frac{2}{1 - e^{2\pi z/\varepsilon}} + O\!\left(e^{-\pi^2/\varepsilon^2}\right)$$

where one chooses a small parameter $0 < \varepsilon < \pi/z$. It turns out that the implied big-*O* constant can be taken to be 3. The following *Mathematica* example shows how to handle precision issues for this remarkable algorithm:

(2.4.4)

```
(* [Chiarella and Reichel 1968] algorithm for
   the error function. *)
prec = 50;
h = 1/Sqrt[prec];
lim = Floor[N[prec] Sqrt[Log[10]]];
erfc[z_] := 1/Pi E^(-z^2) h z * (1/z^2 +
            2 Sum[ E^(-m^2 h^2)/(m^2 h^2 + z^2),{m,1,lim}] +
            2/(1-E^(2 Pi z/h));
N[erfc[1], prec]

0.15729920705028513065877936491739074070393300020337
```

Problem 2.4.5: Implement the above high-precision error function algorithm, and apply it to various calculations mentioned previously in this chapter; for example to zeta function evaluation (parallel or otherwise), or to evaluation of multidimensional sums.

Problem 2.4.6: Estimate the theoretical complexity for resolution of an erfc() value to D good decimal digits.

Problem 2.4.7: Use calculated error function values to create Gaussian normal distributed random variables, suitable for Monte Carlo applications. Start by building a table of values of a certain inverse function $I(z)$, with z in $(0,1)$, with I defined:

$$\frac{1}{\sqrt{\pi}} \int_{-\infty}^{I(z)} e^{-t^2}\, dt \;=\; z$$

Now, for *uniformly* distributed random z in $(0,1)$, determine an approximation to $I(z)$ via linear interpolation, say, on the stored table values of I. The resulting random variable $I(z)$ will be Gaussian normal, with variance 1/2.

Problem 2.4.8: Here is an important, and to the present author's knowledge, open problem: work out an analogous algorithm to (2.4.3) for the incomplete gamma function $\Gamma(a, z)$, whose instance $a = 1/2$ would essentially be the Chiarella and Reichel error function method. The present author feels that one promising approach would be to attempt Poisson summation of an appropriate generalization of the summation in (2.4.3), using at some key juncture in the analysis the integral representation:

$$\Gamma\left(a, z^2\right) \;=\; \frac{2\, z^{2a}\, e^{-z^2}}{\Gamma(1-a)} \int_0^\infty \frac{t^{1-2a} e^{-t^2}\, dt}{t^2 + z^2}$$

The n-th Fermat number is:

$$F_n = 2^{2^n} + 1$$

so F_{22} is, in *binary*, 100000 . . . 000001 where the number of zeros is 4194303. The printed *decimal* digits of F_{22} would comprise a thick book.

Pepin theorem:

F_n for positive n is a prime number if and only if it evenly divides

$$3^{2^{2^n-1}} + 1$$

Squaring chain:

Start with 3 (in binary) and square exactly 4194303 times, always reducing the square modulo F_{22}. Each of the squarings can be performed via a DWT (discrete weighted transform) for maximum speed:

$$00 \ldots\ldots\ldots\ldots\ldots .000000000011 \quad (= 3)$$
$$00 \ldots\ldots\ldots\ldots\ldots .000000001001 \quad (= 9)$$
$$\ldots$$
$$01 \ldots\ldots\ldots\ldots\ldots .011100101010 \quad (= \text{final Pepin residue})$$

If this $\uparrow$ final leading bit were 1, F_{22} would be prime; but the bit is zero, so F_{22} must be composite.

The story of F_{22}, the twenty-second Fermat number. This calculation is perhaps the longest ever performed for a one-bit answer. Using the classical Pepin theorem, about four million squarings of F_{22}-sized integers resulted in a final residue whose leading bit resolved the character of F_{22}. A North American team, and independently a Brazilian team carried out the calculation, with precise agreement on the final residue.

3 Number-theoretical algorithms

This question [whether there be infinitely many Wilson primes] seems to be of such a character that if I should come to life after my death and some mathematician were to tell me it had been definitely settled, I think I would immediately drop dead again.

[*Vandiver, quoted in [Ribenboim* 1988]]

Number theory–might we call it the study of those solemn games at which the integers perpetually play? The noble and satisfying study of the integers has two main branches: theoretical and computational. Herein we investigate some new approaches to open problems, and we do so primarily–but not exclusively– from the computational perspective.

3.1 Primes

Mersenne primes

The current largest explicitly known prime number is the Gage-Slowinski prime:

$$2^{859433} - 1$$

possessed of more than 250000 decimal digits. We convey an idea of scale by mentioning that these digits if printed out in full would essentially fill an issue of a typical magazine. As a member of the class of Mersenne primes, *i.e.* primes of the form $p = 2^q - 1$, such a number is relatively easy to test for primality. In fact we have the Lucas-Lehmer test for such p:

$$(3.1.1)$$

Algorithm (Lucas-Lehmer test) for assessing primality of $p = 2^q - 1$:

1) Set $x_0 := 4$;
2) For $n := 1$ to $q-2$

$$x_n := x_{n-1}^2 - 2 \pmod{p}$$

3) Then p is prime if and only if the last iterate x_{q-2} vanishes $\pmod{p}$.

It is hard to imagine a simpler primality test, as the algorithm requires only $O(q) = O(\log p)$ squarings to provide a definitive conclusion. Still, the reason for the scarcity of known explicit primes in the region of the Gage-Slowinski example is that one would have to do about q squarings, modulo a number of q bits. Furthermore, all of this needs to be done for various primes q until an actual Mersenne prime is found. (It is elementary that if $p = 2^q - 1$ is prime then q is prime.)   One might think that sieving out small prime divisors of candidates $2^q - 1$ would rule out many exponents q, but in practice one can only remove roughly half of all possible prime exponents. One uses the known theorem that if a prime r divides p, then r is necessarily of the form $2kq + 1$. Thus the possible prime factors of a Mersenne primality candidate (that if found would rule out said candidate) are disappointingly scarce. The impressive $2^{859433} - 1$ was found by "casting about" on a supercomputer, testing various prime exponents q that survived some moderate sieving. Because the tested q were not taken from a contiguous sequence, it is not even clear how many Mersenne primes exist up through this largest one, or even whether additional Mersenne primes exist in the neighborhood of this largest known case. (A complete table of what Mersenne primes are known through 1994 appears in [*Projects* 1994], where it also is proposed that a good milestone for the year 2000 would be the complete exhaustion of all exponents q less than one million.)

Since the testing of Mersenne primes comes down to squaring $\pmod{p}$ it is interesting to investigate the relative efficiencies of various squaring and mod methods. First, there is the Mersenne mod technique described in Section 1.2, whereby a Mersenne mod becomes essentially a shift/add operation. Then in Section 1.3 we discussed multiplication enhancements, such as Karatsuba and FFT methods. One should note also, as in Problem 1.3.7, that there exist alternative convolution schemes with which one might in principle perform the requisite squarings.

In the face of these interesting squaring alternatives, we present here a recently developed squaring algorithm specific to Mersenne arithmetic (meaning the manipulation of numbers modulo a Mersenne number 2^q-1). Observe first that if an integer x be written:

$$x = \sum_{k=0}^{q-1} x_k 2^k \qquad (3.1.2)$$

where the $\{x_k\}$ are the binary bits of x, then the square of x (mod p), where $p = 2^q-1$, is given by:

$$x^2 = \sum_{k=0}^{q-1} z_k 2^k \pmod{p} \qquad (3.1.3)$$

where the $\{z_k\}$ are the components of the cyclic autoconvolution of x with itself; that is, the z sequence is defined:

$$z_n = \sum_{i+j=n \,(\mathrm{mod}\, q)}^{q-1} x_i x_j \qquad (3.1.4)$$

In this way we can in principle effect a squaring x^2 (mod p) via a cyclic convolution of a sequence with itself, which sequence being comprised of the binary bits of x. There are two problems with this approach. First, on most machinery, arithmetic operations on single bits are relatively inefficient; and second, the length q of the convolution (3.1.4) is not generally a power of two (the usual convenient length for many convolution algorithms). It turns out that both of these difficulties can be surmounted, and furthermore only one basic observation so surmounts and leads to a successful algorithm. One might look longingly at (3.1.2) and observe that, if we could use not base 2 but an *irrational* base $2^{q/N}$, where N will be a power of two, then the digit representation in the new base, written:

$$x = \sum_{k=0}^{N-1} X_k 2^{qk/N} \tag{3.1.5}$$

will provide the square of x modulo p via the relation:

$$x^2 = \sum_{k=0}^{N-1} Z_k 2^{qk/N} \pmod{p} \tag{3.1.6}$$

where the Z sequence is the cyclic convolution of order N:

$$Z_n = \sum_{i+j=n\,(\mathrm{mod}\,N)}^{N-1} X_i X_j \tag{3.1.7}$$

Now we have a power-of-two length for the cyclic convolution (3.1.7), but the digits X_k for the irrational base expansion are generally irrational themselves. A way around this, which simultaneously yields power-of-two run length and integer digits, is to adopt the "next best thing" to an irrational base; namely, a variable base representation.

To this end, define a variable base according to successive integral word lengths

$$b_k = ceiling\left(\frac{qk}{N}\right) - ceiling\left(\frac{q(k-1)}{N}\right) \tag{3.1.8}$$

for $k = 1, 2, ...$. In such variable base representation, a given x can be represented by unique digits D_i according to:

$$x = D_0 + D_1 2^{b_1} + D_2 2^{b_1+b_2} + \ldots = \sum_{k=0}^{N-1} D_k 2^{\sum_{i=1}^{k} b_i} \qquad (3.1.9)$$

where each D_i is an integer lying in $[0, 2^{b_{i+1}}-1]$. Now this representation, in view of the telescopic nature of the definition (3.1.8), can be written:

$$x = \sum_{k=0}^{N-1} D_k 2^{ceiling(qk/N)} \qquad (3.1.10)$$

It is at this juncture where the notion of weighted convolution comes into play. We cannot simply take the cyclic convolution of (3.1.10), for although this would be an integer convolution, it will not be the Mersenne square. There is, however, a modified convolution that *does* give the correct Mersenne square x^2 (mod p), as follows. Let a so-called weight signal a be defined

$$a_k = 2^{ceiling(qk/N)-qk/N} \qquad (3.1.11)$$

This is generally an irrational number, but there is a numerical convenience: a_k is always relegated to the interval [1,2). Consider now the weighted signal denoted formally $w = a D$, meaning that w is comprised of componentwise products: $w_k = a_k D_k$. It can be shown [Crandall and Fagin 1994] that the square of x is now correctly given by:

$$x^2 = \sum_{k=0}^{N-1} c_k 2^{ceiling(qk/N)} \pmod{p} \qquad (3.1.12)$$

where c is the weighted autoconvolution:

$$c_n = \frac{1}{a_n} \sum_{i+j=n \, (mod \, N)}^{N-1} w_i w_j \qquad (3.1.13)$$

Furthermore it can be shown that each of these c components is an integer.

What we have succeeded in doing is providing a convolution scheme (3.1.13) for x^2 (mod p) that has power of two length. This means that, provided we have means of handling to sufficiently high precision the arithmetic associated with the irrational weights a_k, any of the well known convolution schemes that assume such run lengths may be applied to the problem of Mersenne primality testing. (In particular, if FFTs are used for the convolution, there is no zero padding of any kind in this scheme.) The following *Mathematica* example shows how in this way one may compute a square, in this example, (mod $2^{521}-1$):

$$(3.1.14)$$

```
(* Weighted convolution for squaring modulo a Mersenne
   prime.*)

q = 521; p = 2^q-1; n = 16;
(* Next, the variable base bit lengths. *)
b = Table[Ceiling[q j/n]-Ceiling[q(j-1)/n],{j,1,n}];
(* Next, the signal weights. *)
a = Table[2^(Ceiling[q j/n] - (q j)/n), {j,0,n-1}];
(* Next, a grammar-school cyclic to test the concept. *)
cyc[x_, y_] := Table[Sum[x[[i+1]] y[[1+Mod[m-i,n]]]
        ,{i,0,n-1},{m,0,n-1}];
digits[x_] := Module[{= Table[0,{n}], y = x, r}
                Do[ d[[r+1]] = Mod[y, 2^b[[r+1]]];
                    y = Floor[y/2^b[[r+1]]]
                    ,{r,0,n-1}]
                ];
                d
            ];
undigits[d_] := Sum[d[[r+1]] 2^Sum[b[[k]],{k,1,r}],{r,0,n-1}];

(* Next, choose an x to be squared (mod p). *)
x = 19443399776139590227069989271238943039600788\
    19206228746492652527463695110140703949431520\
    64743634429899282279152972637295012755204078\
```

```
    33280191033309503743297161;
d = digits[x];
Print["The digits of x are:"];
Print[d];
(* Next, the weighted signal and weighted convolution. *)
w = a d;
c = Round[1/a cyc[w, w]];   (* These must be integers! *)
Print["x^2 (mod p) = ", Mod[undigits[c], p]];
```

When this example is run, the choices $q = 521$, $n = 16$ yield the following variable bit-lengths for the digits of x:

$$(3.1.15)$$

$$b = \{33, 33, 32, 33, 32, 33, 32, 33, 33, 32, 33, 32, 33, 32, 33, 32\}$$

giving the chosen input x the digits:

$$d = \{2566293129, 3445994888, 159263879, 5780259887,$$
$$2117979611, 6871835258, 257878631, 2099087185,$$
$$7599433523, 186317888, 5694928729, 3604803920,$$
$$2903761032, 1830661269, 5555530111, 1216478187\}$$

To be clear, we note that all of this means x has a representation:

$$x = 2566293129 + 3445994888 * 2^{33} + 159263879 * 2^{33+33} +$$

$$5780259887 * 2^{33+33+32} + ...$$

The weight signal, which is where all of the irrational numbers in this scheme are "concentrated," reads:

$$a = \{1, 2^{7/16}, 2^{7/8}, 2^{5/16}, 2^{3/4}, 2^{3/16}, 2^{5/8}, 2^{1/16}, \qquad (3.1.16)$$

$$2^{1/2}, 2^{15/16}, 2^{3/8}, 2^{13/16}, 2^{1/4}, 2^{11/16}, 2^{1/8}, 2^{9/16}\}$$

(As we discuss in a moment, an actual implementation for large Mersenne numbers will normally involve floating-point components for a rather than these symbolic ones.) After the step $w := a\,d$ we have a weighted signal w which, due to general irrationality of the a components, must be considered a floating point number or some high-precision equivalent. Note that the Round[ ] function near the end of the program may not be necessary if your processor correctly cancels *symbolically* the involved fractional powers of 2, but the rounding is absolutely necessary if the weighted convolution's final integer result is being achieved via floating point within the convolution algorithm.

To use this weighted convolution approach in a Lucas-Lehmer test, one needs an extra step inserted after each weighted convolution and subtraction of two; *i.e.*, after one obtains a new Lucas-Lehmer iterate. The extra step is that x_n obtained in step (2) of Algorithm (3.1.1) must be given the proper variable-base representation (3.1.9); *i.e.*, with consistent constraints on the digits D_i. One way to effect this constant re-alignment is to perform add-with-carry, immediately after the weighted convolution (step $w := a\,d$ in the *Mathematica* example). For it is here in the whole procedure that the "digits;" that is, elements of w, are generally larger than the allowed magnitudes on the variable-base digits. Aside from this add-carry adjustment, one may use this weighted convolution scheme to effect a complete Lucas-Lehmer test. Using signal length of $N = 2^{16}$ and floating-point FFT-based convolution, it is possible to verify the primality of $2^{859433}-1$, on a typical modern workstation, in about one week.

Problem 3.1.1: Show the theoretical result that, for q prime and N a power of two, the variable-base bit-lengths defined by (3.1.8) take on at most two distinct values, as exemplified by (3.1.15).

Problem 3.1.2: Show the theoretical result that each of the components of the c signal, as defined by (3.1.13), is an integer.

Problem 3.1.3: The *Mathematica* example of Mersenne squaring uses a grammar-school cyclic convolution just for testing the whole concept.

Implement (in some language of choice) a fast convolution algorithm (see Chapter 4) and after that, a complete Lucas-Lehmer test for Mersenne prime candidates.

Problem 3.1.4: Compare the execution speed and memory requirements of various methods for squaring modulo a Mersenne number. For example, as discussed in Chapter 1, there exist standard grammar-school multiply, Karatsuba recursion, FFT-multiply (with zero-padding), the currently considered scheme of weighted convolution, and so on. How slow would be the scheme of literally autoconvolving the binary bits of x, with a length-q cyclic convolution?

Problem 3.1.5: Actually there is a variable-base representation different from (3.1.9) that is in some ways superior. Instead of the constraint that the D_i lie in the stated interval, which we might call a "standard" variable-base scheme; we instead constrain each D_i by:

$$-2^{b_{i+1}-1} \leq D_i < +2^{b_{i+1}-1}$$

This has been called "balanced" representation, and has the important advantage that floating-point (or equivalent fixed-precision) convolutions tend to have reduced error. Therefore the requirement that the elements of c in (3.1.13) be integral can be enforced for longer run lengths N in balanced representation. Implement a floating point Mersenne squaring scheme in which a switch can be toggled between standard and balanced representation, to exhibit this interesting precision phenomenon. Little is known about the precise advantage the balanced scheme conveys, but there have been some conjectures along these lines [Crandall and Fagin 1994].

Wieferich primes

Wieferich primes arise in a natural way in classical analyses of Fermat's "Last Theorem," or (FLT), that

$$x^p + y^p + z^p = 0$$

has no integer solutions x, y, z, p; with $xyz \neq 0$ and prime $p > 2$. Wieferich's main theorem solves–up to a fascinating congruence–a special case (called FLT(I)) which presupposes that p does not divide the product xyz. The Wieferich result is: if the odd prime p does not divide xyz (a product of three integers), then $x^p + y^p + z^p = 0$ implies the congruence:

$$2^{p-1} = 1 \ (\mathrm{mod} \ p^2) \tag{3.1.17}$$

An odd prime p satisfying this congruence (which turns out rarely to be satisfied so far in practice) is called a Wieferich prime. Thus, if an odd prime p is not a Wieferich prime, then the conditions $x^p + y^p + z^p = 0$ and $p \mid xyz$ are mutually incompatible.

It is elementary that for any odd prime p the simpler congruence:

$$2^{p-1} = 1 \ (\mathrm{mod} \ p) \tag{3.1.18}$$

is always satisfied. This means that the Fermat quotient defined

$$q_p(2) = \frac{2^{p-1} - 1}{p} \tag{3.1.19}$$

is always an integer for any odd prime p. But if the Wieferich condition (3.1.17) is to hold, then this integer $q_p(2)$ must in turn be divisible by p. One might say that the "probability" that the Fermat quotient be so divisible is "about" $1/p$. Indeed there is some numerical evidence that this heuristic probability makes sense. To date the only known Wieferich primes are $p = 1093$ and 3511. D. H. Lehmer had searched in vain, over all primes $p < 6 \times 10^9$ by 1981. The present author and collaborators recently searched over $p < 4 \times 10^{12}$, finding no new Wiefrich primes and producing some data on small occurrences of the number A defined as the smallest-in-magnitude solution to:

$$2^{p-1} = 1 + 2Ap \quad (\mathrm{mod}\ p^2) \tag{3.1.20}$$

to lend some support to the probability idea [Crandall *et. al.* 1995a].

It is amusing that *some* primes can immediately be pronounced non-Wieferich on theoretical grounds. It turns out that if the positions of the 1's in the binary expansion of an odd prime p all lie in a single arithmetic progression, then p cannot be a Wieferich prime. Thus, the set of Wieferich primes contains neither Fermat primes ($p = 10...01$ binary) nor Mersenne primes ($p = 11...11$ binary) nor primes such as:

$$\tag{3.1.21}$$

$$p = 100000010000001000000100000010000001 \text{ (binary)}$$

Aside from these numerologically quaint examples of non-Wieferichs, there is no known way to test various p except via a standard binary powering ladder. That is, to test (3.1.17) one raises 2 to an appropriate power, using the binary expansion of $p-1$. But there are various refinements that will speed up the process. First, it is a theorem that if (3.1.17) holds, then

$$2^{(p-1)/2} = \pm 1 \ (\mathrm{mod}\ p^2) \tag{3.1.22}$$

so that one may save a few operations. More significant (depending on the integer precision of one's machinery's) is to use a base-p representation of all integers (mod p^2). If we generally represent any number x (mod p^2) as $x = a + bp$, denoted $\{a,b\}$; with each of a,b lying in $[0, p-1]$, then

$$x^2 = a^2 + 2abp \,(\mathrm{mod}\ p^2) \tag{3.1.23}$$

so that the representation of x^2 becomes

$$\{(a^2)\%p,\ (2ab+[a^2/p])\%p\} \tag{3.1.24}$$

where [ ] denotes greatest integer and % denotes (mod p) reduction. We see thus that:

- Doing x^2 (mod p^2) directly, to full precision, takes 1 square and 1 mod;
- Using (3.1.24) takes 1 square, 1 multiply, 1 divide and 2 mods.

It is not hard to see that for some machinery, the second, base-p alternative will actually be faster because all of the operations are of reduced precision (*e.g.* (mod p) rather than (mod p^2)).

There are further enhancements, for example the steady-state divide/mod as outlined in Section 1.2. It turns out that various enhancements can be used to effect a squaring of a random representation as in (3.1.24) in the equivalent of five "size-p" multiplies, meaning products are of order p^2; and no explicit machine divides or mods.   This five-multiply scheme is very efficient, and coupled with an efficient sieve to form a testing set of primes, is what has allowed searches to extend beyond 10^{12}.   An effective algorithm for exhaustive search runs like so:

$$(3.1.25)$$

Algorithm for Wieferich prime search:

1) Choose an overall search limit L.
2) Store all primes $\leq \sqrt{L}$.
3) For each successive integer block of some convenient length B,
        4) Sieve out, using the stored primes, all composites
          from the block;
        5) For each prime p remaining in that block,
                6)* In a binary powering ladder, use
                (3.1.24) and steady-state divide/mod
                (Algorithm (1.2.5)) to obtain a final
                base-p form:
                $2^{(p-1)/2} = \{C, D\}$ (mod p^2)
              7) If C is neither 1 nor $p-1$, exit with
              fatal error; otherwise report C, D
              noting that a Wieferich prime must
              have $\{C,D\} = \{1, 0\}$ or $\{p-1, p-1\}$.

(Note (*) if one's machine has sufficiently high integer precision for fundamental operations, it may well be better just to effect squaring (mod p^2) directly, or to avoid steady-state ideas, or both.)

One might have thought that the elementary congruence (3.1.18) could be used to isolate probable primes, but there is apparently nothing faster than an incremental sieve as suggested in the above algorithm.

Problem 3.1.6: Prove the theoretical arithmetic progression null criterion, of which (3.1.21) is an example, by starting with the equivalent assumption

$$p = \frac{2^{kt} - 1}{2^k - 1}$$

Then raise 2^{kt} to the $(p-1)/(kt)$ power to show that 2^{p-1} cannot be 1 (mod p^2).

Problem 3.1.7: For Mersenne primes $p = 2^q-1$, and for Fermat primes 2^q+1, find (either by initial numerical experiments followed by rigorous proof, or just by proof) an exact relation for 2^{p-1} (mod p^2) in terms of q; in this way ruling out any possibility of Mersenne- or Fermat-Wieferich primes.

Problem 3.1.8: Implement software that carries out a Wieferich search. The current search limit is 4 x 10^{12}, below which the only Wieferich primes are p = 1093, 3511. Clearly these small Wieferich primes will test the software. But another sharp test is to verify the "close call" [Crandall *et. al.* 1995a]:

$$2^{76843523890} = 1 - 2*76843523891 \pmod{76843523891^2}$$

In other words, for this prime the parameter $A = -1$ in (3.1.20). As small as can be without being a Wieferich instance!

Problem 3.1.9: Argue that, heuristically, the expected number of Wieferich primes that exist in an interval $[x, y]$ should be asymptotic to:

$$\log\left(\frac{\log y}{\log x}\right)$$

How many Wieferich primes did one "expect to find" between the Lehmer bound of 6 x 10^9 and the current bound of 4 x 10^{12}?

Problem 3.1.10: The issue of whether the number of Wieferich primes is infinite is an open one; one might say almost completely open since so little is known. Besides the amusing arithmetic progression criterion, can some other class of primes be ruled out in similar fashion? Note that we do not even know whether there exist an infinitude of primes having all 1's in a single arithmetic progression. It has been pointed out that the small Wieferichs 1093, 3511 have interesting, if inconclusive, binary patterns [Vardi 1991].

Wilson primes

To effect a parallel study to that of the Wieferich primes of the last section, we turn to Wilson primes. Consider the two congruences, for p prime:

$$(p-1)! \;=\; -1 \;(\text{mod } p) \qquad\qquad\qquad (3.1.26)$$

$$(p-1)! \;=\; -1 \;(\text{mod } p^2)$$

As in the Wieferich scenario, it is elementary that the first congruence holds for all prime p (Wilson's theorem); in fact we have Lagrange's converse, that the first congruence of (3.1.26) implies p is prime. However, the second congruence (mod p^2) is apparently rare (and difficult to analyze–to this day the quote atop the chapter still makes a good deal of sense). A prime satisfying the (mod p^2) congruence is called a Wilson prime. The only known Wilson primes are $p = 5$, 13 and 563. There exist no others below 4 x 10^8 [Crandall *et. al.* 1995a].

What might be called the naive approach to searching for Wilson primes is to "multiply up" the factorial in literal fashion: start with 2, and multiply by 3, 4, ... always accumulating (mod p^2) until a conclusion is reached upon multiplication by (p–1) and the final mod. Unfortunately this requires, on the face of it, about p multiply/mods. But, unlike the Wieferich search problem, there exist a host of possible enhancements that render the naive calculation dramatically faster. The Wieferich search enhancements we have described may lend an order of magnitude speed increase, but the Wilson enhancements can yield several orders of magnitude over a "naive" scheme.

Before we investigate ways to compute (p–1)!, it is worth noting that factorial evaluation must in general be problematic. One way to see this is, if we wanted to factor some number N, and if it were easy to find massive factorials $M!$ (mod N), where M is say of order $N^{1/2}$ or even some lower but significant power of N, then one could simply take the GCD of the factorial with N, routinely to produce factors of N. On the belief that factorization is intrinsically difficult, it must follow that so, too is factorial evaluation. Another way to say this is, a factorial $M!$ contains *some* information about every integer not exceeding M.

Now to the enhancements for evaluating (p–1)! (mod p^2). First, it is not necessary to compute the full factorial, thanks to Morley's theorem, a case of which being:

$$(p-1)! \ = \ \left(\left(\frac{p-1}{2}\right)!\right)^2 (1 - 2^p) \ \left(\bmod\, p^2\right) \tag{3.1.27}$$

Thus it suffices to compute ((p–1)/2)! (mod p^2). This cuts the work in half. But one can go further, depending on the value of p (mod 12). Some powerful modern results [Granville 1994][Berndt *et. al.* 1995][Chowla *et. al.* 1986][Coster 1988] give lucrative relations, some of which are discussed in [Vardi 1991]. Consider quadratic form representations:

$$(3.1.28)$$

$$p = 1 \pmod 4 \quad ; \quad p = a^2 + b^2 \qquad ; a = 1 \pmod 4$$
$$p = 1 \pmod 3 \quad ; \quad 4p = c^2 + 27d^2 \quad ; c = 1 \pmod 3$$
$$p = 1 \pmod 3 \quad ; \quad 4p = u^2 + 3v^2 \quad ; u = (-1)^{(p-1)/8} \pmod 3$$
$$v = 0 \text{ or } \pm 1 \pmod 6$$

Then, for $p = 1$ or $7 \pmod{12}$ it can be derived [Crandall *et. al.* 1995a] that:

$$(3.1.29)$$

$$(p-1)! \; = \; \left(\left(\frac{p-1}{6}\right)!\right)^6 \left(-u^3(2^p - 1) + 3pu\right)\left(-c + \frac{p}{c}\right)^{\frac{3^p - 1}{2}} \pmod{p^2}$$

while for $p = 5 \pmod{12}$ we have:

$$(3.1.30)$$

$$(p-1)! \; = \; \left(\left(\frac{p-1}{4}\right)!\right)^4 (3 \cdot 2^p - 4)\left(2a^2 - p\right) \pmod{p^2}$$

while for the outlying case $p = 11 \pmod{12}$ one must, in the absence of further theoretical results, use (3.1.27). These relations, being fascinating algebraic number theory relations in their own right, are complicated. Yet, for a Wilson prime search, the ensuing computational savings are considerable. In fact, for the respective cases $p = 1,7 \pmod{12}$; $p = 5 \pmod{12}$; and $p = 11 \pmod{12}$ the work to resolve $(p-1)!$ involves, rather than the naive p multiply/mods, only about $p/6, p/4, p/2$ such operations. The net savings is on average thus a factor of 48/13, almost a factor of four. Incidentally, the quadratic representations (3.1.28) can, in practice, be obtained "brute force," by simply looping over enough squares, without any serious degradation in performance. Though fast algorithms for seeking out such quadratic forms do exist, such refinement is not significant, such is the extreme complexity of evaluating the remaining factorials themselves.

So the Wilson factorial evaluation problem comes down to that of calculating a reduced factorial of the form $((p-1)/k)! \pmod{p^2}$ for some divisor k. But the story does not end here. It turns out that a factorial can be reduced further in complexity by a technique we shall call "factorial sieving." This method depends on the simple fact that a factorial generally involves a certain redundancy. For example, if N is divisible by 6, we have the identity:

$$N! = \frac{2^{N/3} 3^{N/6} \left(\frac{N}{2}\right)! \left(\frac{N}{3}\right)!}{\left(\frac{N}{6}\right)!} \prod_{\substack{1 \leq k < N \\ (k,6) = 1}} k \tag{3.1.31}$$

where $(k, 6)$ denotes $GCD(k, 6)$. The identity is obtained by considering the multiples of 2 and 3 and both, all less than N. On consideration of how the relevant intervals overlap, it is evident that this $N!$ can be evaluated in (asymptotically in N) no more than $2N/3$ multiplies. One can of course derive progressively more complex identities (with perhaps more restrictions on the divisors of N), to effect yet more reduction. For example, it is possible to reduce the number of multiplies to $283N/768$ [Crandall *et. al.* 1995a]. But it is not yet known how far this factorial sieving can be taken.

Now we employ the previous apparati–the quadratic forms identities and factorial sieving–that enable us to perform the Wilson calculation via the evaluation of the products of various terms lying in arithmetic progression. For example, if we use such as (3.1.31) we require the evaluation of the k-product. Happily this is *two* products, for $k = 1, 5 \pmod 6$ respectively, each of which product involves terms in arithmetic progression. But in Section 1.5, with Algorithm (1.5.2) and Problems (1.5.4), (1.5.7) we have seen fast algorithms for the evaluation of products of terms in arithmetic progression. A special instance of Algorithm (1.5.2) thus arises for a polynomial of the form:

$$p(x) = x(x + b)(x + 2b) \dots (x+(m-1)b)$$

that is, not only the evaluation points but the roots themselves lie in arithmetic progression. It turns out that some extra enhancements are possible in this situation (see Problem 3.1.12).

Using all of these results, it is possible to carry out a Wilson prime search several orders of magnitude faster than one would at first realize with a "naive" factorial scheme. As companion to the Wieferich search algorithm, we present the following:

(3.1.32)

Algorithm for Wilson prime search:

1) Choose an overall search limit L.
2) Store all primes $\leq \sqrt{L}$.
3) For each successive integer block of some convenient length B,
> 4) Sieve out, using the stored primes, all composites from the block;
> 5) For each prime p remaining in the block,
>> 6) As $p = 1,7,5,11 \pmod{12}$, select a quadratic forms reduction formula (3.1.27), (3.1.29), or (3.1.30);
>> 7) Use a factorial sieve identity such as (3.1.31) together with an arithmetic progression evaluator to obtain $(p-!)! = \{C, D\} \pmod{p^2}$;
>> 8) If C is not $p-1$, exit with fatal error; otherwise report D noting that a Wilson prime must have $\{C,D\} = \{p-1, p-1\}$.

There is still a great deal of algorithmic ground to break on this problem. In [Crandall *et. al.* 1995a] there is reported an experiment on a recursive-remainder, $O(p^{1/2}\log^2 p)$ polynomial evaluator (in the style foreshadowed in Problem 1.5.7) that evaluates the polynomial

$$(x+1)(x+2) \dots (x+m)$$

at points $x = 0, m, 2m, \dots,(m-1)m$; in order to obtain $(m^2)! \pmod{p^2}$. The most computationally intensive result achieved in this way was that for the prime $p = 1099511628401$, the Wilson factorial is:

$$(p-1)! = -1 - 533091778023\, p \;(\mathrm{mod}\; p^2) \qquad (3.1.33)$$

To the present author's knowledge, this is the largest p whose Wilson factorial has been calculated $(\mathrm{mod}\; p^2)$; and furthermore the largest p that is thus proven prime by the Lagrange converse of Wilson's classical theorem. It should be remarked that the recursive polynomial evaluation, in practice, did not run faster than the efficient arithmetic progression scheme until the primes under test reached beyond 10^{11}.

The problem of optimizing Wilson factorial evaluation remains quite open. In fact, as one looks into this problem, new enhancements seem to appear naturally and often. One possible source for new algorithms is a theorem [Buhler 1995] that involves a mere $(\mathrm{mod}\; p)$ rather than $(\mathrm{mod}\; p^2)$ congruence. Let p be a prime possessed of primitive root g. Then p is a Wilson prime if and only if:

$$\sum_{k=1}^{p-1} \left\lfloor \frac{g^k}{p} \right\rfloor g^{p-1-k} = 0 \;(\mathrm{mod}\; p) \qquad (3.1.34)$$

On the face of it this theorem appears to require at least p multiplies to effect a Wilson test. But the situation is much better than it might seem: the sum in (3.1.34) can actually be carried out with $O(p \log g)$ adds and *no* multiplies. One thinks of the sum as a polynomial in g, to be evaluated, say, via Horner's rule. In the elegant case when $g = 2$ is a primitive root, the algorithm is especially attractive. The following *Mathematica* example is a rigorous Wilson test for any prime for which 2 is a primitive root:

$$\qquad (3.1.35)$$

```
(* Purely additive Wilson test.
   The final output s is 0 if and only if p is Wilson.
 *)
```

```
p = 563;
g = 2;   (* Two must be a primitive root of p. *)
a = 1; b = s = 0;
While[True,
      a += a;
      b += b;
      If[a >= p, a -= p; ++b];
      If[b >= p, b -= p];
      s += s+b;
      If[s >= p, s -= p; If[s >= p, s -= p]];
      If[a == 1, Break[]];
];
Print[p," ",s," ",Mod[(Mod[(p-1)!, p^2] + 1)/p,p]]

563 0 0
```

Indeed this example proves that $p = 563$ is a Wilson prime; in fact this is the largest Wilson prime known. Note that this *Mathematica* example is entirely devoid of multiplies and even devoid of divides/mods. This is possible because If[ ] statements can be used after additions to effect modular arithmetic. If 2 is not a primitive root, one can in principle use $O(\log g)$ adds and some ancillary If[ ] statements still to render a pure-addition algorithm.

There is yet another merely (mod p) Wilson test, but it is not yet clear how to forge from it a fast algorithm. The theorem is as follows [Crandall *et. al.* 1995a]. For any integer q with $1 < q < p$, denote by $(1/p)_q$ the unique inverse of p (mod q), assumed to lie in $[1, q-1]$. Then p is a Wilson prime if and only if

$$\sum_{q=2}^{p-1} \left(\frac{1}{p}\right)_q = -1 \pmod{p} \tag{3.1.36}$$

There is perhaps the possibility of computing inverses in parallel, for many primes at once, or for many q at once.

Problem 3.1.11: Show, using (3.1.27) and the sieve formula (3.1.31) with $N = 276$, that $p = 563$ is a Wilson prime. The challenge is to use the least possible number of multiplies on the basis of the two formulae.

Problem 3.1.12: By analyzing the Algorithm (1.5.2) for evaluation of a polynomial along points in arithmetic progression, but now in the case where the polynomial roots also lie in an arithmetic progression, show that $N!$ can be computed in

$$O(N) \text{ adds,}$$
$$O(N^\phi) \text{ multiplies}$$

where $\phi = (\sqrt{5} - 1)/2$ is the "Golden Ratio." This peculiar power comes from the notion of recursing in an optimal way on step (1) of the Algorithm (1.5.2). Can this sort of add-multiply complexity be achieved likewise for the [Veljan 1994] refinement discussed in Problem 1.5.2?

Problem 3.1.13: Use the attractive algebraic identity:

$$((x^2-85)^2-4176)^2-2880^2 = (x-13)(x-11)(x-7)(x-1)(x+1)(x+7)(x+11)(x+13)$$

to effect a Wilson test for primes p. The identity allows for 7 multiplies of distinct integers to be done for the price of 4 squarings. Can one establish "higher cascaded forms", that is, where yet more squares are involved on the left?

Problem 3.1.14: Use the following function [Buhler 1995], which evaluates the product

$$f(x) = (x+1)(x+2) \dots (x+16)$$

in only 8 multiplies, to effect a Wilson test for primes p:

```
f[x_] := Module[{t0, t1, t2, t3, t4, t5},
  t0 = (x+4)*(x+11);
  t1 = t0+12;  t2 = t0*t1;
  t3 = t2 - 60*t0 + 540;
```

```
t4 = t2*t3;
t5 = t4-128*(3*t2 - 5*t0 - 165);
t4*t5
];
```

Problem 3.1.15: Implement a Wilson test program, using say Algorithm (3.1.32). At the time of this writing, the region $p > 4 \times 10^8$ is largely uncharted. Such a program should reveal some of the known "close calls," an example of which being:

$$(56151922)! = -1 - 56151923 \pmod{56151923^2}$$

which, in the spirit of Problem (3.1.8), is as close to a Wilson instance as a failure can be!

Problem 3.1.16: Implement a recursive-remainder polynomial scheme to exceed the record Wilson calculation of (3.1.33). One of the open problems in connection with such a challenge is to reduce the memory requirement, which in absence of better algorithms, tends to be stultifying.

Problem 3.1.17: Find means by which the scheme suggested by theorems (3.1.34) or (3.1.36) can be made competitive with the arithmetic progression scheme of Algorithm (3.1.32). One difficulty that renders the pure-additive scheme (3.1.34) less effective is the lack of suitable reduction identities, like the (mod 12) based identities; that is, there is as yet no known way to reduce the numer of summands in these alternative theorems.

Other primes

Beyond the Wieferich and Wilson primes, which should occur (independently?–it is not known) with "probability" about $1/p$ (see Problem 3.1.9), one might consider also primes such as the Wall-Sun-Sun primes which one may well expect also to enjoy the "$1/p$" heuristic. These are primes > 5 such that

$$F_{p-\left(\frac{p}{5}\right)} = 0 \; (\text{mod}\, p^2) \tag{3.1.37}$$

where F_n is the n-th Fibonacci number ($F_0 = 0$, $F_1 = 1$, and the rest of the sequence runs 1,2,3,5,8,13,... on the basis of the recurrence $F_n = F_{n-1} + F_{n-2}$ for $n \geq 2$). Here, the Legendre symbol $(p/5)$ means $+1$ if $p = \pm 1 \; (\text{mod}\, 5)$, otherwise -1. Once again, as with Wieferich and Wilson primes, it turns out that the Wall-Sun-Sun congruence (3.1.37) holds merely (mod p) for all primes > 5. Actually this definition of yet another class of primes is not specious: [Sun and Sun 1992] proved the interesting result that if p is a failing exponent of FLT(I), then p satisfies (3.1.37). Thus a failing exponent p must be Wieferich *and* Wall-Sun-Sun, and as it turns out must satisfy even more congruences we do not cover here. [McIntosh 1995] has found via exhaustive search that there are no Wall-Sun-Sun primes whatsoever below 1.6×10^{12}.

To effect a Wall-Sun-Sun search, one must have efficient means of generating Fibonacci numbers. Actually a typical Fibonacci number that McIntosh has checked near 10^{12}, *e.g.* $F_{999999999988}$ for $p = 999999999989$, has more than 10^{11} digits, but of course mods are continually being taken so magnitudes larger than 10^{48} are never reached in such a computation. Still, the impressive magnitude of such Fibonacci numbers indicates that we cannot merely find subsequent Fibonacci's via direct application of the recurrence $F_n = F_{n-1} + F_{n-2}$. Instead, the following *Mathematica* example shows an indirect method; namely, fast powering ladder computation of the Fibonacci numbers:

$$(3.1.38)$$

```
(* Fast algorithm for computation of Fibonacci numbers. *)
fib[n_] :=
Module[{a = 0, b = 1, q},
    If[n==0, Return[0]];
    bits = IntegerDigits[n,2];
    Do[
        {a,b}= {a^2+ b^2, b(2a+b)};
        If[bits[[q]] != 0, {a,b}= {b,a+b}],
```

```
      {q,2,Length[bits]}
    ];
    b
];
Table[fib[n],{n,0,10}]
fib[1000]
```

{0,1, 1, 2, 3, 5, 8, 13, 21, 34, 55}

```
43466557686937456435688527675040625802564660517371780402\
  481729089536555417949051890403879840079255169295922593\
  080322634775209689623239873322471161642996440906533187\
  938298969649928516003704476137795166849228875
```

This example has printed out the first few Fibonacci numbers and also the number F_{1000}. Of course, in a Wall-Sun-Sun search, one would continually reduce values (mod p^2) within the Do[ ] loop. (One might also benefit from the base-p representation as described for Wieferich and Wilson searches, in this way keeping intermediate products to the size of p^2.)

A classic open number theoretical problem is to prove the (heuristically expected) infinitude of twin prime pairs $(p, p+2)$. Little is known beyond the fact that the sum of the reciprocals of all twin primes converges. The number

$$B = 1/3 + 1/5 + 1/5 + 1/7 + 1/11 + 1/13 + ...$$

is called the Brun constant. R. Brent has given the value $B \sim 1.90216054$ [Ribenboim 1988] (see also [*Projects* 1994]). To the present author's knowledge, the largest known twin prime pairs are:

$$697053813*2^{16352} \pm 1 \qquad \text{[Indlekofer and Ja'rai 1994]}$$
$$1692923232*10^{4020} \pm 1 \qquad \text{[Dubner 1993]}$$

Another interesting computational problem is to find a "non-Mersenne" prime larger, say, than the current largest known primes given in the beginning of this chapter. For example, [Noll *et. al.* 1989] discovered the prime

$$391581 * 2^{216193} - 1$$

which for some months was the largest known prime, and a rare instance over the last decades when an actual Mersenne was not front runner.

There are also Cullen primes, being prime instances of the Cullen numbers:

$$C_n = n2^n + 1$$

It is known that there exist infinitely many Cullen composites. [Keller and Niebuhr 1994] have factored all C_n for $n \leq 300$.

There would seem to be no end to the classification of primes or groups of primes. One of the interesting groupings of primes is into arithmetic progressions. For example, [Pritchard *et. al.* 1995] found a record 21-prime progression; namely, each of

$$5749146449311 + 26004868890 \, k$$

for $k = 0,1,...20$, is a prime number. Furthermore, it is known that this progression has minimum final term, amongst all possible length-21 arithmetic progressions of primes.

Problem 3.1.18: Not a single Wall-Sun-Sun prime $5 < p < 1.6 \times 10^{12}$ exists [McIntosh 1995]. Carry out a search for Wall-Sun-Sun primes somewhere above this limit. (Note however the heuristic chances of a find, on the basis of the considerations in Problem 3.1.9.)

Problem 3.1.19: Discover means by which to compute the Brun constant (to more than 8 decimal places, say), or the twin-prime constant:

$$C_2 = \prod_{p>2}^{\infty}\left(1 - \frac{1}{(p-1)^2}\right)$$

to many (say 100) places. The latter constant arises in heuristic arguments [Hardy and Wright 1979] that conclude: the number of twin primes (*i.e.* counting pairs as one count per pair) not exceeding x is asymptotic to $2C_2 x/\log^2 x$. Of course, in spite of this unproven asymptotic estimate the number of twins may be finite for all we know.

Problem 3.1.20: Find some new twin prime pairs. Note that the forms

$$h\, 2^q \pm 1$$

can, especially for sufficiently small h, be tested easily for primality, on the basis of known theorems [Hardy and Wright 1979]. The usual sequence of computations runs like so:

1) Sieve out, using small primes (say primes $< 2^{16}$ or 2^{32} or an even higher ceiling) as many pairs as possible, from some long interval of choice, where a pair is removed if either of its members is composite.

2) Test the remaining numbers for primality.

It is a very instructive exercise first to work out, for example, how long it would take to find a twin prime pair of certain magnitude on the basis of heuristic statistical assumptions (as discussed in Problem 3.1.19) about the distribution of pairs.

Problem 3.1.21: Discover a large non-Mersenne prime, *e.g.* a prime of the form $h\, 2^q - 1$ with $h > 1$. Again, for suitable h primality proofs are easy [Hardy and Wright 1979]. However, there is one difficulty in the non-Mersenne character of such a number: there is no convenient "fast mod" of the kind discussed in Chapter 1. Instead, one may consider the "steady-state divide/mod" also in that chapter. After the creation of one huge reciprocal of the prime candidate, one can complete an entire, rigorous primality test without a single extra explicit divide.

Problem 3.1.22: Investigate the fascinating world of primality proofs. It is now known [Cohen 1993] that in principle a primality proof may be carried out in polynomial time. But currently the most practical schemes are not quite polynomial time. One of the powerful such schemes, an elliptic curve primality proving method, is due to A. O. L. Atkin and F. Morain, and has been used [Keller and Morain 1994] to settle the primality of, for example,

$$p = \frac{2^{3359} - 1}{6719}$$

which is thus known to be a prime of more than 1000 decimal digits. More recently, Morain has proven the primality of the partition number $p(1840926)$ which has 1505 decimal digits. A good primality proving program should be able to handle arbitrary numbers of this size in a convenient time span (hours or days, rather than months or years). One way to begin a career in primality proving is to peruse the excellent and clear discussions of [Lenstra A, in Pomerance 1990]] and [Cohen 1993]. What is more, if one proceeds with elliptic curve methods for primality proof, much of the attendant software will have direct application in the world of factoring.

Problem 3.1.23: Find an arithmetic progression of primes, which progression being of some length greater than 21.

3.2   *Bernoulli numbers*

Bernoulli numbers and Fermat's "Last Theorem"

Fermat's "Last Theorem," or FLT, that $x^p + y^p + z^p = 0$ has no solutions in non-zero integers x, y, z for $p > 2$, has apparently finally been proved, as is well known by now, by the methods of A. Wiles (at the time of this writing, the proof is evidently in good standing, having been completed in a joint work by A. Wiles and R. Taylor). But there remain interesting related, and open, questions.

A classical expedient for ruling out prime exponents p in FLT is the Kummer theorem, which says: if the odd prime p is regular; *i.e.*, if it does not divide any of the numerators of the Bernoulli numbers

$$B_2, B_4, ..., B_{p-3}$$

then $x^p + y^p + z^p = 0$ has no solutions in non-zero integers. If p does divide the numerator of some Bernoulli number B_{2k}, we say that p is irregular and the pair $(2k, p)$ is an irregular pair. Thus, the study of Bernoulli numbers (mod p) is interesting, but not only for the FLT. Though FLT has been settled, there are open conjectures such as: the number of regular primes is infinite. It is not known whether this be true, yet it is expected on heuristic grounds that a finite fraction of all primes are regular. There is also the Vandiver conjecture, which involves instances of irregular pairs and which just might admit of a numerical counterexample, perhaps even for some prime in the region of 10^7 [Washington 1982].

There are many interesting approaches to the problem of calculating Bernoulli numbers (mod p). One approach [Buhler *et. al.* 1992, 1993] is to use the expansion

$$\frac{x^2}{\cosh x - 1} = -2 \sum_{n=0}^{\infty} \frac{(2n-1)B_{2n}}{(2n)!} x^{2n} \tag{3.2.1}$$

which turns out to be, up to differentiation and a little manipulation, formally equivalent to (2.2.9). (Note that the B_{2n} are related simply to the Riemann zeta function at even integer arguments via (2.2.15).) One may expand the denominator $\cosh x - 1$ of (3.2.1) in a finite power series to degree $(p-1)/2$ in a variable $z = x^2$, with all coefficients of said polynomial evaluated (mod p), and perform Newton method polynomial division (as described in Chapter 1 and exemplified in code (2.2.23)) to obtain the right-hand side to a similar degree. It is possible to carry out in this way calculations of B_{2n} (mod p) for p into the hundreds of thousands on a typical workstation, say. However, one runs into memory problems, such as the storage of several polynomials of the given degree. A technique known as multisectioning reduces the memory requirement, and enables irregular pairs to be recorded for p into the millions. The idea is to evaluate only those B_{2n} lying in some arithmetic progression, then those in another, disjoint progression, and so on until all the required B_{2n} are evaluated. For each arithmetic progression, one uses a certain amount of memory, then reuses it for the next progression, and so on. One possible multisectioning procedure is to derive identities such as:

$$x(\coth x + \cot x) = 2 \sum_{n=0,4,8,12,\dots}^{\infty} \frac{2^n B_n}{n!} x^n \tag{3.2.2}$$

$$x(\coth x - \cot x) = 2 \sum_{n=2,6,10,\dots}^{\infty} \frac{2^n B_n}{n!} x^n$$

Now the left-hand sides can be put into the forms:

$$x\left(\frac{\cosh x \sin x \pm \cos x \sinh x}{\sinh x \sin x}\right) \tag{3.2.3}$$

and the key is, the denominator ($\sinh x \sin x$) is in fact x^2 times a series in x^4.

Specifically, it can be shown that:

$$\sinh x \sin x = \sum_{n=2,6,10,\ldots} (-1)^{(n-2)/4} 2^{n/2} \frac{x^n}{n!} \qquad (3.2.4)$$

Thus the Newton inversion of the relevant finite polynomial in $z = x^4$ only involves degree roughly $p/4$; *i.e.* about half the degree that was required for (3.2.1). In this fashion the memory storage for the whole Newton process is essentially halved.

But one can multisection yet further, and it is a good idea to do so if one is to go beyond the currently resolved (meaning all instances of $B_{2k} = 0 \pmod{p}$ are recorded) range $p < 4000000$. A starting point for general multisectioning is the formula:

$$\omega^k x \cot\left(\omega^k x\right) = \sum_{n=0,2,4,6,\ldots} (-1)^{n/2} 2^n B_n \frac{x^n \omega^{kn}}{n!} \qquad (3.2.5)$$

If we let ω be an N-th root of (-1), for example $\omega = e^{\pi i/N}$ (although the analysis of other roots, such as roots of (-1) modulo certain p, is an interesting research area) then a Fourier sum yields a series involving only those Bernoulli numbers with their indices belonging to certain arithmetic progressions:

$$(3.2.6)$$

$$\sum_{k=0}^{N-1} \omega^{k-2jk} x \cot\left(\omega^k x\right) = N \sum_{n=j \,(\mathrm{mod}\, N)} (-1)^n 4^n B_{2n} \frac{x^{2n}}{(2n)!}$$

Here we see that for a fixed j in $[0, N-1]$, the Bernoulli numbers appearing are

$$B_{2j}, \; B_{2j+2N}, \; B_{2j+4N}, \; \ldots$$

The multisectioning idea turns, then, on the fact that the Fourier-cotangent sum on the left of (3.2.6) involves, for each $j = 0, 1, ..., N-1$; a common denominator series whose structure depends only on N. For the Newton inversion, then, it is enough to compute the coefficients (mod p) in what we might call the "denominator" series:

$$D_N(x) = \prod_{k=0}^{N-1} \sin(\omega^k x) \qquad (3.2.7)$$

where, again, ω is an N-th root of (-1). Note that the sinh-sin product (3.2.4) is essentially just the special case $N = 2$, $\omega = i$; and sure enough the two options (3.2.3) with their common denominator (essentially D_2) split the Bernoulli indices into two disjoint progressions. It turns out that the power series of D_N is always x^N times a power series in x^{2N}. Thus, in computations (mod p) of the Fourier sum on the left of (3.2.6), the common denominator polynomial approximating D_N can be taken to be of degree about $p/(2N)$ in the variable $z = x^{2N}$.

Another area of research is to endeavor to apply alternative representations of the Bernoulli numbers. For example, one might consider using the continued fraction:

$$c(x) = 1 + \cfrac{x}{3 + \cfrac{x}{5 + ... + \cfrac{x}{p-2}}} \qquad (3.2.8)$$

which is a truncated form of the fraction for $\sqrt{x} \coth \sqrt{x}$. It can be shown that

$$\qquad (3.2.9)$$

$$c(X) = \sum_{n=0}^{(p-3)/2} \frac{4^n B_{2n}}{(2n)!} X^n + O\left(X^{(p-1)/2}\right) \quad (\bmod p)$$

so that one may evaluate Bernoulli numbers (mod p) by finding the final convergents $p(x)/q(x)$ for the fraction (3.2.8), and again use Newton inversion for $1/q(x)$. (The big-O notation here means simply that the finite sum will exactly determine all the Bernoulli numbers (mod p) through the stated range on the index n.)   It remains unclear what advantage such a fraction based scheme might have. In particular, it is not clear how to multisection the process, although to figure out how to do same might give rise to a very efficient algorithm for finding irregular pairs.

Yet another interesting approach is to use the following formal fraction due to Bender. Given a prime $p > 5$, consider

$$f(X) \; = \; \cfrac{1}{1 + \cfrac{Xb_1}{1 + \cfrac{Xb_2}{1 + \ldots + Xb_{(p-5)/2}}}} \tag{3.2.10}$$

where the b_n are defined

$$b_n \; = \; \frac{n(n+1)^2(n+2)}{4(2n+1)(2n+3)} \pmod{p} \tag{3.2.11}$$

Then we have

$$\tag{3.2.12}$$

$$f(X) \; = \; 1 + 6 \sum_{n=2}^{(p-3)/2} B_{2n} \, X^{n-1} \pmod{p} + O\!\left(X^{(p-3)/2}\right) \pmod{p}$$

Again, evaluation of the final convergent polynomials to the fraction (3.2.10) would allow computation of Bernoulli numbers (mod p).

A different line of analysis, which has actually brought new results for very large primes p, is that of [Shokrollahi 1994]. The Shokrollahi formula, actually a kind of discrete Fourier transform (DFT), runs as follows. Let g be a primitive root of the prime p, and define the operation $x\%p$ to yield the unique residue of x lying in $[0,\ldots,p-1]$. Further define

$$(3.2.13)$$

$$c_j = \left[\frac{\left(g^{-1} \%p \right)\left(g^j \%p \right)}{p} \right] g^{-j} \quad ; \; j = 0, 1, ..., p - 2$$

Then the set of $B_{2k} \pmod{p}$ can be obtained in terms of a DFT:

$$(3.2.14)$$

$$\sum_{j=0}^{p-2} c_j \, g^{2kj} = \left(1 - g^{2k} \right) \frac{B_{2k}}{2kg} \pmod{p} \quad ; \quad k = 1, ..., \frac{p-3}{2}$$

Thus all relevant irregular pairs $(2k, p)$ can be resolved via a single DFT of length $p-1$; in fact the pairs will correspond precisely with the zeros of the DFT sum. However, because g^2 is a primitive root of order $(p-1)/2$, the DFT length can be decreased for all p, and decreased further for p of special form. For certain p Shokrollahi's method is, in practice, the fastest known for completely resolving the irregular pairs.

Problem 3.2.1: Use the classical generating function for the Bernoulli numbers:

$$\frac{x}{e^x - 1} = \sum_{n=0}^{\infty} \frac{B_n}{n!} x^n$$

to derive (3.2.1) and show that the latter is equivalent, via (2.2.15), to (2.2.9). Prove the Fourier identity (3.2.6).

Problem 3.2.2: Show that the denominator function $D_N(x)$ enjoys the symmetry

$$D_N(\omega x) = -D_N(x)$$

and argue further that indeed D_N is x^N times a power series in x^{2N}. Now observe that the denominator function for N a power of two, say $N = 2^k$, can be computed via the following algorithm (we use *Mathematica* to express the operations here):

```
reflect[f_] := (f /. x-> -x);
star[f_] := (Expand[f reflect[f]] /. x->Sqrt[x]);
p[0] = Normal[Series[Sin[x]/x,{x,0,10}]] /. x ->Sqrt[x];
p[k_] := If[k > 0, star[p[k-1]]];
p[2]


1 - x/9450 + 59 x^2/1302566265000 - ...


w = Exp[Pi I/4];
Series[Product[Sin[w^k x], {k,0,3}], {x,0, 20}]


-I x^4 + I x^12/9450 - 59 I x^20/1302566265000 + ...
```

Show theoretically that D_N can be recursively computed via a sequence of these "star" operations (which in turn involve "reflect" operations as in the code). These observations provide another proof that, when $N = 2^k$, D_N is x^N times a power series in x^{2N}. Finally, work out an algorithm for computation of the N different *numerator* polynomials (exemplified for the special case $N = 2$ by (3.2.3)). It turns out that, if the numerator polynomials $\{A_m(x)\}$ are indexed in a certain, natural order, then they enjoy some nice symmetries, *e.g.*, sums such as $(A_{m+N/2} \pm A_m)$ are especially simple.

Problem 3.2.3: Determine the coefficients in the D_N series for $N = 4$ in terms of a recursion relation amongst said coefficients. For this N the series can be written:

$$D_4(x) \ = \ x^4 \sum_{n=0}^{\infty} \frac{A_n}{(8n+4)!} x^{8n}$$

where the A_n turn out to satisfy $A_n = FA_{n-1} + GA_{n-2}$; $n \geq 2$, for absolute constants F, G. So the problem here is to find F, G. What sort of recursion relation works for $N = 8$ or even some higher N?

Problem 3.2.4: Write a program that uses (3.2.6) for $N = 4$ (the previous two problems may be useful) and thus establishes irregular pairs $(2k, p)$ for various primes p. Note that one also has to evaluate numerator polynomials in (3.2.6), and a useful fact is that each of these will satisfy a recurrence relation analogous to that of the previous problem. Note also that if all the Bernoulli numbers with even indices less than $p-1$ are nozero modulo p, then you have proved FLT for the exponent p.

Problem 3.2.5: Write a program that resolves irreguler pairs $(2k, p)$ via one of the continued fraction formalisms, (3.2.8)-(3.2.9) or (3.2.10)-(3.2.11).

Problem 3.2.6: Assuming p is an odd prime, write the Shokrollahi DFT (3.2.14) explicitly as a DFT of length $(p-1)/2$. Then argue that the DFT is the evaluation of a certain polynomial $f(x)$ at all points $x = g^{2m}$. Since these x are precisely the quadratic residues (mod p), it makes sense to evaluate f modulo the polynomial $(x^{(p-1)/2}-1)$. If $(p-1)/2$ in turn is possessed of conveniently small factors, one may obtain f modulo smaller degree polynomials, and in this way perform rapid polynomial evaluation. Describe the overall evaluation algorithm, and the role that small factors of $(p-1)/2$ play. This evaluation scheme is how Shokrollahi has managed to resolve irregular pairs for some very large primes ~ 20 million.

Problem 3.2.7: To the author's knowledge the largest known regular prime is:

$$67108859$$

which was found using the Appendix code "conlib.c" to calculate a sectioned DFT. Verify the regularity of this prime, or better: find a larger regular prime.

Problem 3.2.8: Write a prime-factor FFT to compute the Shokrollahi DFT (3.2.14). Note that, as intimated in Problem 3.2.6, the length can be taken to be $(p-1)/2$; and that code implementations of prime-factor FFTs can be found in [*Projects* 1994, p. 373].

Problem 3.2.9: Investigate the conjecture that if g is a primitive root of p, then

$$h_n = \sum_{j=1}^{p-1} j^n \left[\frac{gj}{p} \right]$$

vanishes (mod p) if and only if B_{n+1} does. In particular, is this equivalent to the Shokrollahi DFT result? What about the present author's converse conjecture: that if $(2k, p)$ is an irregular pair, then for any $g > 1$ (not necessarily a primitive root) h_{2k-1} vanishes (mod p). If there be anything to this second conjecture, then forcing $g = 2$ may allow a vary rapid test on particular irregular pairs.

Problem 3.2.10: The "irregularity index" of an odd prime p is the total number of irregular pairs $(2k, p)$. An irregularity index of zero signifies a regular prime, and hence a settled exponent for FLT. The largest known irregularity index is seven. Show that the prime $p = 527377$ has index six while $p = 5216111$ and 5620861 have index seven. For example, 5620861 divides the numerator of each of the numbers

$$B_{4907976}, \ B_{1740504}, \ B_{4637100}, \ B_{2357692}, \ B_{1024990}, \ B_{3970642}, \ B_{4979346}$$

Euler numbers

Euler numbers are defined by the generating series

$$\operatorname{sech} x = \sum_{n=0}^{\infty} E_n \frac{x^n}{n!} \tag{3.2.15}$$

and there have been some interesting questions raised. For example, though it is known that if a prime $p \equiv 5 \pmod 8$, then $E_{(p-1)/2} \not\equiv 0 \pmod p$ [Guy 1981]. Yet, there is the question of whether this congruence can hold for $p \equiv 1 \pmod 8$. It seems that if there be a case of the congruence for some p less than, say,

10 million, then it should be findable via the methods outlined in the previous section.

Problem 3.2.11: Using Newton polynomial division as in the previous section where Bernoulli numbers were considered, and preferably with a multisectioning technique, search for instances of $E_{(p-1)/2}$ divisible by p, for p = 1 (mod 8).

3.3 *Factoring*

State of the factoring art

As of this writing, we have the interesting scenario in which various predictions of factoring limits have, over the last decade or two, been considerably off the mark. As described in [Odlyzko 1995b], the records for the digit size of an integer lying at the limit of factorability look like so:

Year	Record factorizations
1964	20 decimal digits
1974	45 decimal digits
1984	71 decimal digits
1994	129 decimal digits

These sizes refer to "random" integers in some sense, for integers of certain special forms are more vulnerable on average. Whereas the celebrated 129-digit cryptographic number RSA129, which is

114381625757888867669235779976146612010218296721242362562561842935706935\
2457338978305971235639587050589890751475992900268795435415 =
34905295108476509491478496199038981334177646384933878439908205775 *
32769132993266709549961988190834461413177642967992942539798288533

was split quite recently into the two large prime factors shown [Atkins et.al. 1995] ; an even larger, 155-digit number $F_9 = 2^{512} + 1$ had been factored several years before. The RSA129 number was factored with a multiple polynomial variation of the quadratic sieve, while F_9 was overcome with the number field sieve [Lenstra and Lenstra 1993] . The current situation–which depends of course both on algorithms and machinery–appears to be as follows. First, the quadratic sieve is the most efficient general purpose method for numbers above 100 digits (though not for more than about 150 digits). The number field sieve was at first applicable mainly to numbers of special form, such as the Fermat numbers or generally "Cunningham" numbers $a^m \pm 1$. But in recent years the number field sieve has enjoyed various improvements, and now can be applied effectively to some arbitrary numbers beyond 100 decimal digits.

It should be stressed that, for much of the factorization work that has been carried out recently for >100 digit numbers, it has become fashionable (if not necessary) to use many computers in parallel fashion. Because the "workhorse" algorithms of today, like the quadratic sieve and the number field sieve, are parallelizable in almost every phase of the factorizations, it is no longer the best idea to apply one very fast scalar supercomputer; rather, to apply networked computers. [Odlyzko 1995b] gives the following table of the effort required for typical record factorizations; without which table the previous table of record digit sizes is conceptually incomplete:

Year	MIPS-Years to achieve record factorizations
1974	0.001 (a few hours at 1 MIP (10^6 instructions/sec.))
1984	0.1 (a MIP running for about one month)
1994	5000 (requiring many machines)

Problem 3.3.1: Study the situation involving the most powerful factoring algorithms, and attempt to forge an estimate of how many digits will be the

factoring limit (for "random and hard" integers) by the year 2000. What about: by the year 2010? This is a hard question, especially in view of the failure of some of the experts to have successfully predicted what has happened in the current decade.

Problem 3.3.2: Based on references in this section, and references therein (and also [*Projects* 1994]), implement a powerful factoring algorithm of modern vintage. This exercise does not make practical sense unless some computational network is available (or unless one develops a new algorithm or variant of an existing algorithm). Still, see the next section for factorizations that yet can be done with moderate resources. Incidentally, an excellent factoring newsletter is periodically issued by S. Wagstaff of Purdue University; which newsletter contains a thorough summary of "most wanted" numbers and recent achievements in the field.

Factoring with limited resources

Even though some of the most spectacular recent factorizations have involved massive network efforts, there is yet a great deal that can be achieved via moderate resources; *e.g.,* smaller networks. Here are some facts that might be useful to anyone contemplating a relatively humble factoring approach:

- We have mentioned that F_9 has been completely factored (in fact via NFS and large network). Just as the present book was going to press, the author was informed of R. Brent's demolition of the number $F_{10} = 2^{1024}+1 = 45592577 * 6487031809 *$ 4659775785220018543264560743076778192897 * prime252. The new 40-digit factor was found via elliptic curves running on a moderate number of workstations. Note that a few years before, Brent had already demolished $F_{11} = 2^{2048}+1$ in similar fashion.

- The elliptic curve method has the tantalizing feature that, unlike the powerful sieves MPQS and NFS, the run time depends strongly on the unfound factor rather than on just the whole number to be factored. On this principle the present author found, in 1991, the two factors 2663848877152141313 and 3603109844542291969 of $F_{13} = 2^{8192} + 1$, using the elliptic curve method on a few dozen machines. Very recently (June 1995) R. Brent found a new factor of F_{13}; namely, 3195460208205516432206725 13, again without using a large network. Thus F_{13} is the product of the three factors just listed, an old factor 2710954639361, and a 2391-digit composite. There is still some possibility that the composite can be broken further with the elliptic curve method and not an untoward number of machines.

• There is an "RSA Factoring Challenge" list put out by RSA Data Security, Inc., many of whose unfactored entries might still be susceptible to attacks via moderate resources.

• The "genuine composite" $F_{14} = 2^{16384} + 1$ (genuine meaning it has been proven composite yet not a single factor is known) remains elusive. Though this number has been hit hard with the elliptic curve and other methods, it may yet harbor a factor of less than 40 digits.

• There is no known factor of $F_{20} = 2^{1048576}+1$, nor of $F_{22} = 2^{4194304}+1$, yet both of these "genuine" numbers are proven composite [Crandall *et. al.* 1995b]. These numbers have been sieved to rule out up to roughly 20 digit factors, but it would not be too surprising if an elliptic curve or $(p-1)$-method approach were to turn up a factor of between 20 and 30 digits for one or both numbers.

• There is still something to be said for outright sieving. In order to sieve out Mersenne prime candidates, for example, it would be lucrative to improve existing schemes for finding small (say less than 15 digit) divisors for numbers in the region of one million bits.

We turn to a few factorization methods that can yield spectacular isolated results, which methods stand distinct from the powerful aforementioned methods that compeletely factor 100+ digit numbers. One method, the Pollard $(p-1)$ method, sometimes achieves sharp results, depending on the "smoothness" of a hidden factor p of N (the number to be factored). A number is said to be s-smooth if none of its prime factors exceed s. When a hidden factor of N is s-smooth for sufficiently small s, the $(p-1)$ method is especially efficient.

Our reason for discussing the $(p-1)$ method is not to begin a tour of the relatively elementary factorization methods. The galaxy of such methods is touched upon in [*Projects* 1994] and references therein, so we shall not develop the many elementary alternatives. Rather, it turns out that the particular $(p-1)$ method can be enhanced dramatically, due mainly to the work of [Montgomery 1992][Montgomery and Silverman 1990] who have developed modern enhancements. We shall ultimately look at the method from the vantage point of other algorithms in this book; notably, along the lines of polynomial evaluation. The present author believes that the full refinement of the method should yet be able to discover new factors of some very large numbers. What is more, [Montgomery 1992] indicates how the same enhancements may be applied efficiently to the elliptic curve method. From the present perspective it is useful to consider the elliptic curve method as a multipronged analogy to the $(p-1)$ method. In the former, one may use the following ideas on a virtually endless succession of elliptic curves, hoping that an elliptic group order be smooth; whereas the $(p-1)$ method depends on one lucky notion: that a hidden factor of N be sufficiently smooth. Of course, the $(p-1)$ approach is much simpler to code in software, so we shall concentrate mainly upon that method in what follows.

An elementary description of Pollard's $(p-1)$ method runs as follows. To find a factor of N, choose an integer a and compute:

$$GCD\left(a^{\prod p_i^{t_i}} - 1, N\right)$$

where the p_i are small primes raised to various powers (usually the smaller primes are raised to the higher powers). The idea is, if a prime p is a hidden factor of N, and if we are lucky enough that the product in the exponent above is divisible by $p-1$, then

$$a^{\prod} = a^{M(p-1)} = 1 \,(\mathrm{mod}\,p)$$

for some multiple M, and the GCD is likely to yield the factor p of N. Thus if $p-1$ be sufficiently smooth (specifically, if one employs the right set of p_i), the product will likely produce the factor p. The following *Mathematica* example is an elementary experiment along these lines:

(3.3.1)

```
(* Pollard (p-1) method for (sometimes) rapid
   factorization. This is "stage one" of a full
   algorithm.
 *)

n = 67030883744037259;
s = Floor[N[Sqrt[n]]];
a = 3;
q = 1;
b1 = 1000; (* Smoothness limit, or stage-one limit. *)
While[True,
   p = Prime[q]; ++q;
   e = Floor[N[Log[p, s]]]; (* Use p-dependent powers. *)
   a = PowerMod[a, p^e, n];
   g = GCD[a-1, n];
   If[g > 1, Print[g]; Break[]];
   If[p > b1, Break[]];
];

373587883
```

Incidentally, a much more compact *Mathematica* implementation can be done with a single function, like so:

```
PollardP[n_, c_, max_] :=
    GCD[PowerMod[c, LCM @@ Range[max], n]-1,n];
PollardP[11111111111, 3, 100]
```

```
21649
```

It is interesting that this example runs in about one second on a typical modern workstation, and it is hard to imagine sieving, say, to find a factor $>$ 10^8 with such speed. The example works, of course, because the discovered prime factor minus one is reasonably smooth:

$$373587882 = 2 * 3 * 31 * 59^2 * 577$$

It turns out that many instances of $(p-1)$ are not especially smooth, but happen instead to be a fairly smooth number times a *single* outlying prime. For such a circumstance, a so-called "second stage" to the $(p-1)$ method is called for. (This second stage idea, like almost every principle we are discussing for the $(p-1)$ method, applies equally well to the fundamentally more powerful elliptic curve method [Montgomery 1992].)

The second stage method works as follows. Assume we have already in stage one calculated $A = a^\Pi$ where Π is a product of primes not exceeding some smoothness limit b_1, but with each prime raised to an appropriate power. After having failed to produce a factor of N with $GCD(A-1, N)$, we may try to compute

$$GCD\left(\prod_{r > b_1}^{b_2} (A^r - 1),\ N \right) \tag{3.3.2}$$

where the product appearing here is carried out over primes r in the interval $(b_1, b_2]$. If a hidden factor p of N has structure:

$$p-1 \; = \; (\text{some } b_1\text{-smooth number}) * r$$

where the outlying prime r is some prime in $(b_1, b_2]$, then (3.3.2) will likely produce the factor p of N.

Because the exponent $r\Pi$ of a implicit in (3.3.2) involves a single prime r, there is an efficient speed-up that works like so [Montgomery 1987]. Assume we can store in a table the successive differences between primes. If q denotes the first prime greater than the stage-one limit b_1, then via stored differences Δ_n we can recover the primes in the interval $(b_1, b_2]$ as:

$$q, \; q + \Delta_1, \; q + \Delta_1 + \Delta_2, \; q + \Delta_1 + \Delta_2 + \Delta_3, \dots$$

Then the following algorithm accumulates terms $(a^{r\Pi} - 1)$:

$$b := a^{\Pi} \quad \text{(already in hand, from stage one)}$$
$$a := b^q \quad \text{(raise } b \text{ to the first prime in the interval } (b_1, b_2])$$
$$c := 1 \quad \text{(initialize)}$$

$$a := a * b^{\Delta_1}$$
$$c := c * (a - 1) \quad \text{(Ultimately we take the } GCD(c, N))$$

$$a := a * b^{\Delta_2}$$
$$c := c * (a - 1)$$
$$\text{etc. } \dots$$

and so on, where each of the multiplication and powering operations is to be followed with a (mod N) to keep values under control. It is clear that an extra advantage is enjoyed if we actually store not the prime differences *per se* but the numbers $\{b^{\Delta}\}$. In practice, the maximum difference does not get too large (apparently no larger than $\log^2 b_2$), and furthermore it is always an even difference.

The following *Mathematica* example shows a second stage factorization of the Mersenne number

$$N = 2^{67}-1 = 147573952589676412927$$

using stage-one and stage-two limits $b_1 = 500$, $b_2 = 10000$ respectively. The previous code is presumed to have been executed with starting number $n = 2^{67}-1$ in (3.3.1). Note how a table of $\{b^\Delta\}$ is formed, using the maximum detected prime difference.

(3.3.3)

```
(* Second stage of (p-1) method.   Intact values of
    n, b1, q, p, a are assumed from stage one. *)

b2 = 10000;
plist = Table[Prime[r],{r,q, PrimePi[b2]+1}];
pdiff = Table[plist[[r+1]]-plist[[r]],{r,1,Length[plist]-1}];
md = Max[pdiff];
c = Mod[a^2, n];
facts = Table[PowerMod[c, r, n],{r,1,md/2}];
a = PowerMod[a, Prime[q], n];
c = 1;
Do[
            a = Mod[a*facts[[pdiff[[q]]/2]], n];
            c = Mod[c*(a-1), n],
            {q,1,Length[pdiff]}
];
g = GCD[c,n];
If[g > 1, Print[g," * ", n/g]];

193707721 * 761838257287
```

The program finds the hidden factor $p = 193707721$ because

$$p-1 = 193707720 = 2^3 * 3^3 * 5 * 67 * 2677$$

Here, the first stage of the *Mathematica* absorbed all the factors through 67 because the smoothness limit b_1 was 500; then the second stage covered the factor 2677 because this is less than the second stage limit $b_2 = 10000$.

But the two-stage idea can be taken yet further, not with a third stage but with more efficient ways of carrying out the second stage. Let us first explore the idea of using not (3.3.2) for the second stage, but something like:

$$GCD\left(\prod_C \left(a^{C\prod p_i^{t_i}} - 1\right), N \right)$$

where C runs over "random composites." That way, if there be an outlying prime r, we may hope to include it by accident, as a factor of some random C. To this end, consider setting $b := a^{\prod}$ as before, but now for some carefully chosen fixed power K accumulate the product:

$$c = \prod_{i,j}\left(b^{i^K} - b^{j^K}\right) \qquad (3.3.4)$$

over various values of (unequal) i, j. Now if there happens to be a congruence $i^K = j^K \pmod r$ for the outlying prime r, then a $GCD(c, N)$ may well produce the factor p of N. Thus it becomes useful to be able to evaluate rapidly numbers of the form

$$x^{n^K} \qquad ; \; x, K \text{ fixed} \quad ; \; n = 1, 2, 3, \ldots$$

Happily, this can be done in a style reminiscent of the evaluation of a polynomial along arithmetic progression values:

Algorithm for evaluation of $x^{1^K}, x^{2^K}, x^{3^K}, \ldots$ for given x and K: $\qquad$ (3.3.5)

1) For $j = 0$ to K
$$z_j := x^{j! \, S_K(j)} ; \qquad (* \text{ This powering and other operations}$$
$$\text{would be done (mod } N\text{) in}$$
$$\text{a factoring problem. } *)$$
where $S_K(j)$ denotes the Stirling number of the second kind. Note the special test values $z_0 = 1$, $z_1 = x$, and $z_K = x^{K!}$.

2) For $n = 1$ to ∞ {

$$z_0 := z_0 * z_1 ;$$

(* Now z_0 is the desired x^{n^K}. *)

$$z_1 := z_1 * z_2 ;$$

...

$$z_{K-1} := z_{K-1} * z_K ;$$

}

Note that the first z table entry z_0 is the one to track for the desired powers, while the last entry z_K never changes. A *Mathematica* implementation of this n^K method is as follows:

(3.3.6)

```
(* n^K second stage method.  Intact values of
   n, a are assumed from stage one. *)

k = 24;
b = a;
z = Table[PowerMod[b, j! StirlingS2[k, j], n], {j, 0, k}];
powtable = {};
numpows = 50;
Do[
  Do[
    z[[q]] = Mod[z[[q]] * z[[q+1]], n],
    {q, 1, Length[z]-1}
  ];
  powtable = Append[powtable, z[[1]]],
  {m, 1, numpows}
];
c=1;
Do[
    Do[
      c = Mod[c (powtable[[j]]-powtable[[i]]), n];
      , {i,j+1,numpows}
    ],
    {j,1,numpows-1}
];
```

```
g = GCD[c,n];
If[g > 1, Print[g," * ", n/g]];
```

193707721 * 761838257287

What this program does in its final double loop is calculate (3.3.4) over a set of indices $i > j$. This is not an optimal way to use n^K powers, as has been noted by [Montgomery 1992]. For one thing, there is some redundancy in the product (3.3.4). For example, if a pair (i, j) have been checked, there is no need to check say $(3i, 3j)$. The reference [Montgomery 1992] discusses means for generating power sequences having less redundancy. In addition, one should check GCD[c, n] periodically within the final double loop, since there is often no reason to continue looping after a factor is found. With just a few such enhancements it is possible to start wielding some real "workstation power" for factoring special numbers. In *Mathematica* it is possible in this way to factor F_8 (see Problem 3.3.4) in one sitting.

There is yet another known second-stage enhancement which in some ways represents the state of the art in the problem of inclusion of "outlying primes." This technique has been used in [Montgomery and Silverman 1990][Montgomery 1992], and amounts to a polynomial evaluation scheme. Say we have, as usual, obtained a first-stage value a^Π where Π is the usual product of primes $< b_1$, raised to appropriate powers. Now for some highly composite number B near to, but not exceeding b_1, consider the collection of values

$$b^{Bm+r_1} - 1, \quad b^{Bm+r_2} - 1, \quad ..., \quad b^{Bm+r_\phi} - 1 \qquad (3.3.7)$$

where m runs through $1, 2, ..., M$ and the r_i are the $\phi(B)$ integers in $[1, B-1]$ that are coprime to B. It is evident that taking the *GCD* of each of the values in (3.3.7) with N will eventually cover any outlying prime r that lies in the second-stage interval $(B, (M+1)B)$. In other words, the set of values $\{Bm + r_i\}$ contains all primes in said interval. But this means we may simply evaluate the polynomial

$$(x - b^{-r_1})(x - b^{-r_2}) \cdots (x - b^{-r_\phi}) \tag{3.3.8}$$

at the set of points $x = b^B$, b^{2B}, b^{3B}, ..., b^{MB}. (Of course, all polynomial arithmetic will be modulo N). To this end, we can use the fact that was mentioned in Chapter 1; namely, a polynomial can be, by way of a certain convolution, evaluated at points lying in a geometric progression. The algorithm one can use is:

$$\tag{3.3.9}$$

Algorithm for evaluation of a polynomial along a geometric progression:

1) Given $f(x) = a_0 + a_1 x + a_2 x^2 + ... + a_n x^n$, where $n = 2^k$; we wish to

   evaluate f at $x = g, g^2, g^3, ..., g^n$.

2) Form the sequences

$$A = \left\{ a_0, a_1 g^{T_1}, a_2 g^{T_2}, ..., a_n g^{T_n}, 0, ..., 0 \right\}$$

$$B = \left\{ g^{-T_{n-1}}, ..., g^{-T_1}, 1, 1, g^{-T_1}, ..., g^{-T_{n-1}} \right\}$$

   where $T_n = n(n+1)/2$ is the n-th triangle number, and the A sequence has been padded with $n-1$ zeros. Thus both sequences are of length $2n = 2^{k+1}$.

3) Compute $C = \{C_0, C_1, ..., C_{2n-1}\}$ as the length-$2n$ cyclic convolution of A and B. Then the desired evaluations of f are:

$$f(g^k) = g^{-T_{k-1}} C_{n+k-1} \quad ; \quad k = 1, 2, ..., n$$

Note that to evaluate such as (3.3.8) (mod N) along a geometric progression with this algorithm, one must obtain the explicit coefficients a_i. Methods for getting from roots to coefficients by "multiplying up" are discussed in Section 1.5. Another observation is, in step (2) of the algorithm, we do not of course need to keep track of the power-of-g prefactors. In other words, after evaluating (3.3.8) via the convolution C, we can simply check

$$GCD(C_{2n-1}C_{2n-2}\ldots C_n, N)$$

hoping for a factor of N.

Problem 3.3.3: Write a Pollard $(p-1)$ program (in a language of choice, hopefully on a fast system) that uses the first- and second-stage techniques exemplified by (3.3.1), (3.3.3). Then enhance the second stage using one or more of the following options:

1) Invoke the n^K method (exemplified by (3.3.7)) or some other method of inducing composite powers.
2) Invoke the polynomial evaluation method.
3) Invoke some parallelism; *e.g.* have various machines handle various disjoint arithmetic progressions for the second stage interval primes.

We remind ourselves that each of these possible enhancements may be effected analogously for the elliptic curve method.

Problem 3.3.4: Use an enhanced Pollard $(p-1)$ method to factor $F_8 = 2^{256}+1$. (This is really getting somewhere with limited resources, since this number was not factored until 1980 by Brent and Pollard (by the Pollard "rho" method).) Two good approaches are:

1) Use stage-one limit $b_1 = 1000$, then use $K = 240$ in the n^K second stage; or

2) Evaluate the polynomial (3.3.8), via the convolution to geometric progression Algorithm (3.3.9), at powers b^{mB}, with $B = 2*3*5*7*11*61$. The present author found this a convenient practical choice for the composite B, because f(B) = 28800, so that the polynomial (3.3.8) can be embedded in one of degree 2^{15}. This, together with the Nussbaumer convolution of Section 4.4, is enough to factor F_8 in a few hours on a typical modern workstation.

Note that both these options (especially (2)) require considerable memory. One way to reduce the memory requirement per machine is to invoke some parallelism.

Problem 3.3.5: Write a factoring program that endeavors *completely* to factor using the following hierarchy of algorithms:

Given a number N to be factored:

1) Try first a sieve, that is rapid division by all primes less than say 2^{16}.

2)* Optionally, try briefly a Pollard "rho" method (see various references such as [*Projects* 1994]) until factors less than some choice like 10^{10} to 10^{15} are ruled out.

3)* Try a first-stage $(p–1)$ method.

4)* Try then a stage two $(p–1)$.

5) Try an elliptic curve method, stage one, then if necessary stage two. In particular, the [Montgomery 1992] polynomial-evaluation second stage for elliptic curves is probably the most efficient scheme available for finding factors up to 40 digits or perhaps more. It should be possible with these steps (1)-(5), with (2)-(4) perhaps avoided, to create a program that will completely factor any 50- or 60- digit number N in a convenient time span.

6) If a remaining unfactored piece lies beyond the modern range of the elliptic curve method (*i.e.*, has 80-to-150 digits, say), consider using multiple polynomial quadratic sieve (MPQS) or number field sieve (NFS).

*Note that some factoring experts recommend avoiding such as (2) (3), (4) and going straight ahead with elliptic curves (5) or the last resorts (6). The usual argument is that in a certain algebraic sense, a $(p–1)$ attempt is like a "one shot" choice of elliptic curve. Yet, the overhead in this one shot is very low (witness the simplicity of the *Mathematica* examples in the preceding text). Thus, if one includes (3) and (4) it is like asking for a lucky smoothness property for $(p-1)$; after which a somewhat slower but virtually endless supply of curve calculations can proceed.

The real task here though, aside from the optimization of some of the simpler factoring algorithms, is to forge a *complete* factoring engine. You have been successful if any number having 30 digits or less is always completely factored, including into multiple prime factors (*i.e.* primes-to-powers), without errors or unreduced composite factors of any kind.

Problem 3.3.6: Prove that Algorithm (3.3.9) works by showing algebraically that the convolution yields the desired evaluations.

3.4   *Fermat numbers*

The story of F_{22}

Fermat's conjecture, that each of the numbers

$$F_n = 2^{2^n} + 1$$

for $n = 0,1,2,...$ be prime, is about as ill-fated as a conjecture can be. It is now known that F_n is prime for $n = 0,1,2,3,4$ but no other Fermat primes have been discovered. In fact, we have proof that the n-th Fermat number is composite for every $5 \leq n \leq 23$, and many other $n > 24$. For many, but not all of these n we know explicit factors [*Projects* 1994]. However, the numbers F_{14}, F_{20}, F_{22} are at the time of this writing "genuine" composites, meaning proven composite yet no explicit factor is known. The smallest Fermat number of unknown character is now F_{24}.

The story of how F_{22} was recently proven composite is an interesting one in that both computational and cultural aspects of the proof emerge. In the published proof of [Crandall *et. al.* 1995b], the definitive Pepin primality test is stated in the following form. For $n \geq 1$, assume F_n is a quadratic non-residue modulo an odd prime q. Then F_n is prime if and only if

$$q^{(F_n-1)/2} = -1 \,(\text{mod}\, F_n) \qquad (3.4.1)$$

One may therefore compute and report the residue, call it R_n, defined by the least non-negative residue:

$$R_n = 3^{(F_n-1)/2} \,(\text{mod}\, F_n) \qquad (3.4.2)$$

Clearly, F_n with $n \geq 1$ is prime if and only if the final Pepin residue R_n has the binary form $R_n = 10000...0$ where there are precisely 2^n zeros.

Let us investigate then the work that was required to prove F_{22} composite. First, $2^{22} = 4194304$, so the algorithm runs:

$$(3.4.3)$$

1) Start with $x := 3$.

2) Square x exactly 4194303 times, always reducing $(\text{mod}\, F_{22})$.

3) Now F_{22} is prime if and only if the leading binary bit of x is "1." Thus the Pepin test literally provides a "one-bit answer" to the primality question.

Of course, what makes the algorithm expensive is that almost every one of the 4-million-plus squarings must be performed on numbers R having about 4 million binary bits each. It turns out that a discrete weighted transform (DWT) approach can perform these Pepin squarings using transform run lengths of only $2^{17} = 131072$. We outline the technique as follows. For any x with $0 < x < F_n - 1$, defined the digits $\{x_j\}$ of x in base $W = 2^m$ by:

$$x = \sum_{j=0}^{N-1} x_j \, W^j \qquad\qquad (3.4.4)$$

where the run length is determined from the word size W and the Fermat number in question by $W^N = F_n - 1$. Now if the squaring were to be performed as an acyclic convolution of $\{x_j\}$ with itself, one might use the standard zero-padding-with-FFT multiply as discussed in Chapter 1. The run length for word size $W = 2^{16}$ would be $2N$ (which for F_{22} would be $2^{19} = 524288$). However, because we already know that $W^N = -1 \pmod{F_n}$, we can simply perform–without zero-padding–the negacyclic convolution of the weighted signal

$$\left\{ x_0, \; x_1 e^{i\pi/N}, \; x_2 e^{2i\pi/N}, \; ..., \; x_{N-1} e^{(N-1)i\pi/N} \right\} \qquad (3.4.5)$$

with itself. (After said auto-negacyclic convolution we "unweight" the result with factors $e^{-i\pi k/N}$, normalize the FFT, and round to integer elements to obtain pure-real digits for the square.) Thus the run length is N instead of padded length $2N$, and furthermore there are ways to render the FFT of a sequence (3.4.5), where each x_j is real, virtually as fast as the FFT of a pure-real sequence [Crandall and Fagin 1994]. Thus the negacyclic idea yields a genuine gain. But one can go yet further, and reduce the run length again by a factor of two, to give $N/2$. In this case we use complex FFTs to perform a "right-angle" convolution. It turns out that the transform $x^\wedge$ defined:

$$x_k^\wedge = \sum_{j=0}^{N/2-1} \left(x_j + i\, x_{j+N/2} \right) e^{\frac{\pi i j}{N}} \, e^{\frac{2\pi i j k}{N}} \qquad (3.4.6)$$

can be used to determine $x^2 \pmod{F_n}$ (see Problem 3.4.1). A *Mathematica* example of a fast algorithm for the Pepin test is as follows:

(3.4.7)

```
(* DWT-based Pepin test for Fermat number primality. *)

n = 8;
f = 2^(2^n) + 1; (* Choose the Fermat number. *)
w = 2^16;  (* Digit size. *)
len = Log[w, f-1]; (* Number of signal digits. *)

fermatSquare[x_] := Module[
    {run = len/2, digx, j, a, xhat, square},
    digx = Reverse[IntegerDigits[x, w]];
    Do[digx = Append[digx, 0] ,{q,Length[digx]+1,len}];
    (* Next, create complex digits. *)
    digx = Take[digx, {1,run}] + I Take[digx,{run+1,len}];
    a = N[Table[Exp[I j Pi/len],{j,0,run-1}]];
    digx *= a; (* Form weighted signal. *)
    xhat = N[InverseFourier[digx]];
    xhat *= xhat; (* Spectral squaring. *)
    xhat = N[Fourier[xhat]];
    xhat *= N[Sqrt[run]/a]; (* Weighted normalization. *)
    digx = Round[Join[Re[xhat], Im[xhat]]];
    square = Sum[digx[[q]] w^(q-1), {q,1,len}];
    Mod[square, f]
    ];
Timing[
x = 3;
Do[
    x = fermatSquare[x],
    {q,1,2^n-1}
];
Print["f_",n," is"];
If[x == f-1,  Print["prime."], Print["composite."]];
Print["The Selfridge-Hurwitz residues are:"];
Print[Mod[x, 2^35-1]," ",Mod[x,2^36]," ",Mod[x,2^36-1]];
]

f_8 is
composite.
```

```
The Selfridge-Hurwitz residues are:
30627284506 46310188723 35403253324
{24.3 Second, Null}
```

This example shows a proof that F_8 is composite, which *Mathematica* proof takes less than one minute on a typical workstation. This type of algorithm should take roughly four times longer for each increment in the Fermat index; for example, on the same system used for the above test F_9 should require about 100 seconds. Note that the *Mathematica* example reports the Selfridge-Hurwitz residues, which are the final Pepin residue modulo the three given numbers. The recording of such numbers is one way to test Pepin residues between people and between machines, without having to move around the sometimes gigantic full residues. The paper [Crandall *et. al.* 1995b] lists all Selfridge-Hurwitz residues of F_n for $n = 5$ through 22.

The interesting cultural aspect of the F_{22} story is the fact of a wholly independent *second* proof. This second proof finished a few months after the effort of the present author and collaborators (which effort we shall call the "American" proof for the moment). The second proof took place:

- in another country
- on another hardware system
- using different software

What happened was, the team of [Trevisan and Carvalho 1994], working at the Brazilian Supercomputer Center used numerical packages written by D. Bailey, to effect their own Pepin test on F_{22}. (The North American team had used a custom DWT program tailored for Pepin tests.) The Selfridge-Hurwitz residues from this "Brazilian proof" were in full agreement with those of the American proof. It is perhaps of interest that neither team was aware of the other until the North American proof was finished. It is hard to imagine a better confirmation of a machine proof of something. It seems fair to say: there can be no doubt that F_{22} is composite.

Problem 3.4.1: Prove that if one takes a length-N FFT of the weighted signal (3.4.5), squares this elementwise, takes an inverse FFT of the result, and unweights and normalizes properly, the resulting signal is a valid set of digits for x^2 (mod F_n). (In practice, one needs to round the digits to nearest integer and add-with-carry so that the digits are reduced to lie in $[0,1,...,W-1]$.) In this way the Pepin test can be FFT-based (see Problem 3.4.7).

Problem 3.4.2: Along the lines of the previous problem, show that the half-length "right-angle" transform $x^\wedge$ defined in (3.4.6), after being properly squared, inverse transformed, unweighted, normalized and rounded, will yield valid real digits of x^2 (mod F_n).

Problem 3.4.3: As of this writing, the character of F_{24} is unresolved. Note that, while F_{22} is something like a book full of decimal digits, F_{24} is more like a book*shelf*. At the rate of proof the "North American" and "Brazilian" teams actually enjoyed on their respective systems, it would take about 10 years to resolve the character of F_{24}. One good problem is to attempt to optimize *some* algorithm in order to bring this time down to say one year. Interesting possibilities abound, such as the possibility of parallelizing the powering stage. There is no known algorithm to compute (on a scalar machine!) the Pepin residues any faster than by successive squaring. However, using Chinese Remainder Theorem (CRT) arithmetic, it is possible to raise a number to higher than the second power on each step, using many machines; perhaps with each machine handling a massive negacyclic convolution modulo its own unique small prime. In such a scenario, the *digits* of the negacyclic convolution would be reconstructed using preconditioned CRT. As of this writing the author knows of no network implementation of this idea that overcomes the network communication overhead. Nevertheless, the CRT approach should give a certain gain in principle (meaning if inter-process communication times were negligible).

Problem 3.4.4: Attempt to find what would be the first known proper factor of one of the still-genuine composites: F_{14}, F_{20}, F_{22}. These numbers are well beyond the current limits for the powerful quadratic sieve and number field sieve. Here is a recommendation: use an elliptic curve method with the Montgomery polynomial evaluation described in the previous section.

Problem 3.4.5: Study the generalized Fermat numbers

$$F_{b,m} = b^{2^m} + 1$$

It was shown by [Dubner and Keller 1993] that any prime factor p of $F_{b,m}$ must be of the form $p = k2^n + 1$, with $n > m$ and k odd. (For the pure Fermat case $b = 2$ we know that $n \geq m + 2$.) It is known that every prime number divides an infinite number of these generalized Fermat numbers. Another good problem: find gigantic Fermat composites, via sieving. For example Dubner found that

$$145 * 2^{7312} + 1 \text{ divides } F_{7309}$$
$$19 * 2^{23290} + 1 \text{ divides } F_{23288}$$

and thanks to Keller it has been known for a decade that

$$5 * 2^{23473} + 1 \text{ divides } F_{23471}$$

A program to find such divisors can of course be tested on these cases.

Problem 3.4.6: Here is an amusing, if not radical approach to finding factors of Fermat numbers. Since every prime factor p of F_n must have the form

$$p = k2^{n+2} + 1$$

we can contemplate the evaluation of the product:

$$\prod_{k \in S} \left(k + 2^{-2-n}\right)$$

where the set S is a certain union of disjoint arithmetic progressions. These progressions would be determined via a sieve of Eratosthenes (perhaps a simple, symbolic such sieve), carried out over some very long interval. The idea is simply that many primes of the proper form would be intrinsically hidden in the product. But we have discussed several ways of evaluating products of terms in arithmetic progression, and perhaps the application of one of these would yield at least some of the celebrated known factors such as the factors of F_7 and F_8. In fact, a worthwhile starting task is to estimate the running time of an arithmetic-progression scheme applied to F_7.

Problem 3.4.7: We have seen that squaring modulo a Fermat number 2^N+1 is equivalent, up to $O(N)$ side operations, to performing a certain negacyclic autoconvolution, namely the negacyclic convolution of the signal (3.4.5) with itself. Does it make sense to avoid FFTs altogether and effect a Pepin test via the Nussbaumer negacyclic convolution discussed in Chapter 4?

Problem 3.4.8: With negacyclic convolution for Fermat number arithmetic there is no zero-padding. Does it therefore make sense to attempt more than just one square at a time in the Pepin test? In other words, why not square two or three times before each carry adjustment of the digits?

Problem 3.4.9: Mount an assault upon (*i.e.*, try to factor) the "genuine composites" such as F_{14}, F_{20}, F_{22} by invoking some modern algorithms:

• Elliptic curve method with second-stage polynomial evaluation;
• DWT arithmetic without zero-padding;
• Parallelism (either in choosing curves, or perhaps even at the DWT stage!);
• Adroit choice of elliptic curves [Montgomery 1987, 1992].

Note that various Fermat cofactors (of F_{19} in particular) are also genuine composites as explained and tabulated in [*Projects* 1994][Crandall *et. al.* 1995b]. Here is an interesting question: if one is factoring with virtually all of one's resources, and one desires some kind of "hit," *i.e.*, just one satisfying factor, does it make sense to handle some collection of genuine composites simultaneously, or should one attack just one "genuine" at a time?

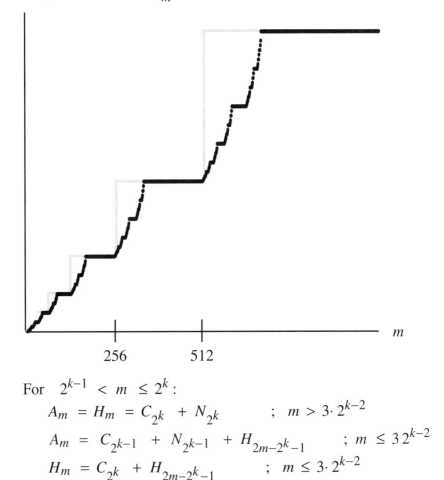

Computational effort A_m

For $2^{k-1} < m \le 2^k$:

$$A_m = H_m = C_{2^k} + N_{2^k} \qquad ; \; m > 3 \cdot 2^{k-2}$$

$$A_m = C_{2^{k-1}} + N_{2^{k-1}} + H_{2m-2^k-1} \qquad ; \; m \le 3\,2^{k-2}$$

$$H_m = C_{2^k} + H_{2m-2^k-1} \qquad ; \; m \le 3 \cdot 2^{k-2}$$

The effectiveness of "devil's convolution." The light gray plot shows the classical effort (via zero-padding and FFTs, say) required to perform an acyclic convolution of length m. The dark plot shows the effort A_m when certain recursion relations involving a "half-cyclic" convolution effort H_m are invoked. The resulting plot is a self-similar devil's staircase fractal.

Transforms

[The fast Fourier transform] has changed the face of science and engineering so much so that it is not an exaggeration to say that life as we know it would be very different without the FFT.

[*Van Loan* 1992]

It is evident from the overwhelming, and apparently never-to-subside, fast Fourier transform (FFT) literature that this most revered grandparent of divide-and-conquer algorithms continues energetically to beget progeny. The many related fast transforms, not to mention special cases of the FFT itself, continue to undergo refinement. Herein we explore some new transform algorithms, wih a view to applications of each.

4.1   *FFT and related algorithms*

FFT review

Let us first review some FFT principles and code examples, for easy reference during the exploration of newer methods. The FFT is a fast algorithm for evaluation of the discrete Fourier transform DFT, which in turn is a transformation of a signal $x = \{x_0, x_1, ..., x_{N-1}\}$ of length N, into a spectrum $x^\wedge = \{x^\wedge_0, x^\wedge_1, ..., x^\wedge_{N-1}\}$:

$$x^\wedge_k = \sum_{j=0}^{N-1} x_j\, e^{-2\pi ijk/N} \qquad (4.1.1)$$

the inverse transform being

$$x_j = \frac{1}{N} \sum_{k=0}^{N-1} x_k^\wedge \, e^{+2\pi i jk/N} \qquad (4.1.2)$$

There are many ways to perform such DFT sums, which is to say there are many types of FFTs. These types in turn depend on the number-theoretic nature of the signal length N, in particular on the prime factorization of N. Here are some types of FFTs commonly in use today:

• Standard Cooley-Tukey and Gentleman-Sande FFTs, for general complex input data having no particular symmetry. Implementations of same usually assume lengths $N = 2^m$, although one can generalize the butterfly structures to other highly composite N.

• Higher-radix FFTs, meaning enhancements of the previous class where the algorithm's internal "butterflies" have modified structure. The run lengths in these situations are usually more specialized, such as $N = 4^m, 8^m$, etc.

• Real-data FFTs, for which one has knowledge that the signal x has all real elements. These FFTs exploit the fact that for run length N even, the transform $x^\wedge$ has Hermitian symmetry; *i.e.*, $x^\wedge_k = x^\wedge_{N-k}{}^*$. Such symmetry allows an asymptotic factor of two speedup in the transform (one can view this intuitively as a consequence of the requirement for half as much spectral data on the basis of the Hermitian redundancy). There are inverse "real-result" FFTs that likewise take Hermitian symmetric input signals and produce a real-only result.

• Split-radix FFTs, possessed of complicated butterfly structure, but tend to be, in practice, among the fastest FFTs known. The combination of split-radix and real-data (or real-result) concepts results in a powerful, practical FFT for real-world data.

• Prime-factor and Winograd FFTs, suitable for signal lengths that, while not perhaps powers of two, are nevertheless products of "small" primes to powers.

• Rader FFTs, of prime length or prime power signal length [McClellan and Rader 1979].

These classes of FFTs are discussed in [*Projects* 1994], along with code examples in *Mathematic* and *C*. For convenience, we list in the Appendix some *Mathematica* examples of forward and inverse standard FFTs. The reader should be advised that in almost any practical situation the speeds of these classical implementations can be beaten. Yet the following standard routines have the distinct advantage that when one moves to different domains (such as polynomial-arithmetic FFTs, number-theoretic transforms, and so on) it is often a good idea to model a more abstract or algebraic FFT starting with these standard loop structures. There is also something to be said for modelling certain problems on the recursive nature of the FFT. Here is a *Mathematica* example of a recursive FFT function:

$$(4.1.3)$$

```
(* Recursive FFT function.
   Signal x's length must be a power of two. *)
fft[x_] :=
   Module[{n, xeven, xodd, g, w},
     If[(n=Length[x]) == 1,Return[x]];
     {xeven, xodd}= Map[fft, Transpose[Partition[x,2]]];
     g = Exp[-2 Pi I/n]; w = Table[g^m,{m,0,n-1}];
     Join[xeven,xeven] + w * Join[xodd,xodd]
   ];

x = {1,1,1,1,-1,-1,-1,-1};
N[fft[x]]

{0, 2. - 4.82843 I, 0, 2. - 0.82842 I, 0,
   2. + 0.82842 I, 0, 2. + 4.82843 I}
```

This recursive example is not optimized for speed. For one thing, it is possible to reduce the computational work by keeping a full table of the powers of the primitive root g, rather than recomputing powers at every recursive level.

Some final review comments seem in order. First, in *Mathematica* the DFT and its inverse (our definitions (4.1.1), (4.1.2)) are given respectively by:

```
Sqrt[Length[x]] InverseFourier[x];  (* Forward DFT of x. *)
Sqrt[1/Length[x]] Fourier[x];       (* Inverse DFT of x. *)
```

Second, perhaps the most important single application of FFTs is in the computation of convolutions. In fact one can at one's leisure move from the world of spectra to the world of convolutions and back. We have the convolution theorem that expresses the cyclic convolution of two signals x and y, both of length N, in terms of their DFT spectra $x^\wedge$ and $y^\wedge$:

$$\sum_{j+k=n\,(\mathrm{mod}\,N)} x_j\, y_k \;=\; \frac{1}{N} \sum_{k=0}^{N-1} x_k^\wedge\, y_k^\wedge\, e^{+2\pi i n k/N} \tag{4.1.4}$$

and in the other direction for N even we have the Bluestein re-indexing trick:

$$\tag{4.1.5}$$

$$x_k^\wedge \;=\; \sum_{j=0}^{N-1} x_j\, e^{-2\pi i j k/N} \;=\; e^{-\frac{\pi i k^2}{N}} \sum_{j=0}^{N-1} \left(x_j e^{-\frac{\pi i j^2}{N}} \right) e^{\pi i (j-k)^2 / N}$$

which reveals that $x^\wedge$ the DFT can be written in terms of a cyclic convolution of two sequences. (For odd signal lengths N see Problem 4.4.21.) As for the convolution theorem (4.1.4), a test of same using the Appendix functions in "FFTs.ma" might go:

```
N[1/Length[a] ffttime[N[fftfreq[a] * fftfreq[b]]]]
(* This gives the cyclic convolution of signals a,b. *)
```

Note that no bit-scrambling is required since ffttime[ ], if given a bit-scrambled result, produces correctly ordered original data. Along the same lines, built-in *Mathematica* functions can be used for the same test, with proper normalization like so:

```
N[Sqrt[Length[a]]] *
    Fourier[N[InverseFourier[a]] * N[InverseFourier[b]]]
(* This gives the cyclic convolution of signals a,b. *)
```

Problem 4.1.1: Implement (on a typical workstation, with a fast, compiled program say) various FFTs. Beyond the standard Cooley-Tukey and Gentleman-Sande FFTs in the Appendix, note that *C* code for various other FFT types is provided in [*Projects* 1994]. Probably the fastest would be (for given real-only data) a split-radix, or Sorenson FFT. A typical, reasonably good workstation benchmark of today is to be able to perform a length-2^{16} real-only FFT in 0.5 seconds or less.

Problem 4.1.2: Prove the convolution theorem (4.1.4) using the definitions (4.1.1)-(4.1.2). Prove an analogous "correlation theorem" where the sum on the left is instead over pairs with $j - k = 0$ (mod N).

Problem 4.1.3: Design and implement an algorithm to compute a prime-length FFT. Call the signal length a prime p. One approach is the following. Note that $x^\wedge_0 = x_0 + ... + x_{p-1}$ and for every k in the remaining set $\{1,...,p-1\}$ obtain $x^\wedge_k$ by assuming a primitive root g of p, so that any member of the set can be cast as some g^m (mod p); whence

$$x^\wedge_{(g^m \%p)} = x_0 + \sum_{h=1}^{p-1} x_{(g^{-h}\%p)} e^{-2\pi i g^{-h} g^m / p} \quad ; m = 1,...,p-1$$

The sum above is a length-$(p-1)$ cyclic convolution of two sequences. This convolution can be embedded in a longer, zero-padded one of length a power of two, whence three FFTs of the new power-of-two length can be used to resolve the convolution. (Alternatively, see the end of this chapter for convolution schemes on non-power-of-two lengths.)   In this way a prime-length FFT can always be performed in $O(p \log p)$ arithmetic operations. How does this Rader trick, which gives a convolution of order $p-1$, compare to invoking the *odd* analog of Bluestein trick (Problem 4.4.21) to obtain a convolution of length p? (Another way to ask this: is there any advantage to the fact of the Rader trick yielding an *even* length?) What about these same questions when the original signal length is a prime power p^b?

Fractional Fourier transform

The fractional Fourier transform (FRFT) of [Bailey and Swartztrauber 1991] is not only of theoretical interest but is also useful in various branches of computational Fourier analysis. Given a signal $x = \{x_0, x_1, ..., x_{N-1}\}$ of length N, define the FRFT to be

$$\hat{x_k}(\alpha) \;=\; \sum_{j=0}^{N-1} x_j \, e^{-2\pi i j k \alpha} \tag{4.1.6}$$

The complex parameter α is not subject to any *a priori* restrictions. Note that the standard DFT and its inverse are both definable in terms of the FRFT:

$$\tag{4.1.7}$$

$$DFT(x) \;=\; \{\hat{x_k}(1/N) \quad ; \; k = 0, 1, ..., N-1\}$$
$$DFT^{-1}(x) \;=\; \frac{1}{N}\{\hat{x_k}(-1/N) \quad ; \; k = 0, 1, ..., N-1\}$$

On the assumption that we have available a suitable FFT algorithm for computing the DFT, the Bailey-Swartztrauber algorithm for the FRFT (4.1.6) runs as follows:

(4.1.8)

Algorithm for computation of the fractional Fourier transform (FRFT):

Given a signal x of length N, and a parameter α;

1) Define two signals y, z each of length $2N$ by:

For $j = 0$ to $N-1$ {

$$y_j := x_j \, e^{-\pi i j^2 \alpha} \; ; \quad z_j := e^{+\pi i j^2 \alpha} \; ;$$

}

For $j = N$ to $2N-1$ {

$$y_j := 0; \quad z_j := e^{+\pi i (j - 2N)^2 \alpha} \; ;$$

}

2) Then the FRFT components are given implicitly by

$$\left\{ x_k^\wedge(\alpha) \, e^{i\pi k^2 \alpha} \; ; \; k = 0, 1, \ldots, N-1 \right\} \;=\; \left(DFT^{-1}[DFT(y)\,DFT(z)] \right)_{\text{left}}$$

where each DFT and the inverse DFT are each of length $2N$, with the notation meaning that the two forward DFTs are multiplied elementwise, while the right-hand half (indices N through $2N-1$) of the final inverse DFT is to be discarded.

The following *Mathematica* example computes the FRFT:

(4.1.9)

```
(* Fractional Fourier transform (FRFT) algorithm. *)

frft[x_, a_] := Module[{v,t,y,z,len = Length[x]},
        v = Table[Exp[Pi I j^2 a],{j,0,len}];
        t = Take[v,{1,len}];
        y = N[Join[x/t, Table[0,{len}]]];
        z = N[Join[t, Take[Reverse[v],{1,len}]]];
```

```
        y = InverseFourier[y]; (* These are forward DFTs.*)
        z = InverseFourier[z];
        y = Fourier[y * z];
        N[Sqrt[2 len] Take[y,{1,len}]/t]
        ];
x = {0,1,2,3,-4,5,6,7,11,13,7,-50};
(* Next, test the routine in the perfect DFT case. *)
a = 1/Length[x];
y = a frft[frft[x,a], -a];
Abs[x-y] . Abs[x-y]   (* Report squared error. *)
4.36995 10^-27
```

The function frft[x, a] will return a numerical fractional transform for signals *x* and arbitrary complex numbers *a*. In the example above, the function is tested on the special case that it is just a DFT (*i.e.*, the parameter *a* is the reciprocal of the signal length).

The FRFT has a powerful application to which we now turn. The problem is to evaluate *continuous* Fourier transforms; *i.e.*, to evaluate numerically an integral:

$$F(x) \ = \ \int_{-\infty}^{\infty} f(t)e^{-itx} dt \qquad\qquad (4.1.10)$$

at some finite set of points $\{x_0, ..., x_{N-1}\}$. The standard, general and powerful numerical integration techniques of today can certainly give very good values for individual points x_i, but to use such numerical methods for the whole set of desired *x* values is wasteful–something like doing a DFT brute-force without a fast algorithm. The Bailey-Swartztrauber recommendation is to do this integral, simultaneously at all the x_i, with an FRFT:

$$(4.1.11)$$

Algorithm for numerical approximation to the continuous Fourier
   transform (4.1.10):

Given $f(t)$, assumed to be of negligible magnitude outside $[-a/2, +a/2]$;
Given N values of f at $t_j = ja/N - a/2$ for $j = 0,1,..., N$;
Given space increment γ and N points $x_k = (k - N/2)\gamma$ for $k = 0,1,...,N-1$;

1) Define a signal y by

$$y_j := f(t_j) e^{ij a\gamma/2}$$

2) Then the continuous transform (4.1.10) approximations can be obtained via
   the FRFT as:

$$F(x_k) = \frac{a}{N} e^{ia\gamma\left(\frac{k}{2} - \frac{N}{4}\right)} \hat{y}_k\left(\frac{a\gamma}{2\pi N}\right)$$

This algorithm is in many ways superior to the more naive approach of simply
calculating an N-point FFT over the support interval $[-a/2, +a/2]$ of f.

The interested investigator will also find of interest the treatment of [Press
and Teukolsky 1989], in which the authors make some valuable observations
about Fourier integration errors.

Problem 4.1.4: Implement an FRFT scheme for numerical evaluation of
continuous Fourier transforms (4.1.10) and investigate the numerical accuracy
for some exactly known cases, such as:

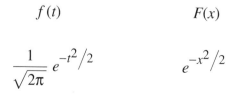

$f(t)$	$F(x)$
$\dfrac{1}{\sqrt{2\pi}} e^{-t^2/2}$	$e^{-x^2/2}$

$$\frac{1}{2} e^{-|t|} \qquad\qquad\qquad \frac{1}{1+x^2}$$

Use the method to guess the absolute constant C in the third example:

$$\operatorname{sech} t \qquad\qquad\qquad C \operatorname{sech} \frac{\pi x}{2}$$

Problem 4.1.5: Work out an FRFT-based algorithm that performs the standard DFT (4.1.1) of *any* positive integer length N in $O(N \log N)$ arithmetic operations. Compare this problem to Problem 4.1.3 for prime lengths.

Discrete cosine transform

Recently a new, recursive approach to calculating the discrete cosine transform (DCT), and particularly its inverse (which had been problematic for hardware designers), was put forth by [Wang Z *et. al.* 1994]. Their algorithm is intended for parallel use, because the recursion calculates one DCT component at a time. However, for a length N DCT, it is hard to imagine anything faster than N parallel machines performing the Wang *et. al.* algorithm for the full transform. Let us first review the motivation and definition of the DCT (we use here the notation in [*Projects* 1994]). A primary motivation for study of this transform is that certain signal processing applications–notably image compression–heavily involve the theory and practice of the DCT. As for notation, we establish the following transform formulae (which are equivalent, up to zeroth component and normalization, to the DCT definitions in [*Projects* 1994]). Given a signal x of length N we define the DCT of x as the signal X whose N components are:

$$X_k = \gamma(k) \sum_{j=0}^{N-1} x_j \cos\left(\frac{\pi k}{2N}(2j+1)\right) \qquad\qquad (4.1.12)$$

for $k = 0,1,...,N–1$; where $\gamma(k)$ is defined to be 1/2 for $k = 0$, otherwise 1. The inverse transform recovers the original data x via:

$$x_j = \sum_{k=0}^{N-1} X_k \cos\left(\frac{\pi k}{2N}(2j+1)\right)$$
(4.1.13)

The new recursion formulae are derived by first rewriting the forward and inverse transforms in the form:

(4.1.14)

$$X_k = \frac{2}{N}\gamma(k)(-1)^k \cos\left(\frac{\theta_k}{2}\right) S_{N-1}(k)$$

$$x_j = (-1)^j \sin(\theta_j) P_{N-1}(j)$$

where $\theta_j = \pi(2j+1)/(2N)$ and the S, P functions are

(4.1.15)

$$S_m(k) = \sum_{i=0}^{m} x_{m-i} V_i(\cos \theta_k)$$

$$P_m(k) = \sum_{i=0}^{m} X_{m-i} U_i(\cos \theta_k)$$

where V, U are the Chebyshev polynomials of the third and second kind, respectively:

$$V_n(\cos \theta) = \frac{\cos\left(\left(n+\frac{1}{2}\right)\theta\right)}{\cos \frac{\theta}{2}}$$
(4.1.16)

$$U_n(\cos \theta) = \frac{\sin((n+1)\theta)}{\sin \theta}$$

Each of V, U satisfies the Chebyshev recurrence:

$$W_{n+1} = 2\cos\theta \, W_n - W_{n-1}$$
(4.1.17)

The Wang *et. al.* recurrence relations, which are to be used to calculate either element (the k-th or j-th respectively) of (4.1.14) now take the form:

$$(4.1.18)$$

$$S_m(k) = x_m + 2\cos\theta_k \, S_{m-1}(k) - x_{m-1} - S_{m-2}(k)$$

$$P_m(j) = X_m + 2\cos\theta_j \, P_{m-1}(j) - P_{m-2}(j)$$

The relations are "ignited" by the assigments: $V_0 := U_0 := 1; V_{-1} := 1; U_{-1} := 0$. [Wang *et. al.* 1994] explain that the recursion cell, for example based on relatively simple silicon circuitry, is therefore simple and easily paralleled.

Problem 4.1.6: Implement a recursive DCT algorithm that, for each index k, starts from the first recurrence in (4.1.18) using given input data $\{x_m\}$, and calculates the correct forward DCT component (4.1.12). A complete implementation would also do the inverse DCT, using the second recurrence in (4.1.18).

Problem 4.1.7: Via the Wang *et. al.* recursive DCT algorithm, how many multiplies are required, given the initial data x of length N, to generate a *single* transform element X_k? On the basis of obvious short-cuts, such as the fact of X_0 being essentially just a sum of initial data, how many multiplies *total* are required to obtain the complete transform X? Of course, in a parallel architecture the time required only depends on the k-channel of maximum complexity. Compare, then, the theoretical performance of a parallel DCT with the fastest $O(N \log N)$ algorithms known for DCT. Note that the typical image processing DCT is an 8-by-8 two dimensional transform, and that there is naturally great interest in rapid implementations, especially for the inverse transform (video playback).

Number-theoretical transforms

We have seen in Chapter 1 that multiplication of large integers may be carried out via FFTs; and that, in Chapter 3, multiplication via Mersenne or Fermat numbers can be carried out with DWTs. One fairly general form of DWT presumes at least a primitive N-th root g of unity:

$$X_k \;=\; \sum_{j=0}^{N-1} x_j\, A^j g^{-jk} \qquad\qquad (4.1.19)$$

whose special cases include the DFT ($A := 1$) and the Fermat-mod DWT ($A :=$ a square root of g) (see Section 4.4).

One may have remarked that each of the previous multiplication methods suggests a floating-point implementation. For one thing, roots such as g and A are easy to generate immediately as forms $e^{\pi i k/N}$ in the floating-point world. However, there is a legitimate complaint: that in doing integer arithmetic (where, say, integer convolutions are being effected via transforms) one has no business applying floating point with abandon; that is, without complete and rigorous knowledge of the attendant errors.

Here are some realistic options for employing transforms to do integer arithmetic, usually integer convolution:

$$(4.1.20)$$

Options for removing floating-point transform errors

• Use balanced digit representation, whereby instead of the usual interval of possible signal element values $[0,1,...,W-1]$ where $W = 2^b$ say, use $[-W/2, ..., W/2-1]$. For reasons not entirely understood, this balanced representation dramatically reduces convolution errors [Crandall and Fagin 1994].

• For sufficiently many i, use a length-N FFT where N is a convenient length such as a power of two, but everything is (mod p_i), where the $\{p_i\}$ are primes each of which is possessed of a respective primitive N-th root of unity. It is sufficient to choose primes of the form $p_i = 1 + k_i N$; $k_i > 1$. In convolution mode one should have the product $\Pi\, p_i$ greater than the maximum allowed theoretical magnitude bound on a convolution component, and thus be able to reconstruct said component from the separate convolutions (mod p_i). If one has need for a DWT; *e.g.*, Fermat-mod arithmetic is being used in the attendant number-theoretic investigation, choosing $p_i = 1 + 2k_i N$ allows for an N-th root A of (-1).

- Use a transform such as a Fermat or Mersenne transform as can be found in the literature. These are transforms that use primitive roots in rings, to effect a pure-integer spectrum. Thus for integer convolution, not only the final result but every intermediate transform step yields a pure-integer result. (See [*Projects* 1994] and the older, but quite excellent and illuminating [McClellan and Rader 1979]).

- Use a "Galois transform," in which primitive N-th roots of unity in $GF(p^2)$ exist whenever N divides p^2-1. Arithmetic (essentially equivalent to complex arithmetic when $p = 3$ (mod 4)) proceeds in the Galois field, yielding transforms with field elements, and ultimately convolutions with exact integer elements.

For the remainder of this section we concentrate on the Galois transform method, because it exemplifies virtually every useful property of number theoretical transforms. This particular transform also has the interesting feature of virtually unlimited precision. In fact, for large enough Mersenne prime $p = 2^q-1$, the field $GF(p^2)$ will have a multiplicative group order $2^{q+1}(2^{q-1}-1)$, so a pure-integer convolution of power-of-two length through 2^{q+1} can be performed. For what follows, we choose the field and a primitive root of h of order $N = 2^{16}$:

$$p = 2^{61} - 1 \qquad\qquad (4.1.21)$$

$$h = 1510466207055935382 \; + \; 120042544849731353 \, i$$

We provide next a *Mathematica* example establishing that h is indeed a root of order 65536 in $GF(p^2)$. Note that any element x of $GF(p^2)$ can be represented as a Gaussian integer $x = a + bi$, with the multiplicative operation being standard complex multiplication. A sufficiently modern version of *Mathematica* will simply perform group operations via Mod[x * y, p]. A different symbolic processor handling only real arithmetic would necessitate something like

```
{Mod[Re[x] Re[y]-Im[x] Im[y],p],
          Mod[Re[x] Im[y]+Im[x] Re[y],p]}
```

for the group product (a pair consisting of the real and imaginary components) of two elements x and y.

$$(4.1.22)$$

```
(* First, exhibit a primitive root of order 2^16. *)
 p = 2^61-1;
 g = 1510466207055935382 + I 120042544849731353;
pow[a_, b_, c_] :=  (* Binary powering ladder in GF(p^2). *)
    Module[{bits = IntegerDigits[b,2], x, q},
        x = 1;  (* Actually 1 + 0 I. *)
        Do[
            x = Mod[x*x, c];
             If[bits[[q]] != 0, x = Mod[x*a,c]]
             ,{q,1,Length[bits]}
        ];
        x
    ];

p
pow[g, 2^15, p]

2305843009213693951
2305843009213693950
```

Since $h^{32768} = -1$ in the field, it is not hard to conclude that h is a primitive root of order 65536. Incidentally, it is interesting that the above binary powering ladder, because of the proper handling of Gaussian integers in the language, is identical to one we could write for $GF(p)$; *i.e.* for simple (mod p) integer powering.

Now because h has power-of-two order we can use appropriate powers of h, say

$$g = h^{2^{16}/N} \quad ; \quad A = h^{2^{15}/N} \tag{4.1.23}$$

to perform any negacyclic convolution (via Fermat-mod arithmetic DWT (4.1.19)) with power-of-two run length $N \le 2^{15}$; or

$$g = h^{2^{16}/N} \quad ; \quad A = h^{2^{14}/N} \tag{4.1.24}$$

to perform a DWT of power-of-two run length $N \le 2^{14}$ for right-angle convolution; or just

$$g = h^{2^{16}/N} \quad ; \quad A = 1 \tag{4.1.25}$$

for cyclic convolution via the DFT:

$$X_k = \sum_{j=0}^{N-1} x_j\, g^{-jk} \quad (\mathrm{mod}\, p) \tag{4.1.26}$$

where $N \le 2^{16}$ is a power-of-two length. Let us discuss first the implementation of the number-theoretic transform itself. The inverse transform will be:

$$x_j = N^{-1} \sum_{k=0}^{N-1} X_k\, (g^*)^{-jk} \quad (\mathrm{mod}\, p) \tag{4.1.27}$$

Happily, for N a power-of-two, and sufficiently large Mersenne prime p, the inverse of N is immediately seen to be $(p+1)/N$, for:

$$N\,((p+1)/N) = 1 \pmod{p}$$

The following *Mathematica* example shows a fast Galois transform and its inverse:

(4.1.28)

```
(* Recursive fast Galois transform. *)
gfft[x_, g_, p_] :=
   Module[{n,xeven, xodd, xsplit, w},
    If[(n=Length[x])==1,Return[x]];
    xsplit = Transpose[Partition[x,2]];
    xeven = gfft[xsplit[[1]],Mod[g^2, p], p];
    xodd  = gfft[xsplit[[2]],Mod[g^2, p], p];
    w = Table[pow[g,m,p],{m,0,n/2-1}];
    Mod[Join[xeven+w*xodd,xeven-w*xodd], p]
    ]

 igfft[x_, g_, p_] :=
        Mod[(p+1)/Length[x] * gfft[x, Conjugate[g], p], p];
```

For a fast implementation (as opposed to a slow elegant one) the investigator should use an FFT with explicit loop and butterfly structure rather than this recursive version. At any rate, we are now in a position to use standard zero-padded FFT multiplication, but with the convolution performed in $GF((2^{61}-1)^2)$:

(4.1.29)

```
(* Integer multiplication via Galois transform. *)
p = 2^61-1;
(* Next, a primitive root of order 2^16 in GF(p^2). *)
g = 1510466207055935382 + I 120042544849731353;
w = 2^16;
gmul[x_, y_] := Module[
    {digx, digy, len, root},
    digx = Reverse[IntegerDigits[x, w]];
    digy = Reverse[IntegerDigits[y, w]];
```

```
len =
    2*2^Ceiling[N[Log[2,Max[Length[digx], Length[digy]]]]];
Do[digx = Append[digx, 0],{q,Length[digx]+1,len}];
Do[digy = Append[digy, 0],{q,Length[digy]+1,len}];
root = pow[g, w/len, p]; (* len-th root of 1 in GF(p^2).*)
digx =
    igfft[gfft[digx,root,p] * gfft[digy,root,p], root, p];
digx
];

x = 64172864713871263741287378126713786123784213784000000001;
y = 72134246712651273561251274356263162143412343333234;
convo = gmul[x,y]
(x * y) - Sum[convo[[q]] w^(q-1),{q,1,Length[convo]}]

{3176990088, 4815130953, 7668701046, 7114005571, 9529829151,
 13076834173, 13150489043, 15462150312, 17593701674,
 18774960319, 17118527179, 15824224267, 13121187083,
 10780360999, 10758438847, 9068866779,6878695394,3443660899,
 1548198930, 18817422, 32781, 0, 0, 0, 0, 0, 0, 0, 0, 0, 0}

0
```

The output of the list "convo" shows pure-integer elements, actually the base-W digits of the product $x*y$; and the final output of "0" indicates vanishing convolution error. As usual for transform-convolution schemes, systematic multiplication that must recur many times requires that the digits in the convolution list be reduced to a standard (or balanced) base-W representation, usually after each convolution.

Problem 4.1.8: Implement a Fermat-mod multiplier that multiplies two large integers x, y (mod F_m) via a negacyclic convolution based on a Galois transform with the choices (4.1.23). Such a multiplier can be used for a Pepin primality test or for factorization of Fermat numbers. Note that an implementation would not require the zero-padding of the *Mathematica* example (4.1.29).

Problem 4.1.9: Can the right-angle convolution based on a Galois transform with choices (4.1.24) be used in a practical way? The idea is to use this particular root choice to halve the run length of the previous problem, meaning that the typical run length of the *Mathematica* example (4.1.29) would be cut by a factor of four.

4.2   *Walsh-Hadamard transform*

Mathematica formulation of Walsh operations

The Walsh-Hadamard transform is described in various references; *e.g.* [*Projects* 1994], so we briefly review here the salient properties and give some *Mathematica* implementations. The Walsh-Hadamard transform of a length-N signal x (we shall assume N is a power of two) and its inverse are taken to be:

$$W_k = \sum_{j=0}^{N-1} x_j \, Wal_k(j) \qquad (4.2.1)$$

$$x_j = \frac{1}{N} \sum_{k=0}^{N-1} W_k \, Wal_j(k)$$

where the Walsh functions $Wal_k(j)$ are defined:

$$Wal_k(j) = Par(j \,\&\, k) \qquad (4.2.2)$$

where $\&$ denotes bitwise "and," while the *Par* function gives the parity of its argument $((-1)$ to the number of binary ones in the argument). Note that, because j and k are interchangeable, the inverse transform to recover the $\{x_j\}$ is, up to the $1/N$ normalizer, identical to the forward transform. The indices k are difficult to interpret physically, but a transformation to "sequency" indices does exist, with the latter denoting the number of zero crossings of the Walsh function. The index transformation is, for s denoting sequency,

$$s = \sim(k \wedge (k \gg 1) \wedge (k \gg 2) \wedge ...) \qquad (4.2.3)$$

$$k = \sim(s \wedge (s \gg 1))$$

where ">>, ^, ~" denote respectively right-shift, exclusive-or, and complement bit operations. Useful *Mathematica* functions for Walsh transform and convolution problems are:

$$(4.2.4)$$

```
(* First, some fundamental bit-oriented functions. *)

FromDigits[list_List] := Fold[(2 #1 + #2)&, 0, list];

Parity[n_Integer] := Mod[Apply[Plus, IntegerDigits[n, 2]], 2];

BitAnd[{i_Integer, j_Integer} , len_Integer] :=
    FromDigits[IntegerDigits[i, 2, len] *
                IntegerDigits[j, 2, len]];

ExOr[{ i_Integer, j_Integer} , len_Integer] :=
    FromDigits[Mod[IntegerDigits[i, 2, len] +
                IntegerDigits[j, 2, len],2]];
```

An example of the use of such functions is the following single line for plotting a particular function $Wal_5(j)$. Note we pass an argument "3" meaning three bits describes any of the j from 0 through 7.

$$(4.2.5)$$

```
Plot[(-1)^Parity[BitAnd[{j,5},3]], {j,0,8}];
```

A second example is the literal, "grammar-school" version of Walsh convolution, by which we mean the left-hand side of a Walsh analog to the classical convolution theorem. Given length-N signals x, y denote by W, V the respective Walsh-Hadamard transforms. Then:

$$\sum_{i \,^{\wedge} j=n} x_i \, y_j \;=\; \frac{1}{N} \sum_{k=0}^{N-1} W_k \, V_k \, Wal_n(k) \qquad\qquad (4.2.6)$$

Note the interesting appearance of exclusive-or (rather than "+") on the summation condition of the left-hand side. A *Mathematica* test version for the convolution is:

(4.2.7)

```
(* Literal, "grammar-school Walsh convolution. *)
walshlit[a_, b_] :=
    Table[
      Sum[
          a[[j+1]] b[[ExOr[{n,j},1+Log[2,Length[a]]]+1]],
          {j,0,Length[a]-1}
      ]
      ,{n,0,Length[a]-1}
    ];
```

Now this is only a test example, because there is, as might be expected, a fast Walsh-Hadamard transform. One implementation is:

(4.2.8)

```
(* Fast Walsh-Hadamard transform.
   The results are scrambled,
   but may remain so during Walsh convolution.
 *)

fwt[x_] := Module[
    {blen = Log[2,Length[x]], s, j, y = x, len = Length[x]},
    For[s = 1, s < len, s *= 2,
      For[j = 0, j < len, j++,
        If[BitAnd[{j,s}, blen] == 0,(* Walsh butterfly. *)
          {y[[j+1]], y[[j+s+1]]} =
              {y[[j+1]] + y[[j+s+1]], y[[j+1]] - y[[j+s+1]]}
        ]
      ]
    ];
    y
  ];
```

This fast transform can be used without regard to bit scrambling in Walsh convolution computations. An example is:

(4.2.9)

```
len = 4;
x = Array[a,len,0]; y = Array[b,len,0];
Expand[fwt[fwt[x] * fwt[y]]/len]

{ a[0] b[0] + a[1] b[1] + a[2] b[2] + a[3] b[3],
  a[1] b[0] + a[0] b[1] + a[3] b[2] + a[2] b[3],
  a[2] b[0] + a[3] b[1] + a[0] b[2] + a[1] b[3],
  a[3] b[0] + a[2] b[1] + a[1] b[2] + a[0] b[3]}
```

Note that the output is the Walsh convolution, the left-hand side of (4.2.6), for the index n in that identity running from 0 through 3. The result is not quite the cyclic convolution, of course, because of the exclusive-or aspect of the index arithmetic. We return to this interesting subject of Walsh convolutions in Section 4.4. For the moment, we notice simply the extremely convenient aspect of Walsh transforms in general: the fast algorithm contains *no multiplication* of any kind; just addition/subtraction. This fortuitous circumstance arises from the fact that the basis functions $Wal_k()$ themselves attain only the possible values ± 1.

Problem 4.2.1: Explain the precise relation between the k-index (in the definition (4.2.2)), the sequency index (also the zero-crossing count), and the output index ordering of the fast algorithm (4.2.8). *C* functions can be found for the relevant transformations, in [*Projects* 1994].

Problem 4.2.2: Here is a fascinating area of exploration. It turns out that certain types of data files tend to be more compressible if Walsh-transformed prior to compression. Work out a compression system which, above all, recovers all data exactly (*i.e.* lossless compression) upon the final inverse Walsh. This is nontrivial because one has to guard against overflow and somehow handle the final normalization for the inverse transform.

 **4.3**　　　*Wavelets*

Wavelet review

The author has written on wavelets in some detail previously, with fairly detailed software code support [*Projects* 1994], so we shall limit ourselves here to a very brief review of the basic wavelet transforms.

There is a theory of continuous wavelet transforms, which transforms stand in analogy to the continuous Fourier transform (4.1.10). For a "wavelet" function W (usually a localized "little wave") and time signal f (assumed to be square-integrable) the formal transform is

$$F(a,b) \;=\; \frac{1}{\sqrt{|a|}} \int_{-\infty}^{\infty} f(t)\; W^*\!\left(\frac{t-b}{a}\right) dt \qquad\qquad (4.3.1)$$

Instead of a frequency-based spectrum, we obtain with the transform a "locale-scale" measure, in the form of F. The locale parameter b indicates *where* disturbances exist in f, while a signifies the *scale* of the disturbance. The inverse transform is, formally:

$$f(t) \;=\; \frac{1}{C[W]} \int_{-\infty}^{\infty}\int_{-\infty}^{\infty} F(a,b)\; W\!\left(\frac{t-b}{a}\right) \frac{da\,db}{|a|^{5/2}} \qquad\qquad (4.3.2)$$

where C is a constant depending on W. In order for the inverse to exist, the wavelet W must satisfy an admissibility condition [*Projects* 1994].

A discrete wavelet transform and its inverse can be cast in the form:

$$(4.3.3)$$

$$F_{mn} = 2^{m/2} \int_{-\infty}^{\infty} f(t)\, W(2^m t - n)\, dt$$

$$f(t) = \sum_{m=-\infty}^{\infty} \sum_{n=-\infty}^{\infty} 2^{m/2} F_{mn} W(2^m t - n)$$

where an orthonormality condition is presumed for the wavelet function:

$$\int_{-\infty}^{\infty} W(2^a t - b)\, W(2^c t - d)\, dt \; = \; 2^{-a} \delta_{ac} \delta_{bd} \qquad (4.3.4)$$

It is a remarkable theoretical discovery, due to I. Daubechies and others [*Projects* 1994], that a discrete wavelet transform algorithm can be developed without precise knowledge of the form of *W*. One may instead use a mother function Φ and a dilation equation for said mother function, to define a wavelet *implicitly* as follows. Assume, for some set of *M* constant coefficients $\{h_0, \ldots, h_{M-1}\}$, the existence of a Φ such that a dilation equation holds:

$$\Phi(t) = \sum_{k=0}^{M-1} h_k\, \Phi(2t - k) \qquad (4.3.5)$$

subject to an orthonormality condition

$$\int_{-\infty}^{\infty} \Phi(t - a)\, \Phi(t - b)\, dt \; = \; \delta_{ab} \qquad (4.3.6)$$

The wavelet function itself is then defined

$$W(t) = \sum_{k=0}^{M-1} (-1)^k h_{M-1-k}\, \Phi(2t - k) \qquad (4.3.7)$$

(Here and elsewhere a coefficient h_m with $m < 0$ or $m \geq M$ is taken to be zero.) It turns out that the resulting wavelet system is consistent, and has all the required properties (such as (4.3.4)), if we adopt the wavelet condition:

$$\sum_{k=0}^{M-1} h_k \, h_{k+2q} = 2\delta_{0q} \qquad (4.3.8)$$

It turns out that, for a consistent wavelet system, the inverse transform of (4.3.3) has an alternative description. In fact for square-integrable functions f there is always an expansion:

$$(4.3.9)$$

$$f(t) = \sum_{k=-\infty}^{\infty} s_k \Phi(t-k) + \sum_{m=0}^{\infty} \sum_{n=-\infty}^{\infty} d_{mn} W(2^m t - n)$$

and we can define a discrete wavelet transform as the collection of the s and d coefficients. Note a key difference between the inverse in (4.3.3) and (4.3.9) : the m sum in the latter starts at $m = 0$. In practice of course we want a finite set of transform values; and as in the standard DFT setting with sin/cos basis instead of the $\{\Phi, W\}$ basis, we presume length-N signals and length-N transforms. The algebra is somewhat involved [*Projects* 1994], so we simply give next the final form for the length-N discrete wavelet transform.

Let a signal x be thought of as a length-N column vector, where N is a power of two. Then the discrete wavelet transform of x is $W_N \, x$, where W_N is a matrix with decomposition:

$$W_N = T'_2(N) \, T'_4(N) \dots T'_{N/2}(N) T'_N(N) \qquad (4.3.10)$$

where each N-by-N T' matrix is defined by:

$$(4.3.11)$$

$$\left(T_n{}'(N)\right)_{ik} = \begin{cases} \dfrac{1}{\sqrt{2}} \displaystyle\sum_{b \in Z} h_{k-bn-2i} & ; \; i = 0, 1, \dots, \dfrac{n}{2} - 1 \\[3mm] \dfrac{1}{\sqrt{2}} \displaystyle\sum_{b \in Z} (-1)^k h_{M-1-k+bn+2i} & ; \; i = \dfrac{n}{2}, \dots, n-1 \\[3mm] \delta_{ik} & ; \; i = n, \dots, N-1 \end{cases}$$

Here is a *Mathematica* construction of the discrete wavelet transform matrix in the case of Daubechies' celebrated set of $M = 4$ coefficients:

$$\{h_0, h_1, h_2, h_3\} \;=\; \left\{ \frac{1+\sqrt{3}}{4}, \frac{3+\sqrt{3}}{4}, \frac{3-\sqrt{3}}{4}, \frac{1-\sqrt{3}}{4} \right\} \quad (4.3.12)$$

$$(4.3.13)$$

```
(* Generate discrete wavelet transform matrix *)

symbolic = False;
order = 4;   (* Number of h coefficients. *)

(* Daubechies (D4) wavelet choice. *)
h[n_] := If[(n<0) || (n>= order), 0,
            If[symbolic, H[n],
                    Which[n==0,(1+Sqrt[3])/(4),
              n==1,(3+Sqrt[3])/(4),
              n==2,(3-Sqrt[3])/(4),
              n==3,(1-Sqrt[3])/(4)]
            ]
        ];

t[n_] := 1/Sqrt[2] *
    Table[If[i<n/2,Sum[h[j-b n - 2i],{b,-1,1}],
            Sum[(-1)^(j) h[order-1-(j-b n - 2i)],
            {b,-10,10}]
          ],
          {i,0,n-1},{j,0,n-1}
    ];

len = 8;   (* Signal length. *)
tp[n_] := Module[{tt, u},
            tt = t[n];
            u = Table[If[(i<=n) &&(j<=n), tt[[i,j]],
                        If[i==j,1,0]
                      ],
                      {i,1,len},{j,1,len}
```

```
                    ];
              u
          ];
w = tp[len]; q = len/2; While[q>1, w = tp[q] . w; q /= 2];
If[symbolic, Print[MatrixForm[w]], Print[N[MatrixForm[w],3]]];
```

```
{0.354      0.354      0.354      0.354      0.354      0.354      0.354      0.354

-0.0647     0.241      0.371      0.548      0.0647     -0.241     -0.371     -0.548

-0.171      -0.0458    -0.137     -0.171     0.354      0.729      -0.0458    -0.512

0.354       0.729      -0.0458    -0.512     -0.171     -0.0458    -0.137     -0.171

-0.129      -0.224     0.837      -0.483     0          0          0          0

0           0          -0.129     -0.224     0.837      -0.483     0          0

0           0          0          0          -0.129     -0.224     0.837      -0.483

0.837       -0.483     0          0          0          0          -0.129     -0.224}
```

The output is numerical (since symbolic := False in the example shown). If symbolic := True we can see the structure of a typical T' matrix:

```
symbolic = True;
MatrixForm[Sqrt[2] tp[8]]
```

```
{H[0]    H[1]     H[2]     H[3]     0        0        0        0
 0       0        H[0]     H[1]     H[2]     H[3]     0        0
 0       0        0        0        H[0]     H[1]     H[2]     H[3]
 H[2]    H[3]     0        0        0        0        H[0]     H[1]
 H[3]    -H[2]    H[1]     -H[0]    0        0        0        0
 0       0        H[3]     -H[2]    H[1]     -H[0]    0        0
 0       0        0        0        H[3]     -H[2]    H[1]     -H[0]
 H[1]    -H[0]    0        0        0        0        H[3]     -H[2]}
```

The beautiful wrap-around structure, together with the decomposition (4.3.10) renders possible a fast wavelet transform algorithm. In fact, such a fast algorithm can be carried out in the impressive count of only $O(N)$ operations, unlike the Fourier class with its $O(N \log N)$ complexity.

A fast wavelet algorithm in *Mathematica* can be effected in the style of the Appendix program "FastWavelet.ma." In that example the Daubechies coefficients are renamed "hh[ ]" and a function h := hh/$\sqrt{2}$ is used within the wavelet loops for convenience.

New wavelet ideas

Various new wavelet-oriented ideas have appeared recently in the literature. Just a few of these are:

• Short-time Fourier transform (STFT) methods, which in some sense bridge the gap between the Fourier and wavelet worlds, have proven to be quite useful in time series analysis. A recent "pruned-FFT" STFT algorithm is in [Paneras *et. al.* 1994].

• Windowed Gabor transforms and continuous wavelet transforms are related also to STFT ideas. It is problematic to work out fast transforms as approximations to the continuous case. Yet some recent work, *e.g.* [Unser 1994] appears promising in this regard.

• Tomography (reconstruction of radiation images; *e.g.* in medical applications) is yet another application field for wavelet transforms, as described in [Yagle 1994].

• For transforms not restricted to power-of-two run lengths, the work of [Taswell and McGill 1994] is of interest.

• A relation between discrete wavelet transforms and the initialization problem for pyramidal processing algorithms is described in [Abry and Flandrin 1994].

• An interesting application of fast wavelet transform algorithms to linear evolution equations is found in [Engquist *et. al.* 1994].

Again, this is an extremely brief sampling of just a few very recent works. Needless to say, there is already a massive wealth of literature going back to the inception of wavelet theory in the early 1980s. [*Projects* 1994] contains a more complete history and development.

For reasons of its beauty and computational applicability, we single out here as a particular new idea the "harmonic wavelet" approach [Newland 1993]. A continuous harmonic wavelet is defined:

$$W(t) \;=\; \frac{e^{4\pi it} - e^{2\pi it}}{2\pi it} \tag{4.3.14}$$

which when applied in a continuous transform of the type (4.3.1) "picks out" octave-resident information. We get a kind of compromise between Fourier spectra and wavelet components, the latter picking out resolution detail for the compact wavelet cases. The full treatment in [Newland 1993] is the best reference; we give here the algorithm for a fast, discrete form of the harmonic wavelet transform:

$$\tag{4.3.15}$$

Algorithm for the fast harmonic wavelet transform:

Given a length-N signal x of real data, where $N \geq 4$ is a power of two;

1) Compute $X = \mathrm{DFT}(x)$.

2) Compute, in-place,
  -the order-2 DFT of $\{X_2, X_3\}$;
  -the order-4 DFT of $\{X_4, ..., X_7\}$;
  ...
  -the order-$N/4$ DFT of $\{X_{N/4}, ..., X_{N/2-1}\}$;

3) Replace respectively the high $N/2-1$ components with
  Hermitian conjugates:
    for $j = N/2+1$ to $N-1$
      $X_j := X_{N-j}{}^{*}$

4) Now the signal X is the harmonic wavelet transform of x.

Problem 4.3.1: Implement a program to calculate the discrete wavelet matrix W_N, and verify both symbolically and numerically that the matrix is unitary, in the sense that the inverse matrix is the transpose.

Problem 4.3.2: Implement a fast wavelet transform algorithm, verify that it gives (perhaps some reordering!) of the matrix-vector product of the previous problem, and study the effects of such a transform on actual signals. The Appendix code "FastWavelet.ma" is a useful prototype. Incidentally, the basic idea of wavelet compression of data is to take a transform, "drop" some small coefficients, and compress the thus-quantized transform. Then reconstruction will be imperfect, but the imperfections depend only on one's hopefully adroit choice of quantization.

Problem 4.3.3: Work out the inverse algorithm for the harmonic wavelet transform; *i.e.* the procedure that reconstructs the real signal x from the output X of (4.3.15).

Problem 4.3.4: Implement a fast harmonic wavelet transform and study empirically (via graphical means, say) how the transform represents octave-resident information about input signals x. One good signal to analyze graphically is a swept-frequency sine wave. The harmonic wavelet components should reveal, in a plot of their absolute values, the notion of "resolution sorting" of the frequency spectrum.

4.4 *Convolution*

Cyclic, negacyclic, and all that

Let us give a brief, unified summary of all the types of transform-based convolutions that are discussed in this book. The discrete weighted transform (DWT) and its inverse are, respectively:

$$(4.4.1)$$

$$X_k = \sum_{j=0}^{N-1} x_j a_j \, g^{-jk}$$

$$x_j = \frac{1}{N a_j} \sum_{k=0}^{N-1} X_k \, g^{+jk}$$

where g is a primitive N-th root of unity in the appropriate algebraic domain. The "weight signal" $a = \{a_j\}$ is introduced trivially in the above, since the two formulae represent essentially the usual forward and reverse DFTs for the signal $\{a_j x_j\}$. What is not so trivial, and in fact quite useful, is the observation we have touched upon at various points in previous sections: that convolutions can be carried out in special instances, on the basis of special choices for the weight signal a. Denote z as one of various types of convolutions of x and y. All three signals x, y, z are assumed to have length N, except in the acyclic case when only z has length $2N$:

$$(4.4.2)$$

Weighted convolution in general:

$$z = x \times_a y \qquad \text{(nomenclature)}$$

$$z_n = \frac{1}{a_n} \sum_{i+j = n \,(\mathrm{mod}\, N)} (a_i x_i)(a_j y_j) \qquad \text{(definition)}$$

Cyclic convolution (or, trivial weights $a = \{1,1,1,...\}$):

$$z = x \times y$$

$$z_n = \sum_{i+j=n\,(\mathrm{mod}\,N)} x_i\, y_j$$

Negacyclic convolution, (or, weights $a_j = A^j$, with A an N-th root of (-1)):

$$z = x \times_- y$$

$$z_n = \sum_{i+j=n} x_i\, y_j - \sum_{i+j=N+n} x_i\, y_j$$

Acyclic convolution (in this case alone, z has length $2N$, and the final element $z_{2N-1} = 0$ always):

$$z = x \times_{Ac} y$$

$$z = \left\{ \frac{(x \times y) + (x \times_- y)}{2}, \frac{(x \times y) - (x \times_- y)}{2} \right\}$$

$$z_n = \sum_{i+j=n} x_i\, y_j \quad ; \ n = 0, 1, ..., 2N-2$$

Right-angle convolution (weights $a_j = A^j$ where A is an N-th root of i):

$$z = x \times_\perp y$$

$$z_n = \sum_{k+j=n} x_k\, y_j + i \sum_{k+j=N+n} x_k\, y_j$$

Finally we introduce a peculiar, but (as we shall witness near the end of this chapter) a powerful variety of convolution; namely, half-cyclic convolution:

$$z = x \times_{Hc} y$$

$$z_n = \sum_{i+j=n} x_i\, y_j \qquad ; \; n = 0, 1, ..., N-1$$

That is to say, the half-cyclic is defined like the acyclic, except the resulting signal z has only N elements instead of $2N$. Though the half-cyclic can obviously be obtained from the acyclic, and hence via a cyclic and a negacyclic, there are sometimes other, more efficient ways to generate a half-cyclic, as we shall see.

We next establish some observations about the applicability and equivalences of the various convolutions. It will be convenient to assume also that N is even.

• The cyclic convolution of two signals is equivalent to multiplication of two polynomials, in a dummy variable t say, each of degree N–1, modulo t^N–1. The signal elements correspond to the polynomial coefficients in the natural way; *i.e.*, the n-th signal element corresponds to the coefficient of t^n. Thus the convolution can be thought of as polynomial multiplication, with the "high" half (meaning the higher degree half) of the product "wrapped around," *i.e.*, slid over flush with the low half and added into that low half.

• The negacyclic convolution of two signals is equivalent to multiplication of two polynomials modulo t^N+ 1. Thus, negacyclic convolution can be thought of as polynomial multiplication, with the high half of the product "wrapped around with minus," *i.e.* subtracted from the low half.

• The acyclic convolution is equivalent to outright polynomial multiplication. Note that because of the way the cyclic and negacyclic convolutions involve the addition/subtraction of the high halves of the polynomial products, the acyclic can be performed with a cyclic and a negacyclic. An acyclic can also be perfomed with either a zero-padded cyclic or a zero-padded negacyclic.

• Right-angle convolution is often useful if one's computing machinery supports efficient complex arithmetic. We have already seen one application of the right-angle convolution, in the form of the Pepin test example (3.4.7). The basic idea is to create one complex sequence out of two real sequences, then perform complex, right-angle convolution; in this way obtaining convolution information about said real sequences.

What makes a strong connection between DWTs and these various convolution types is the generalization of the convolution theorem (4.1.4). Assume the nomenclature (4.4.1) above; so that two signals x, y each of length N have DWTs X, Y respectively. Then the weighted convolution of x and y is:

$$z_n = (x \times_a y)_n = \frac{1}{N a_n} \sum_{k=0}^{N-1} X_k Y_k \, g^{+kn} \tag{4.4.3}$$

Thus we have:

$$\tag{4.4.4}$$

Algorithm for (various) convolutions via discrete weighted transform (DWT):

Given signals x, y each of length N; and a primitive root g of order N in the relevant algebraic domain; set a weight generator A according to the following scheme (if such an A exists in the respective case):

> cyclic convolution: $A := 1$
> negacyclic convolution: $A := \sqrt{g}$ (*e.g.* A is an N-th root of (-1))
> right-angle convolution: $A := \sqrt{(-g)}$ (*e.g.* A is an N-th root of i)

in our current nomenclature then, the weight signal will have elements $a_j = A^j$.

1) Form weighted signals $\{A^j x_j\}$, $\{A^j y_j\}$ and compute their DFTs via, for example, a standard FFT algorithm for signal length N. The respective spectra are the DWTs X, Y. Note that a decimation-in-frequency (DIF) FFT

at this stage does not require post-unscrambling, if a decimation-in-time (DIT) inverse FFT is used for step (3); for in such a scenario the inverse transform accepts input in scrambled order and produces a natural-ordered result.

2) Multiply X and Y elementwise, forming length N spectrum $Z = \{X_k Y_k\}$.

3) Take the inverse DFT of Z, for example via a standard inverse FFT algorithm.

4) Then the convolution in question is

$$(x \times_a y)_n = A^{-n}\left[DFT^{-1}(Z)\right]_n$$

A *Mathematica* set of literal, or "grammar-school" convolutions is always useful for testing any of the fast algorithms:

(4.4.5)

```
(* Literal, "grammar-school" test routines for
   cyclic and negacyclic convolution of Lists.
 *)
neglit[x_, y_] := Table[
                    Sum[x[[i+1]] y[[Mod[m-i,Length[x]]+1]] *
                        If[m < i, -1,1]
                      ,{i,0,Length[x]-1}
                    ],
                    {m,0,Length[x]-1}
                  ];
cyclit[x_, y_] := Table[Sum[x[[i+1]] y[[Mod[m-i,Length[x]]+1]]
                    ,{i,0,Length[x]-1}]
                    ,{m,0,Length[x]-1}
                  ];

a = Array[x,4,0];
b = Array[y,4,0];
cyclit[a,b]
neglit[a,b]
```

```
{ x[0] y[0] + x[3] y[1] + x[2] y[2] + x[1] y[3],
  x[1] y[0] + x[0] y[1] + x[3] y[2] + x[2] y[3],
  x[2] y[0] + x[1] y[1] + x[0] y[2] + x[3] y[3],
  x[3] y[0] + x[2] y[1] + x[1] y[2] + x[0] y[3]}

{ x[0] y[0] - x[3] y[1] - x[2] y[2] - x[1] y[3],
  x[1] y[0] + x[0] y[1] - x[3] y[2] - x[2] y[3],
  x[2] y[0] + x[1] y[1] + x[0] y[2] - x[3] y[3],
  x[3] y[0] + x[2] y[1] + x[1] y[2] + x[0] y[3]}
```

In the above output we have intentionally bolded the "wrap-around" terms which, as is evident, are negated for the second, negacyclic case.

Problem 4.4.1: Prove the weighted-convolution theorem (4.4.3).

Problem 4.4.2: Write an implementation of the Algorithm (4.4.4) that makes internal choices for what convolution to perform, and test the implementation numerically against "grammar-school" forms (4.4.5).

Problem 4.4.3: Design and implement a fast polynomial multiplication program for polynomials with real (or integer) coefficients, which program using cyclic and negacyclic convolutions via Algorithm (4.4.4). In practice, if floating point is used so that $g = e^{2\pi i/N}$ and $A = 1$ or $e^{\pi i/N}$, there are economies (notably the exploitation of real-only polynomial coefficients) that can be realized in both cases (even in the negacyclic case) [Crandall and Fagin 1994].

Small convolutions

One might look longingly at the *Mathematica* output (4.4.5) and wonder, on the basis of the evident rich structure, why one needs all these approaches for convolution. The answer is basically this: to obtain the convolution elements for two initial length-N sequences requires, if grammar-school methods are used, $O(N^2)$ arithmetic operations. On the other hand, Algorithm (4.4.4) shows that each of the various convolutions we have covered can be obtained in $O(N \log N)$ arithmetic operations, because there will be at most three FFTs taken. But these are asymptotic estimates, and it is usually better in practice to use grammar-school, or even some other "non-transform" scheme, for small N. In particular, there seems almost always to be an interesting trade-off between multiply count and add count. We shall see that some methods having very low multiply count suffer from an exorbitant add count.

Two schemes that apply well to certain small convolution lengths are the Toom-Cook and Winograd convolution schemes [McClellan and Rader 1979]. We describe here the Toom-Cook, although both schemes can be elegantly developed along similar lines, by way of polynomial and tensor theory [Knuth 1981]. Say we wish to find the acyclic convolution of two signals x and y, each of length N. If we consider the polynomials:

$$x(t) = x_0 + x_1 t + ... + x_{N-1} t^{N-1} \tag{4.4.6}$$

$$y(t) = y_0 + y_1 t + ... + y_{N-1} t^{N-1}$$

whose coefficients are manifestly the x, y signal elements, then the acyclic convolution elements can be gleaned from the polynomial product $z(t) = x(t)*y(t)$. Note that z has maximum degree $2N-2$. If we calculate, then, the $2N-1$ numbers:

$$\tag{4.4.7}$$
$$z(j) = x(j) * y(j) \quad ; \quad j = -(N-1), ..., (N-1)$$

we should be able to reconstruct the polynomial z and hence the acyclic convolution, in terms of the $z(j)$. (Other sets of j values than this arithmetic progression can be used of course.) The Toom-Cook acyclic convolution algorithm thus reads:

(4.4.8)

Algorithm (Toom-Cook) for computing acyclic convolution of two signals of length N in $2N-1$ multiplies (disregarding absolute constant multiplies):

Given two length-N signals x,y ;

1) Calculate the $2N-1$ values $x(j)$ and the $2N-1$ values $y(j)$ from (4.4.6), using for example the integer j values in $[-(N-1),...,(N-1)]$.

2) Use the $2N-1$ values $z(j) = x(j)*y(j)$ to reconstruct the polynomial z, whose coefficients $\{z_0, ..., z_{2N-2}\}$ comprise the acyclic convolution.

Step (2) of the algorithm is of course the key, and we can employ symbolic processing to generate the steps for small convolutions. The following *Mathematica* example shows how to do a Toom-Cook 3-by-3 acyclic convolution (*i.e.*, $N = 3$). This example is unique, in that the ultimate output is actually a form of in-line code for the Toom-Cook calculation:

(4.4.9)

```
(* Automated Toom-Cook acyclic relation generator.
   Code is generated for the explicit acyclic convolution
   of two length-N sequences in (2N-1) multiplies
   (disregarding absolute constant multiplies).
 *)

len = 3;  (* Initial signal length. *)
f[a_, t_, d_] := If[t==0,a[0],Sum[a[q] t^q, {q,0,d}]];
lo = (xy[-(len-1)] == f[z, -(len-1), 2*len-2] );
Do[
   log = lo && (xy[q] == f[z, q, 2*len-2]);
   lo = log,
   {q,-(len-2),len-1,1}];
sol = Simplify[Solve[log, Array[z,2*len-1,0]]]
```

$$\{\{ z[1] \rightarrow \frac{xy[-2] - 8\ xy[-1] + 8\ xy[1] - xy[2]}{12},$$

$$z[2] \rightarrow \frac{-xy[-2] + 16\ xy[-1] - 30\ xy[0] + 16\ xy[1] - xy[2]}{24},$$

$$z[3] \rightarrow \frac{-xy[-2] + 2\ xy[-1] - 2\ xy[1] + xy[2]}{12},$$

$$z[4] \rightarrow \frac{xy[-2] - 4\ xy[-1] + 6\ xy[0] - 4\ xy[1] + xy[2]}{24},$$

$$z[0] \rightarrow xy[0]\}\}$$

This output, of the acyclic convolution elements z_0 through z_4 reveals the solution for step (2) of Algorithm (4.4.8) in the present case $N = 3$. Note that the *Mathematica* notation xy[j] means $x(j)*y(j)$. But now we carry the code generation idea further:

$$(4.4.10)$$

```
(* Next, generate computer code for the convolution. *)
Do[
    r[q+len-1] = f[x, q, len-1];
    Print["r[",q+len-1,"] = ", InputForm[r[q+len-1]],";"]
    ,
    {q,-(len-1),len-1,1}
];
Do[
    s[q+len-1] = f[y, q, len-1];
    Print["s[",q+len-1,"] = ", InputForm[s[q+len-1]],";"]
    ,
    {q,-(len-1),len-1,1}
];
Do[
    Print["t[",q,"] = r[", q, "] * s[", q, "];"]
```

```
   '
   {q,0,2*len-2}
];
Do[
   cc[q] = (z[q]) /.
       (sol[[1]] /. xy[n_]-> t[len+n-1]);
   Print["z[",q,"] = ",InputForm[Expand[cc[q]] /. p[n_] ->
                                 t[n+len-1]],";"],
   {q,0,2len-2}
];

r[0] = x[0] - 2*x[1] + 4*x[2];
r[1] = x[0] - x[1] + x[2];
r[2] = x[0];
r[3] = x[0] + x[1] + x[2];
r[4] = x[0] + 2*x[1] + 4*x[2];
s[0] = y[0] - 2*y[1] + 4*y[2];
s[1] = y[0] - y[1] + y[2];
s[2] = y[0];
s[3] = y[0] + y[1] + y[2];
s[4] = y[0] + 2*y[1] + 4*y[2];
t[0] = r[0] * s[0];
t[1] = r[1] * s[1];
t[2] = r[2] * s[2];
t[3] = r[3] * s[3];
t[4] = r[4] * s[4];
z[0] = t[2];
z[1] = t[0]/12 - (2*t[1])/3 + (2*t[3])/3 - t[4]/12;
z[2] = -t[0]/24 + (2*t[1])/3 - (5*t[2])/4 + (2*t[3])/3 -
       t[4]/24;
z[3] = -t[0]/12 + t[1]/6 - t[3]/6 + t[4]/12;
z[4] = t[0]/24 - t[1]/6 + t[2]/4 - t[3]/6 + t[4]/24;
```

To avert confusion we say again: the output of this *Mathematica* program (starting right after the last Do[ ] loop) itself looks like output because we are effecting code generation. This output can actually serve as computer code, *e.g.*, C code, for the acyclic convolution of two sequences of length $N = 3$. Note that there are exactly 5 multiplies (of r[ ] s[ ] terms), and we do not count multiplication by absolute constants, for the good reason that these are usually negligible in practice (it is easy to double or quadruple a number by shifts, and almost as easy to divide by a small fixed integer).

To clarify the code generation idea, we can "run" the generated code even in *Mathematica*, as follows:

(4.4.11)

```
(* Next, actual execution of generated code
   for length 3. *)

r[0] = x[0] - 2*x[1] + 4*x[2];
r[1] = x[0] - x[1] + x[2];
r[2] = x[0];
r[3] = x[0] + x[1] + x[2];
r[4] = x[0] + 2*x[1] + 4*x[2];
s[0] = y[0] - 2*y[1] + 4*y[2];
s[1] = y[0] - y[1] + y[2];
s[2] = y[0];
s[3] = y[0] + y[1] + y[2];
s[4] = y[0] + 2*y[1] + 4*y[2];
t[0] = r[0] * s[0];
t[1] = r[1] * s[1];
t[2] = r[2] * s[2];
t[3] = r[3] * s[3];
t[4] = r[4] * s[4];
z[0] = t[2];
z[1] = t[0]/12 - (2*t[1])/3 + (2*t[3])/3 - t[4]/12;
z[2] = -t[0]/24 + (2*t[1])/3 - (5*t[2])/4 + (2*t[3])/3 -
t[4]/24;
z[3] = -t[0]/12 + t[1]/6 - t[3]/6 + t[4]/12;
z[4] = t[0]/24 - t[1]/6 + t[2]/4 - t[3]/6 + t[4]/24;
Simplify[Array[z,2len-1,0]]


{y[0],
 x[1] y[0] + x[0] y[1],
 x[2] y[0] + x[1] y[1] + x[0] y[2],
 x[2] y[1] + x[1] y[2],
 x[2] y[2]}
```

Indeed, the final output is the acyclic 3-by-3 convolution of two sequences. It may seem that all of these manipulations do not yield much, but such a sentiment is misleading. If the multiplications in a problem are *very* expensive, the Toom-Cook approach can save computation time.

Problem 4.4.4: Implement a Toom-Cook extension to the Karatsuba notion of Chapter 1, as follows. For large integers x, y ; split each in thirds using a convenient word size:

$$x = x_0 + x_1 W + x_2 W^2$$
$$y = y_0 + y_1 W + y_2 W^2$$

where each x_j and y_j is of size less than W. Then employ the output code of *Mathematica* example (4.4.10) to effect the multiplication $x*y$ using just five multiplies of W-by-W sized integers. Argue that, ignoring absolute constant multiplies, the complexity of this scheme is $O(N^{\log 5 / \log 3})$ arithmetic operations for N digits each of x, y; theoretically somewhat better than the classical Karatsuba method. Is there any reason to implement a higher order Toom-Cook; for example, should N be greater than 3? Of course as N increases, the complexity of addition, not to mention those absolute-constant multiplies/divides, increases dramatically. See Problem 4.4.7 in this regard. Also note the Appendix code "toomcook.c," in which an order-4 negacyclic convolution was automatically generated in the fashion of the *Mathematica* technique of this section.

Problem 4.4.5: Implement a Winograd convolution [Knuth 1981][McClellan and Rader 1979] code generator, along the lines of (4.4.9)-(4.4.11). The basic and brilliant idea of Winograd is that cyclic (negacyclic) convolution is the multiplication of two polynomials, each of degree $N-1$, modulo ($t^N \pm 1$) respectively. A perfect implementation should reflect the Winogard result; namely, that the total number of multiplies (disregarding absolute constant multiplies) can be brought down to:

$$2N - \phi$$

where ϕ is the number of primitive factors of the polynomial $(t^N \pm 1)$. In particular, a cyclic convolution can always be done in $2N - d(N)$, where $d(N)$ is the number of divisors of N; but in no less than this.

Problem 4.4.6: Show by symbolic processing that the following algorithm calculates the correct, length-4 negacyclic convolution of signals a, b; with final values $\{z_0, z_1, z_2, z_3\}$:

```
c = b[0]+b[2];
d = b[1]+b[3];
e = c+d;
f = c-d;
g = b[0]-b[2];
h = b[3]-b[1];
i = g-h;
j = a[0]+a[1];
k = a[2]+a[3];
l = a[0]-a[1];
m = a[2]-a[3];
q1 = e*(j+k)/4;
q2 = f*(l+m)/4;
q3 = g*(j-k)/2;
q4 = h*(m-l)/2;
q5 = i*(a[3]-a[1])/2;
t1 = q1+q2;
t2 = q3+q5;
t3 = q1-q2;
t4 = q4-q5;
z[0] = -t1-t2 + 2 a[0]*b[0];
z[1] = -t3-t4 + 2 (a[1]*b[0] + a[0]*b[1]);
z[2] = t1-t2 - 2 a[3]*b[3];
z[3] = t3-t4;
```

From the remarks of the previous problem, such an order-4 negacyclic convolution can be done in a smaller number of multiplies, but the example above certainly has convenient absolute constants.   Thus we see a little further into the thicket of convolution complications: not only do multiply and add counts compete with each other, there is a third consideration having to do with the complexity of the absolute constant coefficients.

Problem 4.4.7: The present author has not seen a comprehensive treatment of the number of adds required for a Toom-Cook, or even a Winograd convolution. A good problem is to analyze precisely the number of multiplies (which can be gleaned from the text of this section) *together* with the number of adds. One feasible conjecture is: a length-N acyclic convolution can be carried out in $2N-1$ multiplies and no more than cN^2 adds (again disregarding those absolute constant operations) for some absolute constant c. One should remember that one reason for the paucity of results concerning addition complexity is that, in the beginning of hardware processor technology the multiplies were really very expensive with respect to adds.

Nussbaumer convolution

We have seen that transform methods, notably FFT and DWT, are applicable to convolution problems. We have also noted the unfortunate fact that deep (*i.e.*, high order) roots of unity often necessitate–or at least suggest–floating point implementations. But [Nussbaumer 1981] found a way to perform both cyclic and negacyclic convolution in a recursive, but literal fashion. This kind of convolution presumes *only* an algebraic domain of a ring (technically, with the inverse of 2 defined). Nussbaumer convolution is ideal in situations where a rigorous, pure-integer convolution result is desired.

We begin a tour of the ingenious Nussbaumer scheme by noting a formal identity for reduction of a cyclic convolution. In the nomenclature of (4.4.2) it is not hard to show that, if x_L and x_H denote respectively the low and high halves of a length-N signal (N is assumed even):

$$(4.4.12)$$

$$x_L = \{x_0, x_1, ..., x_{N/2-1}\}$$
$$x_H = \{x_{N/2}, x_{N/2+1}, ..., x_{N-1}\}$$
$$x = \{x_L, x_H\}$$

then the cyclic convolution of two length-N signals x, y can be written:

$$(4.4.13)$$

$$x \times y = \left\{ \begin{array}{l} \dfrac{((x_L + x_H) \times (y_L + y_H)) + ((x_L - x_H) \times_- (y_L - y_H))}{2}, \\[3mm] \dfrac{((x_L + x_H) \times (y_L + y_H)) - ((x_L - x_H) \times_- (y_L - y_H))}{2} \end{array} \right\}$$

This is a lot of notation, but the theme is that a length-N cyclic convolution can be performed via a cyclic of length $N/2$ and a negacyclic of length also $N/2$. This identity is a manifestation of the fact that, for polynomials $x(t), y(t)$ the Chinese remainder theorem for polynomials says:

$$(4.4.14)$$

$$x(t)\, y(t) \left(\bmod\ t^N - 1\right) =$$
$$\frac{1 + t^{\frac{N}{2}}}{2} \left(x(t) \left(\bmod\ t^{\frac{N}{2}} - 1\right) \right) \left(y(t) \left(\bmod\ t^{\frac{N}{2}} - 1\right) \right) +$$
$$\frac{1 - t^{\frac{N}{2}}}{2} \left(x(t) \left(\bmod\ t^{\frac{N}{2}} + 1\right) \right) \left(y(t) \left(\bmod\ t^{\frac{N}{2}} + 1\right) \right)$$

A *Mathematica* example that realizes this decimation of a general cyclic convolution uses, for the moment and for clarity, the literal "grammar-school" convolution neglit[ ] from (4.4.5), as follows:

$$(4.4.15)$$

```
(* Recursive cyclic convolution prototype.
   To effect e.g. Nussbaumer convolution, the
   call to neglit[] should involve a fast negacyclic.
 *)

cycl[x_, y_] :=
    Module[{len = Length[x], a,b,c,d,e,f},
        If[len < 2, Return[cyclit[x,y]]];
        a = Take[x,{1,len/2}];
        b = Take[x,{len/2+1,len}];
        c = Take[y,{1,len/2}];
        d = Take[y,{len/2+1,len}];
        e = 1/2 cycl[a+b, c+d];
        f = 1/2 neglit[a-b, c-d];
        Join[e+f, e-f]
    ];
a = Array[x,8,0];
b = Array[y,8,0];
Expand[cycl[a,b]]

(Output suppressed )
```

Now, if we only had a fast algorithm for the negacyclic, to replace the call to neglit[] in the above *Mathematica* example, we would have a complete system devoid of "grammar-school" convolution operations.

The Nussbaumer idea, then, is to perform a recursive negacyclic convolution using novel ideas from the algebra of rings. An abstract description runs like so [Knuth 1981][Bernstein 1993][Buhler 1995]. Let R denote a ring possessed of an inverse of 2. We know that negacyclic convolution is equivalent to multiplication of two polynomials each of degree N, modulo $(t^N + 1)$. Assume that N can be factored, $N = mr$, with r divisible by m. Now the ring of polynomials

$$S[t] / (t^N + 1)$$

(meaning polynomials with coefficients in the ring S, with all polynomials and their operations reduced negacyclically) in which we shall perform our negacyclic arithmetic, is naturally isomorphic to

$$T[t] / (z - t^m)$$

where T is the polynomial ring

$$T := S[z] / (z^r + 1)$$

The novel idea of Nussbaumer is essentially that T has a natural, built-in $2m$-th root of unity; namely $z^{r/m}$. This is because all arithmetic proceeds order-r negacyclically in T, that is (mod $z^r + 1$), thus $(z^{r/m})^m$ is (-1) in T. The point of the existence of the natural $2m$-th root is: DFT methods may be used to convolve certain length-m signal (*i.e.*, degree-$(m-1)$ polynomials), but with the DFT's root of unity being the "symbolic"–and hence computationally inexpensive–root $z^{r/m}$.

Let us make the theoretical description concrete by showing explicit manipulation of the relevant polynomials. Let

$$x(t) = x_0 + x_1 t + \ldots + x_{N-1} t^{N-1} \tag{4.4.16}$$

and adopt similar notation for $y(t)$, the idea being that the negacyclic convolution of signals $\{x_i\}$, $\{y_i\}$ will be the product of ring elements $x(t)$ and $y(t)$ in $S[t] / (t^N + 1)$. Now decompose $x(t)$ and $y(t)$ as follows:

$$x(t) = \sum_{i=0}^{m-1} X_i(t^m) \, t^i \tag{4.4.17}$$

$$y(t) = \sum_{i=0}^{m-1} Y_i(t^m) \, t^i$$

where each of the degree-$(r-1)$ polynomials X_i, Y_i will be an element of the polynomial ring T. Specifically, these polynomials are constructed from the original signal elements:

$$X_i(z) = x_i + x_{i+m} z + \dots + x_{i+m(r-1)} z^{r-1} \qquad (4.4.18)$$

$$Y_i(z) = y_i + y_{i+m} z + \dots + y_{i+m(r-1)} z^{r-1}$$

Now we multiply $x(t)$ and $y(t)$ by performing the cyclic convolution

$$(4.4.19)$$

$$Z = \{X_0, X_1, \dots, X_{m-1}, 0, 0, \dots, 0\} \times \{Y_0, Y_1, \dots, Y_{m-1}, 0, 0, \dots, 0\}$$

where each signal (having polynomial elements) has been zero-padded to total length $2m$. The point is, this cyclic convolution can be performed via "symbolic" FFTs, in which the usual numerical root of unity is now replaced conceptually by the abstract root $z^{r/m}$. What this means is, butterfly calculations within the FFT structure merely involve shuffling and translating of polynomial coefficients. Now observe that the usual spectral elementwise multiplication that occurs within an FFT-based convolution (*e.g.*, step (2) in Algorithm (4.4.4)) becomes, in the Nussbaumer scenario, polynomial multiplication that occurs *within the ring T*. Thus the elementwise multiplication is itself negacyclic convolution of order r. (One way to see this is to observe that in (4.4.17), the polynomials X_i, Y_i are each of degree $r-1$ in the variable $z = t^m$, and $z^r = t^{mr} = -1$.) After a final inverse FFT, this time using the "symbolic" root $z^{-r/m}$, we obtain the length-$2m$ signal Z (4.4.19) and thus the acyclic product of $x(t)$ and $y(t)$ in the form:

$$x(t)\, y(t) = \sum_{k=0}^{2m-2} Z_k(t^m)\, t^k \qquad (4.4.20)$$

from which we infer the actual negacyclic convolution elements from

$$\sum_{n=0}^{N-1} (x \times_- y)_n \, t^n = x(t)\, y(t) \,\left(\bmod\, t^N + 1\right) \qquad (4.4.21)$$

via some minor final reordering and wrap-around adjustments (using the reduction relation $t^N = -1$). We outline the overall Nussbaumer algorithm as follows:

$$(4.4.22)$$

Algorithm for Nussbaumer cyclic or negacyclic convolution:

Given two signals x, y each of length $N = 2^p$;

Cyclic case:

1) Use (4.4.13), for example in the style of *Mathematica* example (4.4.15), to obtain the cyclic convolution of x, y in terms of a cyclic and a negacyclic each of order $N/2$, and so on recursively. The only remaining phase of the implementation is therefore to develop a recursive negacyclic.

Negacyclic case:

2) Set $m := 2^{\lfloor p/2 \rfloor}$ and $r := N/m$. Thus r/m will be an integer.

3) Create, from the elements of x and y, the polynomials of (4.4.18). The collection $\{X_i\}$ will then be, for example, a set of m arrays each of length r; and the same for the $\{Y_i\}$.

4) Zero pad the collections to get the two signals in (4.4.19); *e.g.*, the collection $\{X_i\}$ effectively becomes a set of $2m$ arrays, each of length r, with the high m of the arrays each consisting of r zeros. (Note as in Problem 4.4.13 that there exists an enhancement in which this zero-padding is avoided.)

5) To compute the cyclic convolution (4.4.19), start by creating the forward length-$2m$ FFTs for each of zero-padded collections. The primitive root of

unity for these forward FFTs will be the "symbolic" root $z^{r/m}$.

6) After the two forward FFTs, each of the two spectra is again a collection of $2m$ arrays, each array being of length r. Now recursively call an order-r negacyclic for each of the $2m$ elementwise spectral multiplications.

7) Perform, on the collection of $2m$ negacyclic results, an inverse FFT with "symbolic" root $z^{-r/m}$. This will yield the $2m$ polynomials Z_i in (4.4.20) (actually the last one Z_{2m-1} is identically zero).

8) Adjust and collect coefficients to infer from (4.4.21) the final negacyclic elements.

The Nussbaumer algorithm is relatively complicated and nontrivial to code, so we give in the Appendix a *Mathematica* implementation, as "Nuss.ma;" and a *C* program version embodied in "conlib.c." The latter performs convolutions modulo a given prime. For convolutions involving integers of arbitrary size, one may do a straightforward rewrite of conlib.c, linking to the older [*Projects* 1994] files "giants.[ch]," with every instance of an operation (mod p) replaced with an arbitrary-precision operation, and every instance of an array of integers (a signal) replaced with an array of giants. The author actually went through such a code translation–from (mod p) convolution to giants convolution–in order to factor F_8 as in Problem 3.3.4(2).

Problem 4.4.8: Implement Nussbaumer Algorithm (4.4.22), along the lines, say, of Appendix code "Nuss.ma," or the program "conlib.c." If one wanted to test "Nuss.ma," an effective approach is both to time and accuracy-test the Nussbaumer recursion:

```
len = 64;
xx = Table[Random[Integer, 1000],{};
yy = Table[Random[Integer, 1000],{};
Timing[cynuss = Expand[cycl[xx,yy]]] [[1]]
Timing[cylit = Expand[cyclit[xx,yy]]] [[1]]
```

```
(cynuss-cylit) . (cynuss-cylit)

3.42 Second
5.65 second
0
```

Not only is the squared convolution error zero (as it should be; the Nussbaumer approach is a pure-integer approach when the initial ring R is an integer ring) but already with run length $N = 64$ we see that the literal, "grammar-school" method is slower.

Problem 4.4.9: Rewrite the Algorithm (4.4.22) in the elegant language and symbology of ring algebra.

Problem 4.4.10: Implement polynomial software for large-degree polynomials using Nussbaumer convolution and the appropriate arithmetic for coefficients (which might also be large!). One key to efficiency is to "breakover" to small convolutions at the optimal point in the Nussbaumer recursion.

Problem 4.4.11: Study the effect of "breakover" in the Nussbaumer recursion (or for that matter in the cyclic recursion, step (1) of Algorithm (4.4.22)) at various lengths for the literal, "grammar-school" convolution. The Appendix code "Nuss.ma" has these breakover points set by variables "cyccut, negcut." Then study a fascinating option: the use of *other* small convolution methods for intermediate run lengths. The author found, with [Buhler 1995], that a proper choice of a Karatsuba negacyclic breakover considerably enhances the Nussbaumer method. Note also the Appendix code "toomcook.c," in which an automatically in-line-generated, order-4 negacyclic is tested. It appears that these, or other small convolution approaches, can be quite effective even with breakover points as large as run length $N = 32$ or 64 or even higher. Thus it is still, and may always be, of interest to develop new forms of small convolution algorithms.

Problem 4.4.12: Use a fast, practical Nussbaumer algorithm to obtain results in one of the following research areas:

• Resolving irregular primes (as in Chapter 3), where large convolutions are called for.

• Factoring; especially, finding factors of very large numbers via, for example, the Montgomery-Silverman method of evaluating a polynomial along a geometric progression via convolution (Algorithm (3.3.9)). For example, F_8 can certainly be factored in this way (Problem (3.3.4)). Even more promising would be a Montgomery polynomial-evaluation ECM scheme employing full Nussbaumer convolution for the polynomial operations.

• Evaluation of large factorials, using polynomial recursion, to assess for example the Wilson property (Chapter 3) or even to find factors of numbers by evaluating rapidly massive products of integers.

Problem 4.4.13: It turns out that the Nussbaumer algorithm can be improved, at least in terms of memory usage. The zero-padded convolution (4.4.19), being an acyclic convolution with the elementary decomposition (4.4.2); can be performed in less memory by doing the unpadded cyclic and negacyclic convolutions

$$\{X_0, ..., X_{m-1}\} \times \{Y_0, ..., Y_{m-1}\}$$

$$\{X_0, ..., X_{m-1}\} \times_- \{Y_0, ..., Y_{m-1}\}$$

with two DWT passes. The cyclic computation can use the m-th root of unity $z^{2r/m}$. Happily, for the negacyclic computation there *does* exist a "symbolic" m-th root of (-1) in the ring T; namely, the old root $z^{r/m}$. This was a $2m$-th root of $(+1)$ in the standard algorithm, but now the unpadded run length is half what it used to be. Implement this idea in a large-integer multiply routine (note that Appendix code "conlib.c" uses this DWT memory savings notion already). Can the memory be further reduced, say to 1/2 of the size needed in the full zero-padding scenario?

A new convolution algorithm

We have seen in Section 4.2 that a certain Walsh convolution, denoted:

$$(x \times_\wedge y)_n \quad := \sum_{i \,\wedge\, j = n} x_i \, y_j \qquad (4.4.23)$$

for two length-N signals x, y; can always be obtained via N multiplies. This is a very small number of multiplies for a convolution (*e.g.*, FFT and Nussbaumer methods take $O(N \log N)$, Toom-Cook and Winograd take closer to $2N$, and so on). Furthermore, because the N-multiply Walsh convolution scheme willl involve a forward and an inverse fast Walsh transform, the adds are kept "under control," to the tune of $O(N \log N)$ adds. Thus the Walsh convolution scheme truly has a low operation count. Of course, the algebraically important and ubiquitous cyclic convolution is *not* what you get in (4.4.23). Let us look at a pictorial tableau for a true 8-by-8 cyclic convolution, followed by its Walsh analog. The symbols "c i j" or "w i j" correspond to the appearance of summand $x_i \, y_j$ in the sum for the n-th convolution element, with n itself appearing in the left-hand column. In the Walsh tableau the boldface entries "**w i j**" indicate those summands that agree with their corresponding true cyclic summands.

```
7 :c0  7   c1  6   c2  5   c3  4   c4  3   c5  2   c6  1   c7  0
3 :c0  3   c1  2   c2  1   c3  0   c4  7   c5  6   c6  5   c7  4
5 :c0  5   c1  4   c2  3   c3  2   c4  1   c5  0   c6  7   c7  6
1 :c0  1   c1  0   c2  7   c3  6   c4  5   c5  4   c6  3   c7  2
6 :c0  6   c1  5   c2  4   c3  3   c4  2   c5  1   c6  0   c7  7
2 :c0  2   c1  1   c2  0   c3  7   c4  6   c5  5   c6  4   c7  3
4 :c0  4   c1  3   c2  2   c3  1   c4  0   c5  7   c6  6   c7  5
0 :c0  0   c1  7   c2  6   c3  5   c4  4   c5  3   c6  2   c7  1

7 :w0  7   w1  6   w2  5   w3  4   w4  3   w5  2   w6  1   w7  0
3 :w0  3   w1  2   w2  1   w3  0   w4  7   w5  6   w6  5   w7  4
5 :w0  5   w1  4   w2  7   w3  6   w4  1   w5  0   w6  3   w7  2
1 :w0  1   w1  0   w2  3   w3  2   w4  5   w5  4   w6  7   w7  6
6 :w0  6   w1  7   w2  4   w3  5   w4  2   w5  3   w6  0   w7  1
2 :w0  2   w1  3   w2  0   w3  1   w4  6   w5  7   w6  4   w7  5
4 :w0  4   w1  5   w2  6   w3  7   w4  0   w5  1   w6  2   w7  3
0 :w0  0   w1  1   w2  2   w3  3   w4  4   w5  5   w6  6   w7  7
```

The reason for the peculiar row ordering is twofold. First, the ordering 7,3,5,1,6,2,4,0 is reverse-complement-binary, which is a ubiquitous permutation in fast algorithm theory and often reveals some pattern when used to re-index a tableau. Second, this ordering happens to show a kind of fractal pattern to the error points (boldface summands in the second tableau). To see an even more convincing fractal structure, one can go to higher orders than 8-by-8, whence the bolded points begin to form something like a Sierpinski gasket fractal.

The author analyzed tableau such as these, and employed a symbolic pattern seeking program to attempt to find a quantifiable correction scheme to convert the Walsh tableau into a true cyclic one. The result is a new cyclic convolution scheme in which an attempt is made to "repair" the convolution (4.4.23). The final formula is somewhat complicated, so to ease that aspect let us adopt the notation that a signal of elements $\{a_c, ..., a_d\}$ be denoted

$$\{a_i\}_{i=c}^d$$

while adjoining of $[T]$ to the signal a creates the polynomial whose coefficients are the signal's elements:

$$a[T] := \sum_{n=0}^{N-1} a_n T^n$$

Knowledge of all the coefficients of a polynomial

$$(x \times y)[T]$$

is thus trivially equivalent to knowing the cyclic convolution of x and y. Now consider x, y signals of length $N = 2^m$. The proposed general convolution formula is:

$$(4.4.24)$$

$$(x \times y)[T] = (x \times_\wedge y)[T] + \sum_{k=1}^{m-1} \left(T^{2^k} - 1 \right) *$$

$$\left(\left\{ \{x_{j+2^{k-1}+p2^k}\}_{j=0}^{2^{k-1}-1} \; [T] \right\}_{p=0}^{\frac{N}{2^k}-1} \times_\wedge \left\{ \{y_{j+2^{k-1}+p2^k}\}_{j=0}^{2^{k-1}-1} \; [T] \right\}_{p=0}^{\frac{N}{2^k}-1} \right) \left[T^{2^k} \right]$$

This proposed scheme for evaluation of the true cyclic convolution involves, in the final, erudite term a Walsh convolution of polynomials. Theoretically, that is allowed: clearly the add/subtract Walsh butterflies have nothing to fear from polynomial operands. Furthermore, the elementwise spectral multiplies will be normal polynomial multiplication.

A formula such as (4.2.24) is sufficiently unwieldy that some examples should be exhibited. To this end, consider the case $N = 16$. For this length the specific identity for order-16 cyclic convolution runs:

$$(4.4.25)$$

$$(x \times y)[T] = (x \times_\wedge y)[T] +$$

$$\left(T^2 - 1 \right) *$$
$$(\{x_1, x_3, x_5, x_7, x_9, x_{11}, x_{13}, x_{15}\} \times_\wedge \{y_1, y_3, y_5, y_7, y_9, y_{11}, y_{13}, y_{15}\})\left[T^2 \right] +$$

$$\left(T^4 - 1 \right) *$$
$$(\{x_2 + x_3 T, \; x_6 + x_7 T, \; x_{10} + x_{11} T, \; x_{14} + x_{15} T\} \times_\wedge$$
$$\{y_2 + y_3 T, \; y_6 + y_7 T, \; y_{10} + y_{11} T, \; y_{14} + y_{15} T\})\left[T^4 \right] +$$

$$\left(T^8 - 1 \right) *$$
$$(\{x_4 + x_5 T + x_6 T^2 + x_7 T^3, \; x_{12} + x_{13} T + x_{14} T^2 + x_{15} T^3\} \times_\wedge$$
$$\{y_4 + y_5 T + y_6 T^2 + y_7 T^3, \; y_{12} + y_{13} T + y_{14} T^2 + y_{15} T^3\})\left[T^8 \right]$$

There is one order-16 Walsh convolution (16 multiplies), plus a Walsh of order 8 (8 multiplies), plus a Walsh of order 4 (4 order-2 acyclics, or 12 multiplies), and a Walsh of order 2 (2 order-4 acyclics; but this last case simplifies down to 1 order-4 acyclic, because $T^{16} = 1$, or 7 multiplies) for a total multiply count of 16+8+12+7 = 43 multiplies. This is somewhat less than $N \log_2 N = 64$.

The new convolution proposal leads to some interesting, "hard-coded" small convolutions of the type we have seen earlier. Here is a *Mathematica* symbolic test of the new scheme for $N = 8$:

$$(4.4.26)$$

```
(* 8-by-8 cyclic convolution in (fundamentally)
   18 multiplies, using new convolution algorithm.
 *)

signal[c_, z_] := c . (z^Range[0, Length[c]-1]);
x = Array[a,8,0]; y = Array[b,8,0];
d = signal[walshlit[x,y], t];
e =
signal[walshlit[{a[1],a[3],a[5],a[7]},{b[1],b[3],b[5],b[7]}],
       t^2];
f = Expand[
       signal[Expand[walshlit[{a[2] + a[3] t, a[6] + a[7] t},
                {b[2] + b[3] t, b[6] + b[7] t}]],
       t^4]];
rule = t^(n_) -> t^Mod[n,8];
convopoly = Expand[d + (t^2-1) e + (t^4-1) f] /. rule;
convo = Join[{convopoly /. t->0},
    Table[Coefficient[convopoly, t^q], {q,1,7}]];
MatrixForm[convo]

(Output suppressed)
```

The output shows the correct, symbolic order-8 convolution of signals *a, b*. Detailed analysis reveals that this $N = 8$ scheme gives rise to an 18-multiply hard-coded small convolution. we know that 18 is not optimal for an 8-by-8 cyclic, but we observe that the absolute constant multipliers are very simple in this Walsh-based case. In a fast, practical implementation for large N, calls to walshlit[ ] (4.2.7) would of course be replaced by a transform based convolution such as (4.2.9).

Problem 4.4.14: Implement (4.2.24) using polynomial multiplication routines in some fast language of choice, to effect an integer convolution scheme (*i.e.,* devoid of floating point errors).

Problem 4.4.15: How many multiplies does (4.2.24) necessitate for $N = 32$? $N = 64$? (Incidentally, one way to find out is to implement, as in the last problem, and count operations in an automated way.) How do these compare with $N \log_2 N$? In this connection see the next problem.

Problem 4.4.16: It is unknown whether the proposed convolution scheme (4.2.24) has asymptotic "fast algorithm" complexity; *i.e.,* $O(N \log N)$ multiplies and adds, as to FFT and Nussbaumer methods. However it seems probable that if this new convolution can be effected in $O(N \log N)$ multiplies, then the adds cannot also be so bounded. Investigate the complexity issue. In particular, what if some of the Walsh convolution's spectral elementwise multiplies are Toom-Cook acyclic convolution? It may be the case that the proposed scheme is a way of keeping adds *somewhat* under control (say to be $O(N \log^2 N)$), so that the result may in some sense lie between the fast algorithms and the low-multiply, but add-expensive small convolvers.

Problem 4.4.17: Prove the author's proposed convolution scheme (4.4.24). There is as yet no rigorous proof, although symbolic processing says the identity is valid for $N \leq 64$. It would be good to have a proof based an algebraic notions–not unlike those for Nussbaumer theory, say–perhaps exploiting the group structure of $C_2{}^N$ (direct product of N copies of the two-cyclic group).

Devil's convolution

The last amongst the host of convolution definitions (4.4.2) is the half-cyclic convolution. This convolution is easy to visualize and turns out to act as a centerpiece to a marvelous recursion for the computation of itself and other convolutions. An explicit example of half-cyclic convolution

$$z = x \times_{Hc} y \qquad (4.4.27)$$

is, for $x = \{x_0, x_1, x_2\}, y = \{y_0, y_1, y_2\}$ the explicit signal of three elements:

$$z_0 = x_0 y_0$$
$$z_1 = x_0 y_1 + x_1 y_0$$
$$z_2 = x_0 y_2 + x_1 y_1 + x_2 y_0$$

It is convenient to think of any half-cyclic as a triangular structure, having as many rows as each of the original signals x, y has elements.

It turns out that the half-cyclic can be used to "break the power-of-two stigma," by allowing the computation of cyclic, ayclic, or half-cyclic convolutions with less zero-padding than is traditionally required. Allow some notational levity for the moment, as we denote the *time* to compute a convolutions by an upper-case letter. Thus

$$C_n, A_n, H_n, N_n$$

are meant to denote the *times* to evaluate cyclic, acyclic, half-cyclic, and negacyclic convolution, respectively; in each case the convolution being of length n. Further, denote by m^- the least power of two greater than or equal to m, and by m_- the greatest power of two not exceeding m; that is,

$$m^- = 2^{\lceil \log_2 m \rceil}$$
$$m_- = 2^{\lfloor \log_2 m \rfloor}$$

(Note that when m is an exact power of two, $m = m^- = m_-$.) Then our claims can be listed, starting with:

$$H_m = C_{m^-} + N_{m^-} \tag{4.4.28}$$

which is to be read: "The half-cyclic of length m can be performed via a cyclic and negacyclic, each of the latter two being of length m^-." Admittedly, this is an old notion; in fact an acyclic can also be done in the same basic difficulty:

$$A_m = C_{m^-} + N_{m^-} \tag{4.4.29}$$

(recall the standard ways to multiply polynomials via convolution) and the half-cyclic is merely part of the acyclic. But now we turn to more sophisticated claims, such as:

$$A_m = C_{m_-} + N_{m_-} + H_{2m-m^--1} \tag{4.4.30}$$

$$H_m = C_{m^-} + H_{2m-m^--1} \tag{4.4.31}$$

$$C_m = C_{m^-} + H_{2m-m^--1} \tag{4.4.32}$$

Note that the similarity of two timing formulae such as the latter two above does not mean the detailed algorithmic steps are the same.

We begin the details by exhibiting an explicit algorithm for the recursive relation (4.4.31):

$$\tag{4.4.33}$$

Algorithm for recursive evaluation of the half-cyclic convolution:
Given x, y each of length m the goal is to return

$$x \times_{Hc} y$$

1) Zero-pad each of x, y to length m^-;

2) Perform the cyclic convolution $c := x \times y$;

3) If$(m > 3m^-/4)$ return $\left\{\dfrac{c + (x \times_- y)}{2}\right\} \Big|_0^{m-1}$ /* Relation (4.4.28). */

4) Set $k := 2m - m^- - 1$ and perform the half-cyclic convolution

$$u := \left\{x \ \Big|_0^{k-1}\right\} \ \times_{Hc} \ \left\{y \ \Big|_0^{k-1}\right\}$$

by calling this very algorithm.

5) Return

$$\left\{u \ \Big|_0^{k-1} \ , \ c \ \Big|_k^{m-1}\right\}$$

A *Mathematica* implementation of this recursive half-cyclic runs as follows:

(4.4.34)

```
(* Recursive half-cyclic convolution. *)

cyclit[x_,y_] := Table[ (* Literal cyclic. *)
        Sum[x[[q+1]] y[[Mod[r-q, Length[x]]+1]],
            {q,0,Length[x]-1}],
            {r,0,Length[x]-1}];


neglit[x_,y_] := Table[ (* Literal negacyclic. *)
        Sum[x[[q+1]] y[[Mod[r-q, Length[x]]+1]] * If[q>r,
-1,1],
            {q,0,Length[x]-1}],
            {r,0,Length[x]-1}];


bar[n_] := Round[N[2^Ceiling[Log[2,n]]]];  (* Least p.o.t. >=
argument. *)


pad[zz_] := Join[zz, Table[0,{bar[Length[zz]]-Length[zz]}]];


hcyc[x_, y_] := Module[{m = Length[x], n,u,v,c, k,z,s,t},
        If[m == 1, Print["cyc1"]; Return[{{x[[1]]*y[[1]]}}]];
```

```
         n = bar[m]/2;
         u = pad[x]; v = pad[y];
         c = cyclit[u,v]; Print["cyc",Length[u]];
         If[m > 3n/2, (* Standard half-cyclic. *)
            d = neglit[u,v]; Print["neg",Length[d]];
            Return[Take[(c+d)/2, {1,m}]];
         ];
         k = 2m -2n -1;
         s = Take[x,{1,k}]; t = Take[y,{1,k}];
         z = hcyc[s,t];
         Join[Take[z, {1,k}], Take[c, {k+1,m}]]
      ];

x = Array[a,3,0]; y = Array[b,3,0];
MatrixForm[hcyc[x,y]]


cyc4
cyc1


a[0] b[0]
a[1] b[0] + a[0] b[1]
a[2] b[0] + a[1] b[1] + a[0] b[2]
```

The output shows that

$$H_3 = C_4 + H_1$$

(where $H_1 = C_1 = 1$ multiply) is the effort required to yield the correct order-3 half-cyclic convolution.

As for relations (4.4.30) and (4.4.32), algorithms for these can be inferred from the *Mathematica* Appendix code "ConvolutionsRecursive.ma."

Now we come to the reason for the topic title "devil's convolution." It turns out that, armed with the various recursions, one can perform convolution for which a sudden "jump" to the next power of two run length does *not* occur when one passes a power-of-two demarcation. For example, consider the multiplication of two polynomials each of degree 133. A classical way to multiply is to form two coefficient signals, each padded out to length 512 (*i.e.*, zero-pad to 256 and zero-pad again to 512), then to take a cyclic convolution. One can also take a cyclic of order 256 and a negacyclic of order 256. Thus we have the basic complexity:

$$(4.4.35)$$

$$A_{134} = C_{512}$$

But with the new recursions, we can expect instead an effort:

$$(4.4.36)$$

$$
\begin{aligned}
A_{134} &= C_{256} + H_{11} \\
&= C_{256} + C_{16} + H_5 \\
&= C_{256} + C_{16} + C_8 + C_1
\end{aligned}
$$

which amounts roughly to half the effort of the classical acyclic reductions (4.4.35). The author plotted the effort calculated on the basis of the recursions, for initial signal lengths $m = 1, 2,..., 1024$ in order to fashion the frontispiece to this chapter. A *Mathematica* example that not only plots the approximate effort vs. signal length, but also shows by its recursive structure how the new convolution actually works, is as follows:

$$(4.4.37)$$

```
(* Plot the complexity of new recursive acyclic. *)

(* First, the least power of two >= argument. *)
bar[n_] := Round[N[2^Ceiling[Log[2,n]]]];

(* Next, half-cyclic complexity count. *)
hc[m_] := Module[{mbar = bar[m]},
            If[m ==1, Return[cy[1]]];
            If[m > 3mbar/4, Return[cy[mbar] + ne[mbar]]];
            cy[mbar] + hc[2m-mbar-1]
        ];
```

```
(* Next, acyclic complexity count. *)
acy[m_] := Module[{mbar = bar[m]},
            If[m == 1, Return[cy[1]]];
            If[m > 3mbar/4, Return[cy[mbar] + ne[mbar]]];
            cy[mbar/2] + ne[mbar/2] + hc[2m-mbar-1]
            ];

le = Table[{k, acy[k]},{k, 1,1024}];
tap = le /. {cy[n_] -> n Log[n], ne[n_] -> n Log[n]};
(* Approximate time to do standard
            convolutions is taken to be just n. *)
ListPlot[tap, Axes->None]
```

The horizontal axis here is the signal length (from 1 through 1024) and the vertical axis is the computational effort for acyclic convolution. Note that in the *Mathematica* example we have assumed that the effort for either a cyclic or a negacyclic of order N is just $N \log N$. Note that for the frontispiece, a different plot–this time it was assumed that a cyclic or negacyclic effort is just N rather than $N \log N$–shows a "cleaner" staircase, as might be expected. The frontispiece plot, then, can be thought of as a plot of *multiplicative* complexity, because we know from polynomial theory that either cyclic or negacyclic can be effected with no more than $2N$ multiplies (actually $2N - d(N)$ for cyclic, and $2N - 1$ for negacyclic).

One can easily see in the frontispiece plot that the crossing of a power-of-two barrier (such as $m = 256$ on horizontal axis) is not catastrophic. There are many small discontinuous jumps but the plotted curve, compared to the classical curves (*i.e..*, involving classical zero-padding) for which the effort for length m is taken for graphical simplicity to be m^-, is looking more like a straight line (which would be ideal) in effort vs. signal length.

Of course we have generated a form of "devil's staircase" fractal. This is why it seems appropriate to call this convolution scheme, based upon the half-cyclic recursion (4.4.31), "devil's convolution."

Note that Appendix code "ConvolutionsRecursive.ma" exhibits various forms of convolution, all based on the recursive half-cyclic.

Problem 4.4.18: Prove, using abstract polynomial algebra, that algorithm (4.4.33) is in fact correct. Again using polynomial algebra, show that the other "effort relations" in the sequence (4.4.28)-(4.4.32) hold. The idea for each relation is to prove the efficacy of an explicit algorithm.

Problem 4.4.19: Argue that the following "effort relations" also hold:

$$H_m = H_{m-1} + m$$

$$C_m = H_m + H_{m-1}$$

$$N_m = H_m + H_{m-1}$$

Problem 4.4.20: Under what further conditions on a, b beyond $a + b \geq 2m-1$ is it possible to fashion a half-cyclic algorithm for which the effort is

$$H_m = C_a + H_b$$

Can the attendant ideas be used to fashion a general acyclic convolution algorithm possessed of a yet finer devil's staircase structure?

Problem 4.4.21: Here we consider DFTs of arbitrary length, in light of the devil's convolution. Recall the Bailey-Swartztrauber (arbitrary length) and Rader (prime length, Problem 4.1.3) DFTs. Then there is also the Shokrollahi DFT (length $(p-1)/2$, Chapter 3). Such DFTs can be done using the following principles:

1) A DFT of length $q\, 2^k$, q odd, can be done with 2^k DFT's each of length q.

2) A DFT of length M can be written as a convolution of the same length M. In particular, let x be a signal of *odd* length M. Then the DFT of x, given by

$$\tilde{x}_k = \sum_{j=0}^{M-1} x_j\, h^{-jk}$$

where h is a primitive M-th root of unity, can be cast in terms of a cyclic convolution:

$$\tilde{x} = \left\{ h^{-T_k} \right\} \left[\left\{ x_j\, h^{-T_{j-1}} \right\} \times \left\{ h^{T_n} \right\} \right]$$

where $T_n := n(n+1)/2$ is the n-th triangle number. The notation means that we perform the indicated length-M convolution, then multiply elementwise (dyadically) by the sequence $\{h^{-T_k}\}$.

Principle (1) follows from the classical Danielson-Lanczos recursion for FFTs, while (2) is essentially the classical Bluestein convolution trick for odd lengths (see (4.1.5) for even lengths). Now consider, especially in light of the devil's convolution, the following tasks:

• Write a high-performance FFT for arbitrary length, which nevertheless only uses power-of-two length FFTs internally.
• Apply these ideas to Bailey-Swartztrauber Fourier integration.
• Apply these ideas to Rader prime-length FFTs.
• Apply these ideas to the Shokrollahi DFT of Chapter 3.

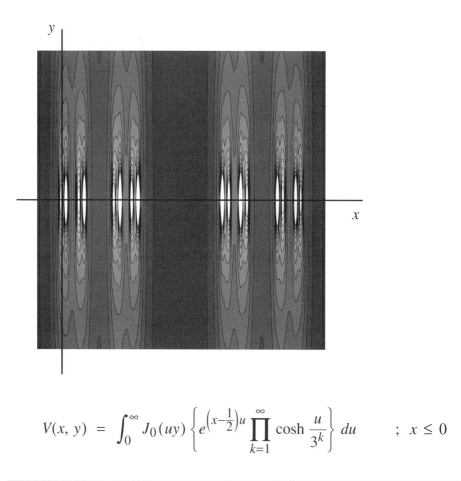

$$V(x, y) \;=\; \int_0^\infty J_0(uy) \left\{ e^{\left(x-\frac{1}{2}\right)u} \prod_{k=1}^\infty \cosh \frac{u}{3^k} \right\} du \qquad ; \; x \le 0$$

Visualization of a fractal electric charge. Above is a contour plot of the potential due to a Cantor set possessed of unit total charge. The set is defined as usual within the unit interval on the x-axis. The potential V(x, y) exists everywhere off that axis. It is known that the potential along the y-axis and near the x-axis behaves–in a certain sense of spatial average–as y^{D-1} where D is the fractal dimension of the Cantor set. The integral representation for V(x, y), with its attractive "self-similar" product, is one way to express such a potential analytically.

5 *Nonlinear & complex systems*

...by revealing to us the fineness of line between order and chaos, [the theories of chaos and of fractals] give us clues for devising new models of artifical creativity, and, perhaps, greater understanding of human creativity as well.

[*Lansdown, in* [*Crilly et. al.* 1991]]

Well known it is that chaos and fractals are, as concepts, inextricably entwined. Also known is that nonlinear systems, such as differential attractor systems, can lead to chaos; but that nonlinearity can also lead to sublime manifestations of order, such as when a neural network successfully "learns" a complex task. This chapter amounts to a brief tour of some modern developments in these various related fields.

5.1 *N-body problems & chaos*

The classical N-body problem of stellar dynamics is to determine the motion of N bodies of respective masses m_k, where the force on the i-th body assumes the Newtonian form:

$$F_i = m_i \frac{d^2 r_i}{dt^2} = -G \sum_{k \neq i} m_i m_k \frac{r_i - r_k}{|r_i - r_k|^3} \qquad (5.1.1)$$

Here, G is the universal constant of gravitation and the r_k are vector positions, usually 3-space vectors. The naive computation of all N forces at each discrete time increment requires $O(N^2)$ evaluations of the summand. In the last decade, great progress has occurred in the computational aspect. It is now possible in practice to evaluate numerically all forces (to some prescribed accuracy) in no more than $O(N \log N)$ operations. Some good introductory articles cover various $O(N \log N)$ schemes, including:

• Hierarchical tree-structure scheme [Appel 1985];
• Iterative potential scheme[Barnes and Hut 1986];
• Parallel hierarchical schemes [Singh 1993] ;
• Parallel mesh schemes [Jessop *et. al.* 1994].

This subject of N-body algorithms and their optimization is complicated. We give here an heuristic approach that at least reveals some of the basic features attendant to such study. Say that we split N bodies into M cells, so that there are about N/M bodies in each cell. This method works well in the fortuitous circumstance that the cells are well separated yet all the bodies in each cell are fairly close together. Then we make the crude approximation that all bodies within a cell (call it the *d-th* cell) gravitate (on all the other centers of mass in all the other $M-1$ cells) as if cell d's bodies are themselves concentrated at the cell d's center of mass. Then we use the simple rule that:

(acceleration on body i in cell c) ~   (5.1.2)
         (accelerations due to the other $(M-1)$ cells)   +
                 (accelerations due to other bodies within cell c)

To resolve the left-hand side acceleration for all $i = 0,..,$ $N-1$, the first parenthetical quantity on the right-hand side takes $O(M^2)$ force calculations for all possible cell pairs, while the second parenthetical requires $O((N/M)^2)$ force calculations to resolve the local interactions in each of M cells. The total effort is thus

$$O(M^2) \;+\; O(N^2/M)$$

force calculations. An approximate optimum should obtain for $M \sim N^{2/3}$, in which case the number of required force calculations is $O(N^{4/3})$. Here is a

Mathematica rendition of this $O(N^{4/3})$ algorithm:

(5.1.3)

```
(*  O(N^(4/3)) force algorithm for the N-body problem.
    We make the simplifying assumptions of unit masses
    and 1 dimension.  The box division is crude here
    and can be considerably improved via a tree method.
    Further recursion can turn this into an algorithm
    of complexity O(N log N).
 *)

n = 125;   (* Number of bodies. *)
(* Next, an inverse square force. *)
g = 0.0002;
v[mass_, distance_] := - g mass *
            If[distance == 0, 0, distance/Abs[distance]^3];
r = Table[Random[Real,1], {n}];   (* Initial coordinates. *)
m = 25;      (* Number of boxes, a divisor of n. *)
boxmass = n/m;
box[j_] := 1 + Floor[(j-1) m/n];
r = Sort[r]; (* Sort the coordinates. *)
boxes = Table[Take[r,{1+j boxmass,(j+1)boxmass}],{j,0,m-1}];
centers = Table[Apply[Plus,boxes[[j]]]/boxmass,{j,1,m}];

Timing[
(* Recurse on this next "m-body"
   function to enhance algorithm. *)
boxaccel = Table[If[i==j,0,
                    v[boxmass, centers[[i]]-centers[[j]]]
                  ],
              {i,1,m}, {j,1,m}
            ];
acc = Table[
          boi = box[i];
          (* Next, do box-box interactions. *)
          Apply[Plus,boxaccel[[boi]]] +
          (* Next, add the within-box interactions. *)
          Sum[If[i==j,0, v[1,r[[i]]-r[[j]]]]
              ,{j, 1 + (boi-1)boxmass, boi boxmass}
```

```
            ],
            {i,1,n}
        ]
][[1]]
(* Next, a literal O(N^2) test.
Timing[
acclit = Table[
            Sum[If[i==j,0,v[1,r[[i]]-r[[j]]]]
                ,{j,1,n}
            ], {i,1,n}
        ]
][[1]]
acc-acclit
*)
```

This program shows a speed dominance over the naive $O(N^2)$ method even for a few dozen bodies. The example has $N = 1000$, and the computation of the full acceleration table takes about one minute on a typical workstation. Note the choice M (variable m in the code) $= N^{2/3}$. There are several things incomplete and unoptimized about the example, the repair of which makes for good exercise (see Problem 5.1.1). But one very important aspect of modern N-body computations is missing in the example; namely, there is no recursion. Consider the parenthetical procedure of (5.1.2) stated:

(accelerations due to the other $(M-1)$ cells)

To get the $O(N^{4/3})$ complexity estimate we have used the fact that this tabulation of all cell-cell interactions (*i.e.,* forces between the centers of mass of pairs of cells) consumes $O(M^2)$. However, this cell-cell problem is *again an M-body problem.* Thus we may recurse on the cell-cell interactions, and obtain, for example with one recursive call for the cell-cell force calculation,

$$O(M^{4/3}) \; + \; O(N^2/M)$$

which leads to an $O(N^{8/7})$ algorithm. This recursion may be continued to a certain degree. In practice, and in theory when we carefully analyze all of the overhead of all the operations, the asymptotic complexity can be brought down in this way to $O(N \log N)$. Notice that, in the style of the above *Mathematica* example, there is no sense trying to "beat" $N \log N$, because even a good implementation of a Sort[ ] function should generally be of that complexity. There are many other ways to understand the ultimate $O(N \log N)$ complexity of the problem, and each of the various methods in the literature tends to arrive at said complexity through a unique argument. In some implementations, the $N \log N$ time obtains, for example, from the overall evaluation of forces as one traverses a tree structure.

Once the accelerations are know, via whatever N-body algorithm, one may perform elementary Eulerian integration to propagate the whole ensemble dynamically. In *Mathematica*, the List "accel" would be used like so:

```
vel += accel * dt;                    (5.1.4)
r += vel * dt;
t += dt;
```

here, "vel" would be a List that had been initialized to the body velocities corresponding respectively to body coordinates.

A fascinating modern research area has been the issue of chaos in the N-body problem. For example, a paper by [Heggie 1991] attempts to quantify the chaos in an N-body stellar ensemble by estimating the sensitivity of macroscopic motion to initial coordinate precision. This is basically the Lyapunov stability notion of chaos theory carried over to stellar dynamics. Heggie reports on interesting historical attempts to conserve certain quantities. For example the total energy

$$E = -G \sum_{i<j} \frac{m_i m_j}{|r_i - r_j|} + \frac{1}{2} \sum_i m_i \left(\frac{dr_i}{dt}\right)^2 \qquad (5.1.5)$$

is exactly conserved in theory, and a good program will not allow this conserved quantity to drift. Another interesting exact physical law is time-reversal symmetry, by which an ensemble in motion, if suddenly time-reversed, should eventually end up at the original configuration.

It turns out that, from the point of view of conserved quantities and absolute physical law, some surprising difficulties arise in N-body computations. The conservation of energy E can be "forced" by constantly renormalizing velocities; *e.g.*, every velocity (dr_i/dt) is multiplied by a constant near 1, so that on the current time increment E is unchanged, and these velocities are used as input for the next iteration. Such renormalization might be tried, for example, between the first and second lines of (5.1.4). But the surprising thing is that this forcing of conserved energy will generally *not* correct body coordinates very well. Apparently [Heggie 1991], one can keep the total energy quite smooth and yet end up with a ludicrous coordinate configuration (ludicrous with respect to the exact Newtonian truth). Similarly, investigators have had a great deal of trouble back-tracking motion, attempting to exhibit time-reversal symmetry, to high accuracy. It appears to take considerable effort even to recover initial coordinates in this way to three significant decimal digits.

Problem 5.1.1: Implement an N-body solver that, first, circumvents the numerical errors in the *Mathematica* example (5.1.3). The chief source of error in the example is that, for simplicity, we have naively sliced up the N bodies' coordinates into M boxes via a mere sort. The problem with this is that a body at an edge of a box can be very close to a body in an adjacent box but near the common edge. Consider sorting into boxes via the following algorithm: take the closest pair of bodies in the whole ensemble, and start the first box with that pair. Then, ignoring this pair, take the next closest pair and that will be the second box, and so on. After thus forming $N/2$ boxes, one may use the same recursion to fuse boxes in order to achieve M total boxes. Can this "closest pair" method be done fast enough? If not, implement a tree scheme in which the basic criterion is met: sufficiently close pairs all reside in common boxes.

Problem 5.1.2: Implement the $N^{4/3}$ example in the text, but with recursion to lower the power 4/3. If this work is properly combined with a better box-creation algorithm as asked for in the previous problem, a good $N \log N$ algorithm should result.

Problem 5.1.3: Develop a theory of the error incurred in the center-of-mass cell-cell scheme of the text. One approach is to use a multipole expansion of the acceleration error, in terms of deviations from center of mass for each particle. (In the one-dimensional setting of the text example, this is just a Taylor expanion of the potential function.)

Problem 5.1.4: Using a simple Eulerian integration scheme such as (5.1.4), and whatever fast N-body algorithm, model two colliding galaxies with $N/2$ particles in each. Provide if possible graphical output. Again if possible, compare the graphical, qualitative results with Euler integration and the naive, $O(N^2)$ literal N-body algorithm. It is interesting that this is basically impossible for N large enough to make "interesting" galaxies, due to the sluggishness of the literal method; one hopes to get good qualitative collisions for $N \sim 100$ say, perhaps then to analyze the behavior of errors in terms of N, then extrapolate error estimates to gigantic N, avoiding the $O(N^2)$ test altogether.

Problem 5.1.5: Study numerically the sensitivity of final coordinates as a function of deviations in initial coordinates. It matters, of course, what is the "class" of the N-body ensemble. There is galaxy class, in which there is a dense core, then cluster class, where the cluster has uniform density at the beginning, and so on.

5.2	*Nonlinear differential systems*

Proof of chaos

A recent breakthrough in the understanding of chaos in differential systems is the computer proof of the existence of chaos in the Lorenz attractor. The Lorenz system, initially pioneered by Lorenz in the form of a weather model, is standardized to be the coupled system of differential equations:

$$(5.2.1)$$

$$\frac{dx}{dt} = s(y-x)$$
$$\frac{dy}{dt} = Rx - y - xz$$
$$\frac{dz}{dt} = xy - qz$$

where the parameters s, R, q are assumed positive. A proof of chaos by [Hassard *et. al.* 1994] runs as follows. The authors state a theorem, that under certain conditions (which can be rigorously checked by computer), there is a solution $\{x(t), y(t), z(t)\}$ such that $x(t)$ has infinitely many zeros for t in $(0, \infty)$, and furthermore dx/dt can have, in a certain sense, virtually any prescribed density of zero-crossing itself between consecutive zeros of x. The authors in fact proved that for the parameter triple

$$\{q, R, s\} = \{9, 76, 10\} \qquad (5.2.2)$$

the theorem thus holds. It is interesting that the authors found reason to use high-precision arithmetic, involving real numbers (as coordinates of vertices of small parallelipipeds in configuration space) with dozens of digits.

Synchronized chaos

Another interesting aspect of modern chaos study is the emergence of the notion of secure communication via synchronized chaos. One form of chaotic communication has an always-noisy communicated data stream which, as described in [Frey 1993] might be generated via a nonlinear digital filter encoder which *even with steady zero input data* produces a chaotic signal. When there is non-zero data presented, the chaos is modified but is still "random" in appearance. At the receiving end, a non-linear inverse filter decoder with closely matched parameters (meaning matched to the sender's filter) can decode the chaotic stream into the proper final output. There is also a certain variant of "synchronized" chaotic communication, based on the very Lorenz equations we just discussed [Cuomo *et. al.* 1993][Johnson and Thorp 1994], and to which we now turn.

Synchronized chaotic communication can be achieved in the following way. Let a transmitter be designed so that a signal $x(t)$ (for example a voice signal to be sent to a remote receiver over a channel) is combined with an output of coupled nonlinear equations:

$$(5.2.3)$$

$$\frac{dU}{dt} = \sigma(V - U)$$

$$\frac{dV}{dt} = rU - V - 20UW$$

$$\frac{dW}{dt} = 5UV - bW$$

$$s(t) = U + x(t)$$

That is, the system of variables $\{U(t), V(t), W(t)\}$ is allowed to free-run as a Lorenz system, with a signal $x(t)$ added to U to create the output $s(t)$. This s signal is sent over a (possibly noisy) channel. Then at the receiving end, a system is driven by s:

$$(5.2.4)$$

$$\frac{du}{dt} = \sigma(v - u)$$

$$\frac{dv}{dt} = r\, s(t) - v - 20\, w\, s(t)$$

$$\frac{dw}{dt} = 5\, v\, s(t) \; - \; b\, w$$

$$X(t) \; = \; s(t) \; - \; u(t)$$

in the hope that X will "track" the desired signal x. It has been found [Cuomo *et. al.* 1993] that a practical choice of parameters (especially when actual electronic circuits are built to model the Lorenz system) is:

$$\sigma = 16 \qquad\qquad\qquad (5.2.5)$$
$$r = 46.5$$
$$b = 4$$

It is of interest that *digital* chaotic communication may be achieved by using the original signal x to drive the b parameter of the first system. One still recovers $X = s - u$ in the same fashion (5.2.5) but the error X should now have two values, as b is modulated plus or minus a fixed digital amount.

A *Mathematica* example of synchronized chaotic communication runs as follows:

$$(5.2.6)$$

```
(*  Synchronized chaotic communication experiment.
    In all such chaos computations one should wonder
    whether the attendant floating-point
    precision is sufficient.  Such is the intrinsic and
    natural computational demand of chaotic dynamics.
*)

sig = 16; r = 46.5; b = 4;
dt = 0.001;
len = 4096;
```

```
x[q_] = N[Sin[q/20]];    (* The signal to be sent. *)

U = V = W = 1.0;
s = Table[0,{len}];
Do[
   dU = sig (V-U);
   dV = r U - V - 20 U W;
   dW = 5 U V - b W;
   {U,V,W} += {dU, dV, dW} dt;
   s[[q]] = x[q] + U,
   {q,1,len}
];
(* Next, show the transmitted signal. *)
ListPlot[s, PlotJoined->True, Ticks->None]

(* Next, run the receiver using List s as the input. *)
u = v = w = 1.0;
r = 30;
X = Table[0,{len}];
Do[
   du = sig (v-u);
   dv = r s[[q]] - v - 20 s[[q]] w;
   dw = 5 s[[q]] v - b w;
   {u,v,w} += {du, dv, dw} dt;
   X[[q]] = s[[q]] - u,
   {q,1,len}
];
(* Next, show the final detected signal. *)
ListPlot[X, PlotJoined->True, Ticks->None]
```

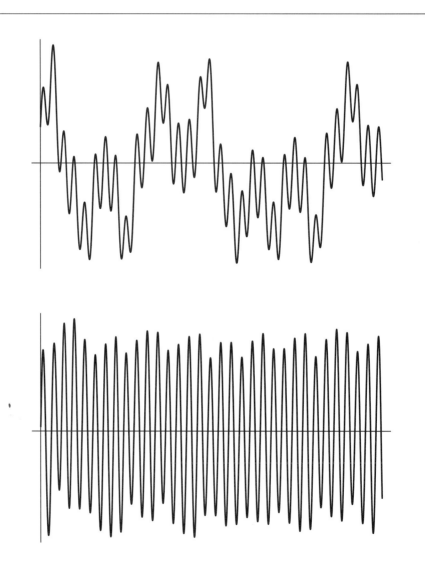

The first output is a Lorenz attractor's first coordinate (U in this case) modulated additively by the original x signal. The receiver system accepts as input this modulated transmitter output. The second plot shows the final detected signal, which is close to a steady sine wave, as desired.

Chaotic pulses

Another interesting new discovery in the field of non-linear differential equations is that there exist differential systems that produce pulse trains. This is interesting because a continuous system is sending out, in some sense, "quanta," or packets of energy. One such system recently studied is [Balmforth *et. al.* 1994]:

$$\frac{d^3x}{dt^3} + \mu \frac{d^2x}{dt^2} + \frac{dx}{dt} - cx + x^n = 0 \qquad (5.2.7)$$

where μ, c are real parameters and $n = 2$ or 3. Here is a *Mathematica* test of the differential system for the parameters $\mu = 1/\sqrt{2}$, $c = 1.92847$, and $n = 2$:

$$(5.2.8)$$

```
(* Irregular pulse-train generator,
   after [Balmforth et. al. 1994].
 *)

m = N[1/Sqrt[2]];
c = 1.92847;
n = 2;
len = 4096;
dt = 0.01;
x = Table[0,{len}];
pos = 0.002; jerk = accel = vel = 0.0;
Do[
     jerk = -m accel - vel + c pos - pos^2;
     accel += jerk*dt;
     vel += accel*dt;
     pos += vel*dt;
     x[[q]] = pos,
     {q,1,len}
 ];
ListPlot[x, PlotJoined->True];
```

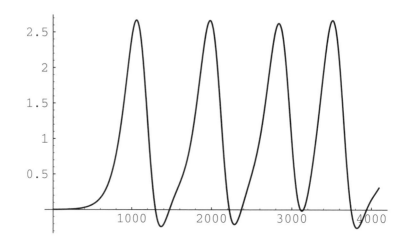

The pulse train output is irregular, meaning the period "dithers," which is very interesting because in certain neurobiological systems similar pulses occur, also with irregularity. This irregular behavior stands in contrast to other differential systems, such as the periodic-pulse system defined by:

$$\frac{d\theta}{dt} = 1 + \cos\theta$$

and variants of same, as discussed in [*Projects* 1994].

Problem 5.2.1: Attempt to work out computer proofs of chaos in other non-linear systems than the Lorenz system.

Problem 5.2.2: Implement *analog* synchronized chaotic communication software in which a random noise signal is added to the channel. Study the signal reconstruction errors empirically, with and without the noise channel.

Problem 5.2.3: Implement a *digital* synchronized chaotic communication system, in which the b parameter at the input stage (or for that matter the σ or r parameter) is modified by a "0-1" input signal.

Problem 5.2.4: Analyze, either theoretically or numerically or both, the "security" of a synchronized chaotic communication system. What is meant is, how does the reconstructibility for the final output at the receiver depend on the "secret" choice of the Lorenz parameters (σ, r, b)? (We assume a security model here for which both sender and receiver agents have a common, secret set of such parameters that said agents employ at each end.)

Problem 5.2.5: In practice, one difficulty with the [Balmforth *et. al.* 1994] chaotic pulse train system (5.2.7) is that, to render a steady (but irregularly spaced) pulse system requires delicate tuning of the differential system parameters. Work out a more "robust" system (perhaps by modifying the differential terms so that they cannot diverge so easily) in which these pulse trains are the rule, rather than the delicate exception.

5.3   *Fractal analysis*

Charged fractals

It is elementary that a charge distribution of integer dimension D generally gives rise to an external electrostatic potential with behavior:

$$V(r) \; \sim \; \frac{1}{r^{1-D}} \tag{5.3.1}$$

Special cases will bring this notion home (the zeroth power r^0 is interpreted as a logarithmic dependence):

$$\tag{5.3.2}$$

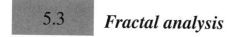

$$
\begin{array}{lll}
\text{point charge } (D = 0) & V(r) \; \sim \; 1/r \\
\text{line charge } (D = 1) & V(r) \; \sim \; \log r \\
\text{planar charge } (D = 2) & V(r) \; \sim \; r
\end{array}
$$

where generally r denotes the closest distance from the charge set. In recent times the situation of *fractal* charge sets has been a subject of scrutiny. We provide here an explicit construction of a fractal charge set. For an integer N, place charges at points $j/3^N$, where j is in $[0,...,3^N-1]$, except that the ternary expansion of integer j is always to be devoid of 1's. Thus, for $N = 3$, we have charges at:

$$(000)_3\,/27, \quad (002)_3/27, \quad (020)_3/27, \quad (022)_3/27, ...$$

where $(\ )_3$ means ternary (base-3) representation. For $N = 3$ we thus have exactly eight charges at

$$0/27, 2/27, 6/27, 8/27, 18/27, 20/27, 24/27, 26/27$$

Furthermore let us normalize the charges, for given N, by assigning charge $1/2^N$ to each point. In this way we have a total charge of unity, for any N. Now the potential at the point $(0, y)$ can be written:

$$(5.3.3)$$

$$V_N(0,y) \sim \frac{1}{2^N} \sum_{\substack{j=0 \\ (j)_3 \text{ is 1-free}}}^{3^N-1} \frac{1}{\sqrt{y^2 + (j/3^N)^2}}$$

A student of fractals will recognize the limiting charge point set as $N \to \infty$ as the celebrated Cantor set in $(0,1)$. We contemplate, then, a total unit charge distributed in this fashion over the Cantor fractal. From the algebraic identity

$$\sum_{\substack{j=0 \\ (j)_3 \text{ is 1-free}}}^{3^N-1} z^j \;=\; \prod_{k=0}^{N-1}\left(1 + \left(z^2\right)^{3^k}\right) \qquad (5.3.4)$$

it is possible to derive from (5.3.3) the result that, as $N \to \infty$, the limiting potential at $(0, y)$ is

$$V_\infty(0, y) \;=\; \int_0^\infty J_0(uy) \left\{ e^{-\frac{u}{2}} \prod_{k=1}^\infty \cosh \frac{u}{3^k} \right\} du \qquad (5.3.5)$$

where J_0 is the standard Bessel function of order zero.

An interesting paper [Dettman and Frankel 1993] treats this charged Cantor set scenario from several points of view. They show that an asymptotic leading term in a certain expansion of $V(0, y)$ is:

$$V_\infty (0, y) \ \sim \ \frac{P\left(\frac{\log y}{\log 3}\right)}{y^{1-\frac{\log 2}{\log 3}}} \tag{5.3.6}$$

where P is a periodic function of period one. Note the striking apperance of the known fractal dimension of the Cantor set, namely $D = (\log 2 \, / \log 3)$. It is not yet known how to derive such a result from an integral representation such as (5.3.5). For one thing, the leading term (5.3.6) is evidently oscillatory, so–because the potential must be monotonic decreasing in y–one expects any oscillations to be cancelled by the missing error terms in the asymptotic expansion.

Other progress on fractal charge distributions has been made by [Jones *et. al.* 1994], who give a fast algorithm for the solution of the Laplace equation on fractal boundaries. One of the interesting aspects of their treatment is the notion that a well-posed Laplacian problem can be approached via nonsingular matrix decomposition.

Fractal dimension

Of course by now the research literature on fractal dimension theory and measurement is vast. Here we mention a very few interesting excerpts from that literature.

There has been progress in the fascinating domain of fractal-dimension assessment via wavelet algorithms. Various rudimentary approaches to such study are discussed in [*Projects* 1994]. One new development is the realization that wavelet transforms of multifractals tend to have maxima that define self-similar curves in the scale-resolution transform plane [Hwang and Mallat 1994]. Another development is the technique of estimating the fractal dimension of a random process (*e.g.* a Gaussian process) via a counting of level crossings [Feuerverger *et. al.* 1992]. This is a fascinating study, involving analysis, matrix algebra, and eigenvalue theory.

Problem 5.3.1: Analyze (5.3.5) numerically, endeavoring to reveal a behavior y^{D-1}, where $D = (\log 2 / \log 3)$ is the fractal dimension of the Cantor charge set. This problem is more difficult than may first appear; convergence for very small y is problematic.

Problem 5.3.2: Attempt to analyze (5.3.5) analytically, perhaps to show an anticipated y^{D-1} behavior consistent with the results of [Dettman and Frankel 1993].

Problem 5.3.3: Implement a [Jones *et. al.* 1994] fast Laplacian solver, and apply it to various fractal charge distributions. Those authors use a two-dimensional Cantor charge set as their canonical problem, but the technique should also shed some light on the one-dimensional Cantor charge problem.

Problem 5.3.4: Use graphics to study wavelet transforms of multifractals, in the style of [Hwang and Mallat 1994].

Problem 5.3.5: Work out an algorithm and write a program to measure empirically the fractal dimension of a Brownian fractal signal. Can this be done merely by counting zero-crossings? In this connection see [Feuerverger *et. al.* 1992]. Algorithms for generating Brownian fractal time series are exhibited in [*Projects* 1994].

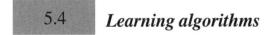
5.4   *Learning algorithms*

Neural network computations

Again the subject is quite broad and by now deeply entrenched in library references. We note just three interesting developments. First, there is the work of [Wu *et. al.* 1994] in the use of neural networks to achieve results in matrix algebra. The authors give a dynamical equation approach, suitable for neural network computation, to find pseudoinverse matrices.

Second, there is an interesting hardware specification for fuzzy neural networks [Kuo *et. al.* 1993]. The present author feels that their idea would make for a superb software simulation study of such networks.

Third, there have appeared in recent years fascinating mixes of deterministic dynamics and learning algorithms. For example, [Banzhaf 1989] describes a novel dynamical approach to the dreaded "traveling salesman problem" (TSP) of computer-scientific and complexity-theoretical fame. The TSP is one of those problems easily put into English, but formidable to solve. The problem is simply: find the shortest traveling route over which a salesman can visit each of N cities. One could also cast this problem in terms of minimum telephone wiring to interconnect N cities, and so on. The fascinating central idea is to use a dynamical system embodied in the coupled nonlinear differential system:

$$\frac{\partial d_{ij}}{\partial t} = d_{ij}\left(1 - 2\sum_{h=1}^{N}\left(d_{ih}^2 + d_{hj}^2\right) + 3d_{ij}^2\right) \qquad (5.4.1)$$

where the $\{d_{ij} : i,j = 1,2,...,N\}$ can be thought of as elements of a real N-by-N matrix. Now under very general conditions, an initial matrix with each element d_{ij} in [0,1] will–and this is the surprising, delightful result–move toward an equilibrium in which every matrix row has one element converging to 1 and the rest to zero. Furthermore, each column ends up with a single 1 and the rest zero elements. In other words, we get a permutation matrix whose 1's correspond in a certain way to the relative maxima of the initial d matrix. A *Mathematica* implementation of the dynamical system (5.4.1) runs like so:

$$(5.4.2)$$

```
n = 3;
d = Table[Random[Real,1],{n},{n}];
ddot = d; (* Just to initialize the ddot list. *)
dt = 0.1;
MatrixForm[Round[10000 d]/10000.0]
Do[
 Do[
   Do[
       ddot[[i,j]] =
           d[[i,j]] *(1 -
           2 Sum[d[[h,j]]^2 + d[[i,h]]^2,{h,1,n}]+
           3 d[[i,j]]^2),
       {i,1,n}
   ],
   {j,1,n}
 ];
 d += ddot*dt,
 {k,1,60}
];
MatrixForm[Round[10000 d]/10000.0]


0.0712    0.7555    0.4085
0.6431    0.4662    0.6498
0.6585    0.9199    0.565


0         0.9996    0
0.0024    0         0.9914
0.9837    0.0002    0.0011
```

The output shows first the random initial d matrix, then the "min-max" permutation matrix after 60 iterations of the differential system. The

[Banzhaf 1989] approach to the TSP is to sandwich this dynamical system in between coding and decoding neural layers. Independent of the TSP, however, there are many nonlinear, difficult problems that can make good use of this "automatic" scheme for forcing an initial matrix to saturate, to converge to a permutation matrix.

Artificial life and genetic algorithms

One recent advance in artificial life theory is quite welcome, in the present author's opinion, as a proper complement to the surfeit of numerically-bound approaches over the past decade. The works of [Adami 1994][Adami *et. al.* 1994] are especially interesting in that therein are combined the following ideas:

- Statistical mechanics of self-replicating systems;
- Fractal nature of evolutionary models;
- Information theory.

It seems fair to conjecture that a great deal of good must come of this synthesis in coming years. One might expect the emergence of a brace of new algorithms for modeling evolution.

Genetic algorithms, in some sense a "converse" to artificial life, use certain quantifications of the notions of mutation and selection to solve difficult problems. The previous work [*Projects* 1994] gives explicit code examples of how to set up a genetic algorithm using a fractal curve to sample the relevant vector space of solutions. An interesting problem which admits of genetic algorithmic solution is posed below, and the genetic algorithm as possible resource in signal compression is mentioned in Chapter 6. An excellent survey work in the field is [Mitchell 1992].

Problem 5.4.1: Use the neural network approach of [Wu *et. al.* 1994] to solve some dynamical system problem other than their matrix pseudoinverse problem.

Problem 5.4.2: Implement a model of genotype propagation, along the lines of [Adami *et. al.* 1994], in which, under appropriate assumptions on mutation and propagation, one expects $1/n^D$ for the number of genotypes with n living copies, where D is fractional.

Problem 5.4.3: Study the evolution of organisms within an artificial life context. One good introduction is [Bedau 1995].

Problem 5.4.4: Study the new and somewhat controversial "no free lunch" (NFL) theorems. The essential goal is to show that, in the words of [Wolpert and Macready 1995], "all algorithms that search for the extremum of a cost function perform exactly the same, according to any performance measure, when averaged over all possible cost functions." This subject is an effective mix of the tenets of genetic algorithm research and standard computational complexity theory.

Problem 5.4.5: Apply the dynamical min-max system (5.4.1) to the TSP or alternatively to a chosen problem of pattern recognition.

Problem 5.4.6: Here is an interesting rigorous formulation of *learning*, in the context of neural networks. As in [Wendemuth *et. al.* 1995] one posits a pattern and a set of targets as follows:

$$\text{pattern:} \quad \vec{x}_1, \vec{x}_2, \vec{x}_3..., \vec{x}_p \qquad ; \ \vec{x}_k \in R^N \ , \ |\vec{x}_k|^2 = N$$

$$\text{targets:} \quad t_1, t_2, t_3..., t_p \qquad ; \ t_k = \pm 1$$

In other words, the pattern consists of p vectors, each vector of dimension N and of Euclidean magnitude $\sqrt{N}$; while the targets are "bits," except that the allowed values are ± 1. The goal of learning is then: find a vector J such that

$$\text{sgn}(J \bullet \vec{x}_k) = t_k \qquad ; \ k = 1, 2, ..., p$$

that is, such that the sign of the dot-product agrees respectively with the targets.

Some research tasks might run as follows. First, explain in detail how the solution vector J can be used in pattern recognition, *e.g.* recognition of ASCII character images. (To effect the explanation one needs to state precisely what the patterns and targets mean in practice.) Second, work out an algorithm that actually learns (tries to find J), either for character recognition or some other learning problem. Note that [Wendemuth 1995] gives "robust" learning algorithms, meaning that one expects convergence (to some J', say) even if no solution J exists.

Problem 5.4.7: Here is a curious and difficult problem [Graffagnino 1995] that was brought to the author's attention and which, on the basis of successful subsequent experiments, is known to be susceptible to an elegant, genetic algorithm attack. A "program" is to be defined as a set of functions whose total memory size is say R. Consider N positive real numbers $r_0, ... r_{N-1}$ that sum to R, with these r_i representing the respective memory sizes of the functions. Let us say that our "compiler" has the option to place the r_i in any order it wishes, for example the memory might be laid out like so:

$$r_3, \ r_{17}, r_8, ...$$

In other words the compiler may consecutively stack the functions in any conceivable permutation of their indices. So far so good. But now we posit a measure of badness, a "paging rate" P, which rate we want to be as small as possible. The rate P depends on an N-by-N calling matrix F, whose entries specify which function calls which with what frequency. The paging rate is defined essentially as the total absolute length of "hopping" amongst the functions in memory, and is given by the expression:

$$P = \sum F_{ij} |s_i - s_j|$$

where s_i is the distance from the program memory origin to the function i, or

$$s_i = \sum_{\pi(j) < \pi(i)} r_j$$

where π denotes the permutation of the function order. Thus P is an expected hopping distance which presumably measures real-world performance in a virtual memory system for which too much memory hopping is expensive.

A wonderful genetic algorithmic approach to minimizing P is to establish "parents," each parent being simply a permutation on N symbols. Each of a parent's children is then the parent's permutation *with an extra transposition (mutation)* on said permutation. Thus a parent's progeny will compete for lowest P, and some subset of the best children will become the new parents, and so on.

5.5   *An old & beautiful nonlinear system*

And we might also say, "a system which connects physics, mathematics, and computation at a deep level." We speak of the true pendulum, a system that has settled–after several hundred years of physics–into two almost entirely disparate educational niches.   On the one hand, the simple harmonic approximation to the nonlinear "true pendulum" equation is often a key component of a first-year college physics course. Such a simplified system is of course exactly solvable in every aspect. But the true nonlinear system is to this day shrouded in a certain mystery, especially if one asks detailed questions about the quantum mechanical setting.   The nonlinear classical equation of motion for the true pendulum is taken to be

$$\frac{d^2 x}{dt^2} = -\frac{g}{L} \sin x \qquad (5.5.1)$$

where x is the pendulum's angle from vertical, g is acceleration of local gravity, and L is pendulum length. In what follows we envision the pendulum as a mass bob on a *rod* (not on a string), so that motion over the top pivot is possible. It is the approximation $x \sim \sin x$ that ignites the complete solution of the elementary harmonic approximation. But if we do not tamper with the sin x term, the classical situation is much, much more complicated; and as we intimated the quantum mechanical situation is not even completely understood.

First we review some classical results previously expressed in [*Projects* 1994], and add some new observations. The reason we exhibit the various formulae is that many computational issues pertain. First, the period of motion for an initial release angle x_0, with release from rest, is given exactly by:

$$(5.5.2)$$

$$P(x_0) \;=\; \sqrt{\frac{8L}{g}} \int_0^{x_0} \frac{dx}{\sqrt{\cos x - \cos x_0}}$$

$$=\; \sqrt{\frac{16L}{g}}\; K\!\left(\sin \frac{x_0}{2}\right)$$

$$=\; \frac{2\pi \sqrt{\frac{L}{g}}}{AG\!\left(1,\, \cos \frac{x_0}{2}\right)}$$

The beautiful relations between elliptic integrals such as K (the elliptic integral of the first kind) and the arithmetic-geometric mean function AG are discussed in [Borwein and Borwein 1987]. It is evident that for zero release angle the period attains its elementary harmonic-approximation value, namely $P = 2\pi\sqrt{L/g}$, as expected. From the aforementioned theory of elliptic integrals one may derive interesting exact periods, as follows:

Initial release angle $x_0 = \pi/2$:   (5.5.3)

$$P\left(\frac{\pi}{2}\right) = 2\pi\sqrt{\frac{L}{g}} \; \frac{\sqrt{\pi}}{\Gamma^2\left(\frac{3}{4}\right)}$$

Initial release angle $x_0 = 2\sin^{-1}[(\sqrt{3}-1)/\sqrt{8}]$:   (5.5.4)

$$P(x_0) = 2\pi\sqrt{\frac{L}{g}} \; \frac{3^{1/4}\Gamma^3\left(\frac{1}{3}\right)}{\pi^2\, 2^{4/3}}$$

Initial release angle $x_0 = \sin^{-1}[(12-8\sqrt{2})(3\sqrt{2}-4)^{1/2}]$:   (5.5.5)

$$P(x_0) = 2\pi\sqrt{\frac{L}{g}} \left(\sum_{n=-\infty}^{\infty} e^{-2\pi n^2}\right)^2$$

This last release angle is about 19.7 degrees. A wonderful property of this release angle is that $2P(x_0) = P(\pi-x_0)$, which means that the period for release at the complementary angle is exactly twice that of the release at angle x_0. Upon realizing this, the author commissioned the construction of a pendulum pair, to see the "2:1 resonance" occur when one pendulum is released at 19.7 degrees and the other released at 160.3 degrees.

The quantum mechanical scenario for the true pendulum is described by a Schroedinger equation:

$$-\frac{1}{2}\psi'' - (A\cos x)\,\psi = E\psi \tag{5.5.6}$$

Let us also invoke a formally equivalent Mathieu equation in standard notation [Abramowitz and Stegun 1965]:

$$\frac{d^2 f}{dv^2} + (a - 2q\cos 2v)f = 0 \tag{5.5.7}$$

and tabulate all the parameter relations, both for previous and future parameters of this topic, thus:

(5.5.8)

$$
\begin{aligned}
h &= 2\pi \\
m &= 1 \\
A &= gL^3 \\
q &= -4A \\
a &= 8E = -4K^2
\end{aligned}
$$

This tabulation maintains consistency between the classical and quantum pictures, whether the latter is supported by the Schroedinger or Mathieu equation.

The author has alluded to the extreme complexity inherent in the quantum system. What is meant precisely is that such fundamental entities as the quantum Green's function $G(x, x_0, E)$ seem to be intractable. Furthermore, there is another, different sort of obstacle to complete understanding. It is well known that certain Mathieu functions, *i.e.*, solutions to (5.5.6) satisfying the pendulum boundary condition $\Psi(x) = \Psi(x+2\pi)$, are the eigenfunctions of the system, and that the corresponding energy eigenvalues E are related to certain Mathieu eigenvalues. However, when one actually tries to calculate the eigenvalues, or plot the eigenfunctions, there is immediate trouble. The author is unaware of any scheme to calculate the Mathieu eigenfunctions *reliably*, meaning that roundoff and explosion errors (particularly for large principal quantum number) are avoided. And, there is plenty of motivation for plotting the eigenfunctions. For example, in some asymptotic sense of small amplitudes the Mathieu eigenfunctions *must of necessity* approach the Hermite eigenfunctions of the simple harmonic oscillator; for after all, the small-amplitude classical picture is that of such an oscillator. Thus in some regime the n-th eigenfunction for the true pendulum should behave as:

$$
\Psi_n(x) \sim H_n\left(xA^{1/4}\right) e^{-\frac{x^2\sqrt{A}}{2}}
$$

(5.5.9)

where H_n is the n-th Hermite polynomial. Thus, visual plots of actual

Mathieu functions can lend some understanding as to just how this mysterious asymptotic behavior occurs. Incidentally, as a technical matter these asymptotic issues evidently turn on only two questions:

1) What is n, the principal quantum number (the eigenfunction's index)?
2) What is A, the "pendulum structure constant?"

Consistent with (5.5.8) the full physical description of the dimensionless A is:

$$A = \frac{4\pi^2 m^2 L^3 g}{h^2} \qquad\qquad (5.5.10)$$

One can identify six separate physical regimes, according to the following table, indexed by the structure constant and the principal quantum number n ("true" here means true pendulum in which the sin x term has some effect, while "rotor" means gravity is negligible):

$$(5.5.11)$$

	$n \ll |A|^{1/2}$	$n \sim |A|^{1/2}$	$n \gg |A|^{1/2}$
large n	classical harmonic	classical true	free rotor
small n	quantum harmonic	quantum true	quantum rotor

Further interpretation of these six regimes is relegated to the problems below.

Aside from the difficult computational and asymptotic-interpetation dilemmas lies the aforementioned Green's function dilemma. In [Crandall 1993] it is shown that the Green's function for a potential $-A \cos x$ can be cast as an infinite formal perturbation series. In particular, denote by O the "double shift" operator, that is

$$O(f(n)) = f(n+1) + f(n-1)$$

Then the true pendulum's Green's function can be written:

(5.5.12)

$$G(x, x_0, E) = -\frac{1}{\pi} \sum_{n=-\infty}^{\infty} \frac{e^{inx}}{n^2 + K^2} \sum_{j=0}^{\infty} A^j O \frac{1}{n^2 + K^2} O \frac{1}{n^2 + K^2} \dots O \frac{e^{-inx_0}}{n^2 + K^2}$$

where it is understood that every operator O operates on everything to its right (n is the parameter to be left-, right-shifted), and that j occurrences of O correspond to the factor A^j, with the single exception that for $j = 0$ the whole O-chain becomes the term $e^{-inx}0$. Technically, G is the quantum amplitude to move from angle x_0 to angle x with energy E. But all we need to know for the computational issues at hand is that *the energy eigenvalues of the pendulum should be the poles of G.* Likewise, the residues at the poles should be the eigenfunction products $\Psi_n(x) \Psi_n(x_0)^*$.

The problem of somehow "evaluating" the Green's function (5.5.12) is formidable. There may be little hope of a closed-form solution; for one thing such a closed form would contain somehow all of the Mathieu eigenvalues as poles, and these eigenvalues as we have mentioned are themselves difficult to compute. Still, the perturbation series (5.5.12) has various features of interest, which features are discussed in the problems below. Before we move on to the problems, we state exact continued fraction relations for the quantum eigenvalues:

(5.5.13)

To get even state eigenvalues $E = -K^2/2$, solve for K in:

$$0 = K^2 - \cfrac{2A^2}{K^2 + 1^2 - \cfrac{A^2}{K^2 + 2^2 - \dots}}$$

(the numerators here continue on forever as $A^2, A^2, \dots$).

To get odd state eigenvalues, again as $E = -K^2/2$, solve for K in:

$$0 = K^2 + 1^2 - \cfrac{A^2}{K^2 + 2^2 - \cfrac{A^2}{K^2 + 3^2 - \ldots}}$$

Problem 5.5.1: Prove (5.5.3)-(5.5.5) by referring to known evaluations of certain elliptic integrals.

Problem 5.5.2: For the "unit pendulum" $L = g = 1$, is it ever the case that both $(\sin x, P(x))$ are algebraic? What about $(x, P(x))$? What about $(\sin x, P(x)/(2\pi))$? There is at least one solution to this last question: the pair $(0,1)$. A certain amount of numerical study could be applied here. For example, using the PSLQ algorithm of Section 2.3 one should be able to find a quartic polynomial with integer coefficients for which the sine of the angle x_0 in (5.5.5) is a zero. Then the period for that angle could be "ruled out" to some degree; *i.e.*, in terms of a bound on the Euclidean norm of polynomial coefficients.

Problem 5.5.3: By resolving high-precision values of the relevant elliptic integrals, verify numerically the "period doubling" claim for the special angle in (5.5.5). Alternatively, model the 2:1 resonance via a Runge-Kutta dynamical solver.

Problem 5.5.4: Verify by numerical computation that the period $P(\pi-\varepsilon)$ as a function of very small ε behaves in a certain exponential fashion. The physical notion is that for very small ε, the pendulum takes a very long time even to "just get going."

Problem 5.5.5: Work out means for visualizing Mathieu eigenfunctions. Using plots of same, explain in more detail the qualitative features of the physics tableau (5.5.11). One point of this whole topic is that the present problem is more challenging than one might think, because there is evidently no easy way to obtain reliable Mathieu plots (at least no such way known to the present author).

Problem 5.5.6: Show that the Green's function series (5.5.12) indeed leads, at least formally, to the eigenvalue fraction rules (5.5.13) for the energy poles. Hint: write G as:

$$G = \sum_{n=-\infty}^{\infty} g_n(x_0)\, e^{in(x-x_0)}$$

and develop a recursion relation for the g_n.

Problem 5.5.7: Work out a *symbolic* relaxation method that finds approximate *symbolic* zeros of the continued fraction(s) (5.5.13). For example, to solve for even state eigenvalues, iterate:

$$K^2 := \frac{2A^2}{F(K)}$$

where you have chosen a clever starting K (such as $2A^2$ itself), and $F(K)$ is a continued fraction that you evaluate to certain precision in A. The trick is to maintain a steadily increasing precision for subsequent iterations. Here is one correct series development: the ground state eigenvalue is given through $O(A^{10})$ by:

$$\dot{E}_0 = -A^2 + \frac{7}{4}A^4 - \frac{58}{9}A^6 + \frac{68687}{2304}A^8 - \frac{123707}{800}A^{10} + \dots$$

So even the ground state energy appears difficult to render to high precision. It is not even clear whether the series converges in any sense, even for A small.

Problem 5.5.8: Here is a difficult but valuable excursion. Attempt to develop symbolically the Green's function series (5.5.12), attempting at each perturbation stage j to contract terms that can obviously be algebraically contracted. The author believes that if one then plots the number of unreducible terms with respect to j, one obtains a fractal graph, probably a class of Morse-Thue fractal. If this be true, the fact of a fractal perturbation series structure is yet another testimony to the profundity of the true pendulum.

Problem 5.5.9: Study one or more of the veritable multitude of chaotic aspects of the driven true pendulum. It is a fascinating thing that the preservation of the (sin x) term in Newton's law of motion leads–when driving forces are applied–to chaotic regimes. In addition, one can discover fractal basins and so on for certain kinds of driving forces [Dobson and Delchamps 1994]. In addition, the literature contains studies of quantum chaos in kicked pendula [Lan and Fox 1991], discrete quantum pendula [Bobenko *et. al.* 1993], and spherical pendula [Guillemin and Uribe 1989].

Problem 5.5.10: Investigate for the pendulum, or for that matter any other completely-bound quantum system, the "quantum zeta function," which is a sum involving all the bound state energy eigenvalues E_n:

$$Z(s) \;=\; \sum_n \frac{1}{E_n{}^s}$$

A canonical case is the simple harmonic pendulum, for which the energy levels are spaced along an arithmetic progression, so that Z can be evaluated immediately in terms of the Riemann zeta function. But $Z(s)$ is sometimes possible to evaluate even if we do not know each energy eigenvalue E_n [Berry 1986]. One may start with the Green's function $G(x, x_0, E)$ satisfying:

$$-\frac{1}{2}G'' + V(x)\, G \;=\; EG - \delta(x - x_0)$$

and ponder the formal solution:

$$G(x, x_0, E) \;=\; \sum_n \frac{\Psi_n(x)\, \Psi_n{}^*(x_0)}{E - E_n}$$

It is immediate that the quantum zeta function at $s = 1$ can be written:

$$Z(1) \;=\; -\int G(x,x,0)\,dx$$

Similar "trace relations" hold for larger integer s (one may use derivatives of G or multiple integrals, and so on). For example, using results of [Voros 1980] one can show that for the quartic oscillator, with Schroedinger equation:

$$-\frac{1}{2}\Psi'' + x^4\,\Psi \;=\; E\Psi$$

the quantum zeta function at $s = 1$ is given exactly by:

$$Z(1) \;=\; \frac{3^{2/3}}{8\pi^2}\,\Gamma^5\!\left(\frac{1}{3}\right)$$

One excellent and fairly difficult numerical exercise is to verify a few places of this exact evaluation via some independent means of assessing quartic eigenvalues. One valuable application of the quantum zeta function is the estimation of ground state energies. These estimates are sometimes surprisingly good. If $Z(1)$ is known, one may use the identity:

$$\frac{1}{E_0} \;=\; Z(1) - \sum_{n=1}^{\infty} \frac{1}{E_n}$$

to estimate the ground state energy E_0, the trick being to use, say, a WKB-class formula for the higher energies. For the quartic oscillator, the first-order WKB estimate is:

$$E_n \;\sim\; \left(\sqrt{8\pi}\,\frac{\Gamma\!\left(\frac{7}{4}\right)}{\Gamma\!\left(\frac{1}{4}\right)}\left(n+\frac{1}{2}\right)\right)^{\frac{4}{3}}$$

So one instructive computational problem is: use this WKB approximation for $n = 1,2,3,...$; take the known exact value of $Z(1)$ above, and estimate in this way the ground state energy E_0. Note that the sum over n converges very slowly, and that Euler-Maclaurin methods are indicated.

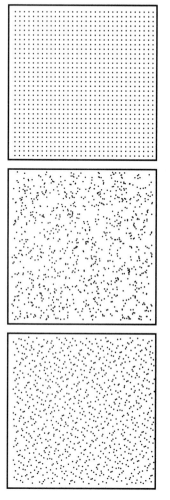

Grid

$$(x_n, y_n) \;\; = \;\; \left(\frac{n \; \% \; N}{N}, \; \frac{\lfloor n/N \rfloor}{N} \right)$$

Monte Carlo

$$(x_n, y_n) \;\; = \;\; (\mathrm{random}(1), \mathrm{random}(1))$$

quasi-Monte Carlo

$$(x_n, y_n) \;\; = \;\; (d_2(n), d_3(n))$$
$$d_p(n) \;\; := \;\; 0.b_0 b_1 b_2 ...$$
$$\text{where} \;\; n \;\; = \;\; b_0 + b_1 p + b_2 p^2 + ...$$

Three image sampling methods. In the bottom figure, two quasi-Monte Carlo discrepancy sequences yield the x, y coordinates. This scheme has attractive properties: speed, lack of pattern aliasing, and lack of random "clumping." What is more, one may use the method in vector quantization (VQ) algorithms, to effect "fair" sampling in high-dimensional spaces.

6 *Data manipulation*

Herb Caen, a popular columnist for the San Francisco Chronicle, *recently quoted a* Voice of America *press release as saying that it was reorganizing in order to "eliminate duplication and redundancy." This quote both states a goal of data compression and illustrates its common need: the removal of duplication (or redundancy) can provide a more efficient representation of data and the quoted phrase is itself a candidate for such surgery.*

[*Gersho and Gray* 1992]

Herein we concentrate primarily on sound and images, although some observations will be made with respect to more general data.

6.1 *Signal synthesis, detection and modeling*

Fractal sound

It is instructive and entertaining to use computing machinery to generate self-similar waveforms or frequency patterns. A good starting point in the study of such "fractal sound" is to contemplate the function

$$n(t) = \sum_{k=1}^{K} (-1)^{\lfloor a^k t \rfloor} \qquad (6.1.1)$$

where t is time, K is an integer of choice, and a is a real scale parameter. Note first that because the greatest integer in $a^k t$ is to be taken, the result $n(t)$, being a sum of ± 1's, is always an integer. Now imagine assigning integer values to successive notes in a well-tempered or other convenient scale. Then (6.1.1) represents a musical "score" which might be rendered audible as a sine wave tone whose instantaneous frequency corresponds to the integer "note" $n(t)$. A plot of the musical score for $a = 2$, $K = 24$ is shown below. Because t is a continuous variable, the actual plot here is of $n(x/63)$, where the x-coordinate runs through positive integers:

We remind ourselves that the above plot is a musical score, without the standard horizontal score lines drawn in, and without other standard notation for timing, key, and so on. But even in this rudimentary form, a soundfile created according to the score can be quite interesting. A simple way to create the final product is to write say a *C* program that generates a steady sine wave, via some line such as:

```
data[j] = sin(j * phase);
```

then to perturb the floating-point variable "phase" every so often according to the fractal music score, which in tabular form appears thus:

```
int note_table =
{12, 9, 8, 5, 8, 5, 4, 1, 8, 5, 4, 1, 4, 1, 0, -3, 8, 5,
  4, 1, 4, 1, 0, -3, 4, 1, 0, -3, 0, -3, -4, -7, 8, 5,
  4, 1, 4, 1, 0, -3, 4, 1, 0, -3, 0, -3, -4, -7, 4, 1,
  0, -3, 0, -3, -4, -7, 0, -3, -4, -7, -4, -7, -8, 11,
  8, 7, 4, 7, 4, 3, 0, 7, 4, 3, 0, 3, 0, -1, -4, 7, 4,
  3, 0, 3, 0, -1, -4, 3, 0, -1, -4, -1, -4, -5, -8, 7,
  4, 3, 0, 3, 0, -1, -4, 3, 0, -1, -4, -1, -4, -5, -8,
  3, 0, -1, -4, -1, -4, -5, -8, -1, -4, -5, -8, -5, -8}
```

The only tricky aspect of such a program is the task of properly perturbing "phase" with the entries of "note_table." One way to make the final sound especially pleasing is to use well-tempered mapping; *i.e.*, let "phase" take on only values:

```
phase = con * exp(note_table[m] * log(2.0));
```

where "con" is a constant, actually an overall pitch tuning of the entire score; while "m" is an integer that counts slowly through the note_table array. In this way one achieves only notes lying on a well-tempered scale.

Upon listening to such a fractal musical piece, the self-similarity is evident as a kind of nested sequence of descending themes. Observe that the *C* struct "note_table" is a numerical representation of the score plot. Now one may either inspect the numerical patterns within the exhibited *C* struct, or alternatively "crush" the graphical plot by a horizontal factor of *a* itself:

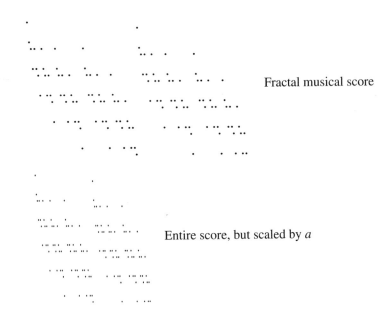

Fractal musical score

Entire score, but scaled by *a*

So here we have a piece within a piece, in that parts of the piece represent the whole piece and vice versa!

As explained in [*Projects* 1994], it is also possible to generate an audible sound on the basis not of frequency domain self-similarity, but time-domain self-similarity. The basic idea is extremely simple: given a signal $x(t)$, superimpose as follows:

$$X(t) = \sum_{k=1}^{K} x(a^k t) \qquad\qquad (6.1.2)$$

The self-similarity comes from the approximate scaling relation $X(t) \sim X(at)$. What is especially appealing for sound generation is that the error terms in this approximate relation can be rendered themselves inaudible! Thus it is possible to create a subjectively precise fractal sound that *sounds basically the same* on different time scales.

Out of sheer curiosity the author, after having generated various fractal superpositions $X(t)$ in software, commissioned the construction of a tape recorder with electronic variable motor speed control. He then taped the computer sound output of an X signal, later to be able to slow down or speed up the tape motor upon playback. The effect if done carefully is astounding: at a motor speed higher or lower by the scale factor a, the effective "pitch" (we use quotes because of course there generally exist a great many frequencies) is indeed subjectively invariant.

Problem 6.1.1: Generate visual and audible representations of a fractal musical score, starting with the self-similar integer function (6.1.1). Does the human ear prefer certain scale factors a above others?

Problem 6.1.2: Generate a fractal sound file $X(t)$, starting with (6.1.2) and fundamental signal $x = \sin(bt)$ for constant b. Work out a value of b that will render the error terms in the self-similarity relation virtually inaudible. The resulting superposition X should sound "the same" if the time scale is changed by a factor of a.

Problem 6.1.3: Here is an amusing experiment. Take some real music, such as a jazz piece with various distinctly audible instruments, and use *that* as the fundamental x in the superposition (6.1.2). Now you have a crazy, cacaphonous piece that nevertheless has themes from the entire piece all working in coexistence at all moments!

Mathematically motivated sound

Computing machinery can also be used to turn mathematical functions into sounds. In this way one can sense the spectral properties of a function. Here are four interesting exemplary classes of functions that give rise to interesting sounds:

- Brownian signals
- Zeta functions
- Weierstrass functions
- Theta functions

Let us discuss each of these classes in turn, with a view to programmatic generation of sound files and spectral data representations. First, a Brownian noise signal $x(t)$ can be generated according to:

$$x(t) = \sum_n \frac{x_n^\wedge}{n^{H+1/2}} e^{int} \qquad (6.1.3)$$

where H is a Hurst exponent related as we shall see to the fractal dimension of the signal, while the coefficients are independent Gaussian normal random variables of unit variance. We may assume, especially when generating sound, that $x(t)$ is real-valued. One way to assure this is to generate the sum in (6.1.3) as a DFT, making sure that the coefficients $x_n^\wedge$ satisfy an appropriate Hermiticity requirement. It is not hard to show, at least heuristically, that a law of microscopic expectations holds:

$$< |x(t+T) - x(t)|^2 > \quad \propto \quad |T|^{2H} \qquad (6.1.4)$$

Note that the case of $H = 1/2$ is classical Brownian motion. In that case (6.1.3) when formally differentiated gives classical white noise. The spectral power density can be shown to be:

$$P(\omega) \propto \frac{1}{\omega^{2H+1}} \qquad (6.1.5)$$

Again, in the classical Brownian case $H = 1/2$ we have power behavior $1/\omega^2$; indeed we can argue heuristically that white noise (of uniform power density) when integrated gives the Brownian walk, whose amplitudes in turn behave as $1/\omega$, whence the result $1/\omega^2$ for power. Finally, the fractal dimension of the graph of the signal $x(t)$ is given by:

$$D = E + 1 - H \qquad\qquad (6.1.6)$$

where E is the topological dimension of the signal space. For (6.1.3) this is the vector dimension of the random coefficients $x^\wedge_n$. For a classical one-dimensional Brownian motion construction (*i.e.,* the coefficients in (6.1.3) are scalars such as complex numbers) we have from (6.1.6) a dimension $D = 3/2$. In this sense, a Brownian walk graph is "more than a line" but not quite two-dimensional-space-filling.

Next we turn to zeta function signals. It is interesting that certain features of the Riemann zeta function of complex argument can be uncovered via sound generation. Start with a generic zeta function, written formally thus:

$$\zeta(\sigma - it) \;=\; \sum_n \frac{e^{it\log n}}{n^\sigma} \qquad\qquad (6.1.7)$$

with real σ, t. To yield a Riemann zeta function for $\sigma > 1$, the index n runs from 1 to infinity; while for smaller σ we infer ζ as usual via analytic continuation. Now think of $Re(\zeta(\sigma - it))$ (or for that matter, $Im(\zeta(\sigma - it))$) as a signal, with σ fixed and t denoting time. When generating an actual sound signal according to (6.1.7) we can take n from 1 to a suitably large $N-1$. When performing a necessary, real-world cutoff N, we are, of course, only approximating the Riemann zeta function. However, various rigorous bounds on the accrued error have been established [Titchmarsh 1967]. So for any real σ, one can construct by direct summation, having chosen a cutoff N, a sound signal corresponding to the real or imaginary part of (6.1.7). These sounds are quite interesting and, as perhaps expected, they vary qualitatively as σ varies.

We now ask an interesting question: does the zeta signal (real or imaginary part of (6.1.7)) enjoy a spectral power law, something like (6.1.5)? The answer is yes and no. No, there is no power law, but yes in a certain heuristic sense one can argue that an exponential spectral relation exists:

$$P(\omega) \;\; \propto \;\; \frac{1}{e^{\omega(2\sigma-1)}} \tag{6.1.8}$$

It is amusing that this heuristic law gives "white" behavior–that is, uniform P regardless of ω–in the theoretically critical case $\sigma = 1/2$, *i.e.*, in the setting of the Riemann Hypothesis. Some explanation of the rather brash leap (6.1.8) is in order. There is a general heuristic relation that yields the above exponential power law in the Riemann zeta case. Consider a general signal in the form:

$$x(t) \;\; = \;\; \sum_{n} A_n e^{it\omega(n)} \tag{6.1.9}$$

where–and this is a crucial assumption–the angular frequency function $\omega(n)$ is monotonic increasing and differentiable in n. Denote by $n(\omega)$ the inverse of the ω function. We now define a certain heuristic quantity called:

Generalized heuristic power density:

$$P(\omega) \;\; = \;\; \left| \frac{A_n^{\,2}}{\frac{\partial \omega}{\partial n}} \right|_{n\,=\,n(\omega)} \tag{6.1.10}$$

The author was motivated to define this formula to aid in the selection of classes of experimental sounds for this chapter. The idea behind the formula is this: $|A_n|^2$ would be a legitimate Fourier power density if frequencies were equally spaced. In general, though, $\omega(n)$ will not be linear in n, so the weighting of frequency bands must be taken into account. Thus the usual Fourier density $|A_n|^2$ must be normalized by a Jacobian factor. A little thought reveals that $\partial n / \partial \omega$ is the correct such factor. Note that the generalized power density for in both the Brownian case (6.1.5) and the Riemann zeta case (6.1.8) follow from the law (6.1.10). Of course, in statistical constructions such as the Brownian ones, we take the expectation of (6.1.10) to yield an explicit spectral law.

A third class of interesting signal is what we shall call the Weierstrass class:

$$x(t) \ = \ \sum_{n} \frac{e^{ia^n t}}{a^{n(2-D)}} \qquad (6.1.11)$$

Here, $a > 1$ is a positive real parameter and D is a dimension parameter lying in $(0,2)$. This signal is reminiscent of the Brownian signals, except that there are no stochastic coefficients. Instead, a Weierstrass sound is "noisy" simply because of the chaotic interplay of the frequency terms in the Fourier representation (6.1.11).

Yet a fourth class of interesting sound is what we shall call the theta class. A general theta signal is

$$x(t) \ = \ \sum_{n} \frac{e^{in^b t}}{n^a} \qquad (6.1.12)$$

where a and b are positive real parameters. The name "theta" we use because a special case $a = 0, b = 2$ yields a form of Jacobi theta function. In fact, for any a with $b = 2$, the signal is the value (at the origin, say) of a quantum-mechanical wave function of a particle in a one-dimensional box. It is fascinating to hear such a signal, and in this way get a new kind of glimpse of the world of quantum behavior: the origin signal is not chaotic *per se*, but it is very complicated.

Problem 6.1.4: Use (6.1.3) to generate a real-valued Brownian signal in the following way. Choose a cutoff integer N (ideally, a power of two) so that the summation index will go from 0 to $N-1$ inclusive. Then choose independent Gaussian random reals $x^\wedge_0, x^\wedge_1, ..., x^\wedge_{N/2}$. Now force Hermiticity via the assignments $x^\wedge_j := x^\wedge_{N-j}$ for $j = N/2+1, ..., N-1$. Now $x(t)$ can be obtained via a standard inverse FFT, and will be real-valued–or nearly so–and the real part can simply be taken as the signal. The constructed signal can be used for graphics or turned into a sound file.

Problem 6.1.5: Is it possible to guess accurately the dimension (6.1.6) of a Brownian signal by listening to that signal? Can one likewise guess, by listening, the power $2H+1$ in the spectral law (6.1.5)? One might guess that the latter challenge is fairly easy, on the idea that perhaps humans evolved with consummate skill to extract *any* spectral data, extracted even from noise.

Problem 6.1.6: Derive the microscopic expectation law (6.1.4) at least heuristically, using the inverse Fourier expansion (6.1.3) as a starting point. Hint: allow the summation index in the Fourier sum to run from 0 to $N-1$ inclusive, and attempt to write the expectation (6.1.4) as a double sum.

Problem 6.1.7: Derive, at least heuristically, the spectral law (6.1.5) starting from the Fourier representation (6.1.3). This is a tricky derivation, with careful assumptions required along the way. There is a discussion of power density derivation in [*Projects* 1994], which discussion may be helpful.

Problem 6.1.8: Derive the zeta signal's generalized power density (6.1.8) from the heuristic law (6.1.10). Further, show that for the Weierstrass signal the power density is

$$P(\omega) \propto \frac{1}{\omega^{5-2D}}$$

and that for a theta signal we have

$$P(\omega) \propto \frac{1}{\omega^{\frac{2a+b-1}{b}}}$$

Problem 6.1.9: From the previous problem we now have heuristic power densities for each of the four classes of sound: Brownian, zeta, Weierstrass, and theta. Synthesize and listen to actual sounds, demonstrating in some qualitative sense the respective power laws. Two cautions are in order. First, one must sample any of these signals at sufficiently dense point sets. For example, to create a zeta sound, one should use points on the graph of (the real or imaginary part of) $\zeta(\sigma - it)$ that are closer together than lie typical zero crossings of the (real or imaginary) part. In signal processing theory one says that meaningful sampling rates are those exceeding the Nyquist rate, which is twice the essential bandwidth of the signal. Second, note that special assumptions must be made in order to allow proper interpretation of the spectra of these strange sounds. For example, we have mentioned that in the sense of definition (6.1.10) the generalized power density for $\zeta(1/2 - it)$ is "white." If one plots the FFT of the signal $Re(\zeta(1/2 - it))$ for some finite number of (sufficiently dense) sample points on the t axis, the resulting power spectrum appears like so:

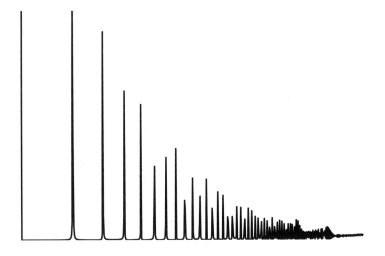

There are vertical power spikes at logarithmic spacing on the horizontal frequency axis, as expected on the basis of the exponent in the definition (6.1.7). However, the power (vertical axis) behaves in just such a way that in a weighted sense the power is spread uniformly. For instance, if we graph the running sum of the Fourier power value, that is a graph of the integral of the above graph, we obtain something like this:

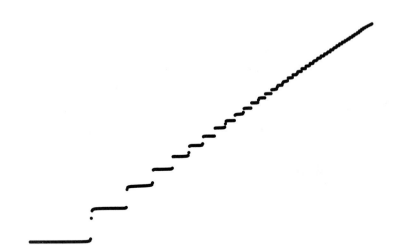

When one listens to a critical half-line zeta sound, it does not sound like white noise, but it certainly does have components of many frequencies competing in complicated ways. The above graphs suggest that there is an overall even weighting of frequencies. Finally, we ask: what is a rigorous analytic formulation of the apparent fact of the above integral graph approaching a straight line as $\omega \rightarrow \infty$? The author does not know of such a formulation, but it would seem that a successful analysis will involve asymptotic properties of the absolute square of

$$\frac{1}{T} \int_{-T/2}^{T/2} \zeta\left(\frac{1}{2} - it\right) e^{-i\omega t} dt$$

as both $\omega, T \rightarrow \infty$.

IFS sound

Iterated function systems [Barnsley 1988] may find modeling application whenever a signal is expected to enjoy self-similarity properties. Indeed, an IFS can be used to generate interesting sound. One way to generate such sound is to imagine a signal consisting of sampled points, so that we have a discrete two-dimensional plot of points at $(t, x(t))$. Imagine applying a tranformation T_1 to every point (t, x), with T_1 defined by:

$$T_1\begin{bmatrix} t \\ x \end{bmatrix} = \begin{bmatrix} a_1 & 0 \\ c_1 & d_1 \end{bmatrix}\begin{bmatrix} t \\ x \end{bmatrix} + \begin{bmatrix} e_1 \\ f_1 \end{bmatrix} \qquad (6.1.13)$$

where a_1, c_1, d_1, e_1, f_1 are constants. For visualization purposes it helps at this point to fix the time scale, so let us say that t is always to be in a unit interval $[0,1]$. Now the entire time axis $[0,1]$ is transformed under T_1 to the interval $[e_1, a_1 + e_1]$. Therefore, if we can construct a set of transformations $T_1, ..., T_m$ such that $[0,1]$ is covered by the whole collection of subintervals $[e_i, a_i + e_i]$, then the union of all the transformed graph points will create a new set of graph points whose time coordinates not only lie in $[0,1]$ but will generally be reasonably distributed over this unit interval. An example of a complete system is the following for $m = 2$ transformations:

$$(6.1.14)$$

$$T_1\begin{bmatrix} t \\ x \end{bmatrix} = \begin{bmatrix} \frac{1}{2} & 0 \\ -\frac{1}{2} & -2 \end{bmatrix}\begin{bmatrix} t \\ x \end{bmatrix} + \begin{bmatrix} 0 \\ 0 \end{bmatrix}$$

$$T_2\begin{bmatrix} t \\ x \end{bmatrix} = \begin{bmatrix} \frac{1}{2} & 0 \\ \frac{1}{4} & 1 \end{bmatrix}\begin{bmatrix} t \\ x \end{bmatrix} + \begin{bmatrix} \frac{1}{2} \\ 0 \end{bmatrix}$$

In this example we start with say N signal graph points $\{(t_k, x_k): k = 0,1,...,N-1\}$, and after one pass of the system $\{T_1, T_2\}$ we obtain a union of the point sets:

$$\{T_1(t_k, x_k)\} \cup \{T_2(t_k, x_k)\} \qquad (6.1.15)$$

for a total of $2N$ points. There is nothing fundamentally wrong with iteration of this scheme to get subsequent signal sets having $4N, 8N, ...$ total points. In practice, however, we would like to keep the number of points under control. To this end, we can continually sub-sample the union (6.1.15), always keeping the total point count at N.

Algorithm for IFS-generated sound: (6.1.16)

1) Start with a set $S = \{t_k, x(t_k)\}$ of N signal points where $t_k := (k-1)/N$ for $k = 0,..., N-1$.

2) Choose m affine transformations $\{T_1, ..., T_m\}$ each defined in the style of definition (6.1.13), and such that the subintervals $[e_i, a_i + e_i]$ as i runs through $1, 2,..., m$ are ordered and by their union cover $[0,1]$.

3) Form the union $R := \{T_1 S, ..., T_m S\}$ which will have mN total points.

4) Perform an m-fold subsampling S of R, for example assign the k-th point (meaning the k-th in temporal order) in the subsampling S to be the (km)-th point of R. Now S has N points.

5) Go to (3), until the system appears to have sufficiently converged.

The following *Mathematica* example shows the generation of a sound via the above algorithm with $m = 2$, with affine transformations (6.1.14). We start with a sine wave which evidently converges to a vowel-like sound:

                                                                      (6.1.17)

```
(* Iterated Function System (IFS) sound
   generation.  An initial sine wave is subject to
   affine transformations until the signal is
   visually stable.
 *)

x = Table[{m/256.0,Sin[m/6]},{m,0,255}];
mat1 = {{1/2, 0},
         {-1/2, -2}};
e1 = {0,0};
mat2 = {{1/2, 0},
         {1/4, 1}};
e2 = {1/2, 0};
```

```
subsample[z_] := Table[z[[q]],{q,1,Length[z],2}];
Do[
    ListPlot[x, PlotJoined->True, Axes->None];
    len = Length[x];
    y = Join[Table[mat1 . x[[q]] + e1,{q,1,len}],
        Table[mat2 . x[[q]] + e2,{q,1,len}]];
    x = subsample[y],
    {w,1,14}
 ];
```

original signal set

first iteration

second iteration

. . .

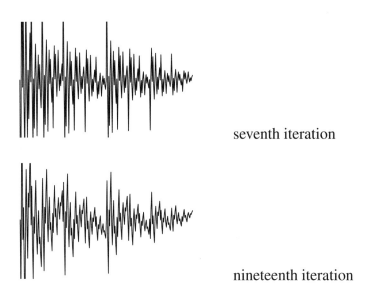

seventh iteration

nineteenth iteration

Evidently the signal set converges to an interesting, vowel-like signal (meaning that there are spikes and damped harmonics visible). A general algorithm for modeling signals with IFS transformations, in which the inverse problem of finding the IFS that converges to a given signal, is found in [Zhu *et. al.* 1994].

Problem 6.1.10: By generating various IFS sounds via algorithm (6.1.17), try to establish (by listening) transformation definitions that yield the various classes of human speech: vowel, fricative ("s", "th", "f"), consonant, etc. Alternatively, use a scheme such as that of [Zhu *et. al.* 1994] automatically to solve the inverse problem; that is to find appropriate IFS transformations on the basis of a *recorded* parcel of speech. It goes without saying that such study may lead to efficient sound compression algorithms: one would simply store a set of affine transformations, together with a minor amount of side data, all of this later to be reconstructed as IFS sound.

Silence detection

Beyond the interesting problems of signal synthesis and modeling, there is the formidable problem of detection. One can with impunity use "formidable" here, as evidenced by the continuing failure of speech recognition systems to satisfactorily act on a par with humans. The recognition problem is just so very hard.

In the speech recognition problem, one of the hard parts among many is the problem of silence detection. One needs accurately to bracket words and phrases with their silence boundaries. To see how hard be this detection, consider the following quote from the modern literature [Junqua *et. al.* 1994]. The reader is urged to understand that the paper is excellent; no fun is being poked at those authors (rather, the idea is just to read the following to attain a feeling for how complex must be the problem, for experts to write this way!). So here is a glimpse into the intricate, troublesome world in which the experts now live:

> *As a first step, we compared the performance of three recently developed word boundary detection algorithms to an algorithm...based on energy levels and durations, which is enhanced by automatic threshold setting...We report their performances when integrated with a commonly used speech recognizer; vector quantization-based hidden Markov model (VQ-based HMM). The VQ-based recognizer used first and second order regression features...extracted from the index weighted cepstral coefficients derived from the twelfth model order of perceptually based linear prediction analysis...The training was done on clean speech produced in a normal environment (without background noise) and the testing on Lombard or noisy-Lombard speech. Accuracy was judged by recognition rates.*

It is evident that special knowledge is required for this special problem. In the referenced paper, incidentally, is an excellent summary of parameter considerations for the silence detection problem. One may use one or a combination of the following parameters in an attempt precisely to demarcate the onset of speech; conversely, the onset of silence (although the onset of silence presumes speech is underway so the two recognition tasks are not entirely symmetrical):

• Signal energy, which is the sound power over some chosen time interval; perhaps weighted into the past.
• Zero-crossing rate; which is the number of crossings the signal makes with its own DC average, over a selected time interval.
• Duration, a measure of how long the signal energy (or other parameter) has stayed above a chosen threshold.
• Other error energies, for example the discrepancy between the current signal and its linear prediction as gleaned from the recent past.

As [Junqua *et. al.* 1994] point out, there is an empirical tendency for algorithms that use one parameter to be necessarily more complex in order to achieve the performance of multiple-parameter detection algorithms.

Problem 6.1.11: Implement a silence detection algorithm, using either real-time speech input or pre-recorded speech. Investigate in particular the respective worthiness of the various parameters listed above. A good working program might for example light an indicator or print to a terminal window during "speech," and otherwise print something else if there is "silence." Another approach is to fabricate a genetic algorithm which has no particular bias towards good or bad parameters, but uses a natural selection measure such as actual time-domain errors in word boundary detection in order to evolve a good system. A reference for genetic algorithms is [Mitchell 1992]. Specific code examples are given in [*Projects* 1994].

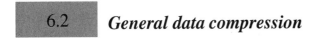

6.2 *General data compression*

BSTW methods

One of the very simplest and most elegant of modern compression techniques is BSTW compression [Lelewer and Hirschberg 1987]. The simple idea is to keep a stack of characters from the input plaintext, always *moving to front of stack* every new character as it appears. BSTW thus has the advantage of requiring no transmission of tables, or at least the transmission of only relatively small tables. This is because the move-to-front operation can be performed also at the decompressor phase, so that the permutations on small internal tables in the decompressor will match precisely the same machinations that occurred in the compressor. The notion of compression of the input plaintext is embodied in the hope that the sequence of *positions* of characters (just before they are moved-to-front) is easily compressed, for example with an entropy-based encoder. One way to keep tables out of the picture even for the entropy encoding of the stack positions is to use some sort of invariant encoding, such as Elias coding, in which each integer 0,1,2,... has a unique variable-bit-length pattern. Elias coding is discussed and working code presented in [*Projects* 1994].

Algorithm for a BSTW compression variant: (6.2.1)

1) Initialize a stack $T = \{0,1,2,...\}$ where every possible plaintext input value appears in said stack.
2) Get next value V from plaintext.
3) Find out where lies V in T. Let $P :=$ said position of V.
4) Report P ; /* Output token representing position. */
5) If(at end of plaintext stream) exit algorithm.
6) Perform a circular permutation of those elements of T from the first through V, such that V ends up at first position of T.
7) Goto (2).

Here is a *Mathematica* example of BSTW compression and decompression:

(6.2.2)

```
(* BSTW experiment. *)

plaintext = {1,0,4,17,8,0,7,7,6,5,6,4,5,4,3,4,3,2,1};
bstwtab = Table[m-1,{m,1,256}];
q = 0;
outlist = {};
While[True,
        ++q;
        c = plaintext[[q]];
        p = Position[bstwtab, c][[1]][[1]];
        outlist = Append[outlist, p];
        If[q == Length[plaintext],
            Break[];
        ];
        bstwtab = Join[{c}, Delete[bstwtab, p]];
 ];
outlist
bstwtab = Table[m-1,{m,1,256}];   (* Re-initialize for
                                     decompress phase. *)
q = 0;
inlist = {};
While[True,
        ++q;
        c = outlist[[q]];
        p = bstwtab[[c]];
        inlist = Append[inlist, p];
        If[q == Length[outlist],
            Break[];
        ];
        bstwtab = Join[{p}, Delete[bstwtab, c]];
];
inlist
```

Note that about midway through this *Mathematica* example, "outlist" is reported. It is this list of integers that one eventually encodes into a compressed stream in a practical BSTW program.

The Appendix code "bstw.c", "ibstw.c", "bstwlib.c" comprises a working example of a BSTW system in which a variant of step (6) in algorithm (6.2.1) is employed (see Problem 6.2.2). Experiments with this particular BSTW system show that a typical machine executable is compressed by 35% in size. There are compressors that can do better than this, but usually at the expense of massive internal tables. Again, one advantage of BSTW schemes is the fact that the internal workings are largely self-constructed in real time. For example the Appendix code when compiled can be expected to occupy a few kbytes of executable, with negligible memory growth during execution.

Problem 6.2.1: Work further with the *Mathematica* BSTW implementation (6.2.2) by assessing the entropy of the "outlist." Note that BSTW works especially well when the input plaintext stream has many regions in which only a few characters interplay (and thus move around near the front-of-stack). In such a situation the assessed entropy should be relatively small.

Problem 6.2.2: Implement and try to improve upon the Appendix code scheme (embodied in "bstw.c", "ibstw.c", "bstwlib.c"). Note that the author selected intentionally for the Appendix scheme a variant of the circular permutation rule; that is, effectively replacing step (6) of algorithm (6.2.1) with:

6) Perform a circular permutation of those elements of T from the n-th element through V, such that V ends up at the n-th position of T.

The pivot position, the n-th, is specified in the Appendix code as a certain *fraction* of the position of V itself. In this way, values from the plaintext stream "migrate gracefully frontward" within the stack, rather than simply jamming themselves at the front. The overall effect of this "migration" variant is that after a great many characters from the plaintext have been processed, there tends to be in practice an exponential distribution of stack positions to emanate as compressed output. Such exponential distributions are especially convenient to entropy-encode. Even so, the Appendix code does *not* use variable-length encoding, rather a simple byte-oriented scheme. Thus one immediate improvement over the Appendix code would be to invoke a more complex entropy-based encoding.

There is another important area of performance improvement for practical BSTW compressors: eliminate the circular permutations by not allowing elements to be moved. Use pointers and linked lists instead, simply to change the order of stack elements rather than shuttling them around. This data structure problem is fairly easy for the standard move-to-front scenario of BSTW, but is more difficult for the "fractional move-to-front" case of the previous paragraph

LZW methods

Lempel-Ziv-Welch compression has, in the last two decades, realized a certain vogue. Many compressors standard to a specific operating system are based on some variant of LZW. Even so, possibilities abound for more improvement in the existing galaxy of LZW implementations. For one thing, LZW does not do well on certain kinds of sounds and images. Indeed the original Lempel-Ziv construction was intended for text, or at least for "alphabetical" files. Yet, as we shall see later, LZW can often provide an excellent "back end" to a signal compressor.

The fundamental idea of Lempel-Ziv was to take into account substrings of characters as they are discovered in a character stream. To make everything simpler, assume that we have an initial table $T = \{a,b,c,...\}$ containing *single* characters. Assume also we have a character string–called the "root" R–initialized to be empty, or $R = \{\}$. Denote by "plaintext" an input character string to be compressed. Now proceed by appending plaintext characters to R, continually checking whether the appended form appears in T.

Algorithm for elementary Lempel-Ziv substring generation: (6.2.3)

1) Initialize single-character table $T = \{a,b,c,...\}$ and an empty root $R = \{\}$;
2) Get next character C from plaintext;
3) $R' := R \cup C$; *i.e.* append C to the root to make a new root;
4) If (R' is not in T) $T = T \cup R'$; /* Append new root to current table. */
    else {
            $R := R'$;
            if(not at end of plaintext) goto (2)
    }
5) Report R ; /* Output a token representing root. */
6) If(at end of plaintext) {
        If($R \neq R'$) report $\{C\}$;
        exit algorithm;
   }
7) $R := \{C\}$;
8) Goto (2).

In this algorithm we expect the table T to grow. In the line that reads:

      Report R ;

resides much of the freedom of LZW variant implementation. The reporting is not to be the string R itself but an integer token representing somehow the *position* of R in the table T (or the position in some other sense–see problems below). In order to achieve good compression, one hopes to report various many-character roots with only a few bits each. Thus the final design step for an LZW variant is often to find a good Huffman coding or other entropy-based coding so that the "Report R" steps are efficient.

In the present author's opinion, the best approach to implementation of one's own LZW variant is to start from a bare-bones experimental example, such as the following:

(6.2.4)

```
(* LZW substring experiment. *)

plaintext = {a, b, c, b, c, c, b, b, b, b,
         b, b, b, a, a, a, c, a, c, a};
root = {}; lzwtab = {a,b,c};
q = 0;
While[True,
  While[True,
        ++q;
        newroot = Append[root, plaintext[[q]]];
        If[!MemberQ[lzwtab, newroot],
              lzwtab = Append[lzwtab, newroot];
              Break[]
        ];
        root = newroot;
        If[q == Length[plaintext], Break[]];
  ];
  Print[root];
  If[q == Length[plaintext],
    If[root != newroot, Print[{plaintext[[q]]}]];
    Break[];
  ];
  root = {plaintext[[q]]};
];

{}
{a}
{b}
{c}
{b, c}
{c, b}
{b}
{b, b}
{b, b, b}
{a}
{a, a}
{c}
{a}
{c, a}
```

Note that the output, after the first empty list, is nothing but entries from the table "lzwtab." Of course, in a practical compressed stream one would have translated these table entry outputs into integer position tokens.

Note that there is a more practical, *C* version of a bare-bones LZW experiment, named "lzw.c" in the Appendix code. That *C* example is suitable as the beginning of an actual implementation. One caution: "lzw.c" has, for purpose of clarity, various points of extreme inefficiency. For example, deciding whether a root is a member of the current table is much better done via a hash function rather than character-by-character compares. The program "lzw.c" does, however, do something that the *Mathematica* example above does not: in the *C* program, unrestricted growth of the table is gracefully avoided: in "lzw.c" the entire table is reset to single character entries whenever it grows too large. Of course, an advanced implementation would abort the current table on certain additional criteria, such as poor current entropy measure. When "lzw.c" was compiled and run with an executable object (technically, a NEXTSTEP objective-*C* application) of size 600 kbytes as input, the distribution of table indices (the table positions of reported roots *R*) appeared like so:

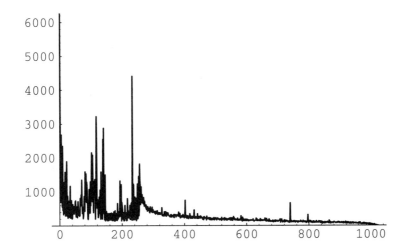

the horizontal being index into a length-1024 table of strings, and the vertical being number of occurrences of given index. The total number of table indices required was about 300k, and the calculated entropy of the above graph was about 9 bits. Thus, a compressed file created via an ideal entropy compressor (which is usually well-approximated by a standard Huffman coder in this context) will have (300k)(9/8) or about 340kbytes, for a compression percentage of (340/600)(100) or 57%. That is almost a factor of 2 compression ratio, typical of a decent LZW implementation.

Problem 6.2.3: Write a *Mathematica* decompressor, that accepts the substring outputs of (6.2.4) and reconstructs the exact input plaintext.

Problem 6.2.4: Starting with the *Mathematica* LZW substring experiment, add code in order to report the entropy of the distribution of table indices. In other words, every time a non-empty root (which by definition is always findable in the strings table) is output in the example, you should record that instance of table index. In this way build up a histogram and, over elements $h[q]$ of the histogram, report total entropy E as the sum of $-h[q] \log_2(h[q]/H)$, where H is the sum of all elements (H is also the total number of nonempty roots output). This E will be an approximation to how many total bits are needed to represent the original input string.

Problem 6.2.5: Starting with "lzw.c" in the Appendix, fashion a complete, efficient LZW compressor. Thus the two basic tasks are first, find the points of inefficiency of the C code; and second, implement entropy coding of table indices.

Problem 6.2.6: Here is a fundamental question relevant to the efficiency of actual practical LZW implementations. As in Problem 6.2.3, one may entropy-encode the table indices to form the compressed output stream. However, one may also try to use positions of the table entries in the original input stream. So the question is: when is it better to emanate, into the compressed output stream, substring positions of the original plaintext, as opposed to table indices *per se*? If one attempts the former option, then as table entries are encountered and/or appended, some record must be kept as to original stream positions. But this is easy to do.

Problem 6.2.7: Here is a wonderful problem in the field of compression research: combine the notions of BSTW and LZW compressors. One approach is to fashion a hybrid that performed BSTW *simultaneously* with table construction, for example only performing move-to-front on the simpler regions of the table. Note for example that the first 256 indices in the above table-index-occurrence histogram plot have a noisy distribution that would undoubtedly become more regular (hopefully exponentially decreasing) with some BSTW scheme invoked for the dense region of the histogram.

Problem 6.2.8: The BSTW and LZW compressor classes were presented in this section as useful, fundamental classes. Implement some other compressor class, such as block coding, arithmetic coding, adaptive Huffman coding, or the like. A basic reference is [Bell *et. al.* 1990].

6.3   *Sound and image compression*

Alphabetization principle

The author feels–and has stated before, *e.g.,* in [*Projects* 1994]–that the following principle is fundamental both to the past and to the future of media compression technology: the *alphabetization* of sound and image data is a valuable first step toward compression. Recall that in the previous section the compressor classes discussed were alphabet-oriented, meaning that tables of symbols are constructed. But when the human ear perceives meaningful sound, the "alphabet" lies in the Fourier domain rather than in the signal domain (technically, the configuration domain). So the alphabetization principle for sound compression reads something like this: "Fourier transform the sound and use an alphabetical compressor (such as LZW) on the resulting Fourier coefficients." Why should such a scheme work? The answer is simple: apparently the human ear is fundamentally and physiologically Fourier-based. Internal membranes literally vibrate in frequency-dependent regions.

For images, it is hard to find a physiological analogy to the vibrating ear membranes. However, in spite of the continuing mystery of the exact nature of the human eye-brain signal processing mechanism, it is well known that the eye is very sensitive to spatial correlation, intensity and its derivatives, and so on. Thus, a transform such as the discrete cosine transform (DCT) or a wavelet transform will generate a set of transform coefficients that, by carrying correlation, intensity, and intensity derivative information represent in some sense a stream of alphabetical characters. Again a promising strategy is to transform an image into such a stream and then use an alphabetical compressor.

Algorithm for "alphabetical" compression of signals: (6.3.1)

1) Given a signal x, break the signal into blocks each of length N (which in turn will be a transform length, usually a power of two).
2) For some selected transform T, perform $x^\wedge := Tx$ to yield N transform data.
3) Select a positive quantization integer q and adjust the transform data according to:
$$a_k := \text{Round}(x^\wedge_k / q) \qquad ; k = 0,1,...,N-1$$

Note that the $\{a_k\}$ can be thought of as symbols (integers) taken from an alphabet (all integers for the known data range).
4) Attempt lossless compression of the alphabetical stream $\{a_k\}$, using for example LZW compression.

Algorithm for decompression: (6.3.2)

5) Decompress to obtain the alphabetical stream $\{a_k\}$.
6) Construct $x^\wedge_k := qa_k$; for $k = 0,1,...,N-1$.
7) Take the inverse transform to yield a (lossy) reconstruction of $x = \{x_k\}$.

The reader may have noted that the above compress/decompress procedure is merely what is done almost universally today with media data such as sound or image data. The author believes, however, that it is instructive and worthwhile to write out the general algorithm in this way, in particular to show exactly where an alphabet-based stream is constructed. This happens in step (3): as soon as the quantization integer q is chosen, one has created perforce a meaningful alphabet $\{...,-2, -1, 0, 1, 2, ...\}$ from which transform elements each inherit one symbol per datum.

Problem 6.3.1: Attempt sound compression in the following way. For every block of chosen length $N = 2^k$ of sound data, take an FFT of said block. *A priori* this yields N complex numbers, but the sound data are assumed real so that the data have Hermitian symmetry. (One can also have used a real-signal transform as given in *C* code form in [*Projects* 1994], in which case only a redundancy-free set of coefficients results.) Thus the transform can be thought of as comprised of N real numbers. Now attempt to quantize the Fourier block of N reals as in step (3) of algorithm (6.3.1). One of course must choose the quantization integer q so that the fidelity of the decompressed and inverse Fourier constructed sound has sufficient fidelity.

Problem 6.3.2: Attempt sound compression via a Walsh-Hadamard transform (Chapter 4). There is also a new, interesting square-wave transform that may be useful for compression [*Projects* 1994]. One might think of the Walsh and square-wave transforms as belonging to a "multiply-free" class; that is, only multiplication by ±1 is required during the fast transform butterflies, which is not really multiplication after all.

Problem 6.3.3: Attempt image compression via a two-dimensional transform. There is the discrete cosine transform (DCT) which is employed in the prevailing JPEG image compression standard. There is always the Fourier transform, although block-boundary effects are known to be a problem for the FFT as opposed to the better behaved DCT. There are also wavelet transforms which have the special attraction of enjoying only $O(N)$ complexity rather than the typical $O(N \log N)$.

Problem 6.3.4: Is the new harmonic wavelet transform of Section 4.3 suitable for image compression? Sound compression?

Problem 6.3.5: Is LZW really a good "back-end" stage of an alphabetical compressor or is there a better, all-purpose lossless back end? Is it possible that there is a best back end for sound compression and a best back end for image compression? The question is compounded by the fact that even simple Huffman encoding has found great success in, for example, the compression of DCT coefficients within the JPEG standard. Is there any reason to use more than a simple entropy-encoder?

Problem 6.3.6: Here is a fascinating and largely untapped research problem: fashion a deepest-possible predictor-corrector compressor. This is discussed somewhat in [*Projects* 1994] but now there are some brand new approaches. In this context, the "transform" is the generation of scan-based differences. Let us work with images, although some of what we say here should apply to sound. Say that three pixels of an image are known:

$$A\ B$$
$$C\ ?$$

and that the pixel ? is to be predicted. The predictor we define as

$$P = B + C - A$$

The "transform data" in this case is P minus the actual pixel value at ?, call that D, so what we want to quantize and send to the back end compressor is just

$$P - D = B + C - A - D$$

If the "corrector" P–D is good enough (*i.e.*, generally small enough) we may achieve good compression in this way. Small correctors accrue of course when the image pixels vary slowly or linearly. This predictor-corrector technique is an old and sometimes effective one, but you might say that all we are doing is performing the transform $\{A, B, C, D\} \rightarrow B + C - A - D$, with the understanding that each pixel neither on the first scan line nor on the left column gets transformed. That is true, we are just implementing a form of algorithm (6.3.1), but consider the possibility of dynamical adjustment of the predictor-corrector scheme depending on the local image properties. For example, one might contemplate a (massive) predictor-corrector scheme:

$$A\ B\ C\ D\ E\ F$$
$$G\ H\ I\ J\ K$$
$$L\ M\ N\ O$$
$$P\ Q\ R$$
$$S\ T\ ?$$

Furthermore, one is free to create a predictor for the above pixels as:

$$P = aA + bB + ... + tT$$

where $a, b, ...,t$ are coefficients not restricted to ± 1 as before. The complexity of such a scheme–given the large number of operations per pixel and the problem of selecting coefficients–might appear stultifying. But here is an idea: use a genetic algorithm to find "very good" predictor scenarios. For various regions of an image, one would generate "parents" each of whom was a predictor scenario, say a collection of data structures:

$$\{N \text{ (number of predictor pixels)},$$
$$\text{configuration of the } N \text{ pixels},$$
$$\text{set of } N \text{ predictor coefficients}\}$$

Then the parents beget mutated offspring (mutated in one or more of the defining structure elements), who compete for compression efficiency; whence the "selection" extinguishes all but a few survivors, and so on.

Problem 6.3.7: Attempt to work out theory and implementation for a *two-dimensional* BSTW compressor intended for image compression. The idea would be to maintain a two-dimensional stack and to index into it in some manner for every pixel, or for every pixel pair, or even for pixel tuples. There may be some good compression efficiency to be had by marrying BSTW with predictor-corrector methods of the previous problem.

Problem 6.3.8: Implement a sub-band image compressor. The sub-band formation is simlar to wavelet transformation, except the sub-band idea involves general filter banks through which one runs pixels. An implementation of the sub-band scenario of [Odegard *et. al.* 1994] is promising; in fact those authors claim that their filter bank scheme removes a good deal of common artifacts that arise in other compression schemes.

"Magic dust" compressors

We have seen that lossy compressors having an alphabet-oriented back end (such as LZW) can be used to compress media data. But there are times when one prefers a *lossless* media compressor. These times are rare (because there is usually sound or image information that just does not matter) but important nonetheless. One might for example have a commercial guarantee of fidelity to uphold and one's firm's legal division might be able to sleep at night because one's compressors are lossless. Then there is the cultural importance of preserving classic art and media, without modification of any kind.

The author coins the term "magic dust" for compressors that are lossy but carry with them enough side information to reconstruct exactly the original media data. This side information is the "magic dust." At the decompress phase, one has the option of taking the lossy reconstruction and–if you will–"sprinkling" on the magic dust to render a perfect reconstruction.

Algorithm for "magic dust" compression: (6.3.3)

1) Denote the original image by I, the chosen transform by T, and the quantization operation by Q. For a chosen lossless compressor (such as the back end compressor chosen for algorithm (6.3.2)) denote by C the lossless compression operation and D the decompression.
2) Create, via transforming and quantizing, the data stream QTI.
3) Create and store the (lossy) compressed data stream

$$L := CQTI$$

So far the operations have followed generic Algorithm (6.3.2).
4) By performing the inverse transform T^{-1}, and subtracting from the original image, create and store a *second* compressed stream:

$$M := C(I - T^{-1}QTI)$$

We call this the "magic dust."

Algorithm for decompression:

5) Given lossy compressed storage L and "magic dust" storage M, create decompressed data DM and DL.
6) Create the data

$$DM + T^{-1}DL$$

which will be (losslessly!) the original image I.

The algorithm is admittedly simple, but there are difficult and fascinating variants of the magic dust idea. For one thing, in step (4) the construction of magic dust M can in principle use a *different* lossless compressor, call it C', in which case its associated decompression operation D' will figure (along with D) into steps (5), (6) of the decompression phase. For another, one may consider recursion on the whole magic dust idea. Indeed, there is nothing preventing experiments in which one does:

$$M := C(I - T^{-1}QTI) \qquad\qquad (6.3.6)$$

$$M' := C(M - T^{-1}QTM)$$

in order, creating perhaps finer and finer versions of the magic dust. The idea of course is to think of an image minus its (lossy) reconstruction as a noisy "dust" image. Then the "dust image" is treated in the same fashion, leaving second-order dust, and so on. The problem of when such a recursion actually converges to a stable state appears to be a profound one.

Problem 6.3.9: Implement a "magic dust" compressor for sound. Can one achieve 2:1 lossless compression in this way, say for 22 kHz sample rate, linear-digitized string quartet music? What about second-order dust (the M' in (6.3.6)? Should it even be created?

Problem 6.3.10: Implement a "magic dust" compressor for images. Can one achieve 2:1 lossless compression for typical video capture images? Also consider the second-order dust issue, as in the previous problem.

Problem 6.3.11: When implementing a "magic dust" compressor for color images in particular, is it best to handle the three channels R, G, B separately? presumably not, because they tend to be correlated. Instead consider a *YUV* transformation [*Projects* 1994], or better yet (with extra computation) find the optimal matrix operation on R, G, B triples such that the compressor behaves optimally on the transformed pixels. The beauty of the whole lossless approach is that *anything* you do to the color pixels will be exactly corrected; one simply needs the correct variant of step (4), Algorithm (6.3.3).

Other image compressors

We briefly mention two powerful image compressor classes, both of which having achieved a certain vogue in modern times. These are characterized by the replacement of a classical transform (such as a single matrix multiply, as in FFT or wavelet, and so on) with some sort of operation that provides low entropy. There is nothing preventing the use of these "non-transform-based" methods in algorithm (6.3.3)–one simply interprets the entity QTM, or perhaps the lossy compressed stream $L = CQTM$, as the result of one of these other compressors. One non-transform class is the vector-quantization (VQ) class. The idea is to create vectors (tuples of pixels) in a table, and simply emanate table indices into the compressed stream.

A second class is that of fractal image coding, in which one seeks iterated function system (IFS) parameters the collection of which allows one to reconstruct the image by a series of transformations.

Problem 6.3.12: Implement a vector-quantization (VQ) compressor, using as a basic reference a text such as [Gersho and Gray 1992]. The present author would be irresponsible not to mention that, as one attempts to search large vector spaces for "best" pixel tuples, there is considerable advantage to be gained by first studying the N-body problem of Chapter 5.

Problem 6.3.13: Here is an elegant method for extremely simple VQ image compression. Using a two-dimensional quasi-Monte Carlo discrepancy set (as described in [*Projects* 1994], or in one-dimensional mode in Section 2.1, or more generally in [Niederreiter 1992]), sample the image over its defining rectangle. From each discrepancy-sampled point, take and store a pixel (1-tuple) or a quad of pixels (4-tuple) or even more pixels per sample; in this way building up a VQ table of some chosen size. Then to compress the image, one emanates as usual into a compressed stream the "best" table index for a given tuple of pixels. Advantages of the quasi-Monte Carlo approach are: speed, and a certain "fairness" across typical images. The fairness occurs because the discrepancy set is basically what one might call "pattern-free," so unfortunate aliases (with patterned images) and/or gaps (as with true Monte Carlo random sampling) do not appear.

Here is a simple *Mathematica* example of quasi-Monte Carlo sampling as pictorialized in the frontispiece to this chapter:

```
(* quasi-Monte Carlo sampling example. *)

(* First, define for prime p the van der Corput
   discrepancy function d[p, n] for n = 0,1,2,3,...
 *)

d[n_, p_] := Module[{lis},
              lis = IntegerDigits[n, p];
              lis . (p^Range[-Length[lis],-1])
            ];

spray = Table[{d[n,2],d[n,3]}, {n,0, 1023}];
ListPlot[spray, AspectRatio->1]
```

For higher-dimensional work such as VQ algorithm development for pixel tuples, one may use longer vectors {d[n, 2], d[n, 3], d[n,5], ...}, where the second argument to d[ ] is always prime.

Problem 6.3.14: Implement a fractal encoding image compressor. A useful review article is [Jacquin 1993]. Another good treatment is [Frigaard *et. al.* 1994].

Appendix

This Appendix is an alphabetical listing of support code sources. See the Preface: Support Software section (pp. *vi–vii*) for instructions on how to obtain these Appendix sources via network connection. Also network accessible in the same manner are topic-specific sources, as well as sources too voluminous to list on paper.

bstwlib.c

```
/* Library for BSTW compression/decompression of executable files.
 */

#include<stdio.h>

#define QLEN 255
#define F1 12
#define F2 12
#define ABOVE ((F2 * QLEN) >> 4)
#define METHOD_17_JUL_95 666

unsigned int que[QLEN];

unsigned int
ex_decompress(unsigned char *in, unsigned char *out)
/* Returns actual number of bytes emitted as decompressed stream
'out.'
   Note that the 'in' stream contains this byte count already.
 */
{
    unsigned int c, j, k, jmatch, jabove;
    unsigned int length, even_length, word, token, version;
    unsigned char *outorigin = out;
    int *a, *b;

    version = *in++;
    version = (version<<8) | (*in++);
    version = (version<<8) | (*in++);
```

```
      version = (version<<8) | (*in++);

      if(version != METHOD_17_JUL_95) {
        fprintf(stderr, "Incompatible version.\n");
        return(0);
      }

      length = *in++;
      length = (length<<8) | (*in++);
      length = (length<<8) | (*in++);
      length = (length<<8) | (*in++);

      for(c=0; c < QLEN; c++) que[c] = c;
      even_length = 2*(length/2);
      while((int)(out-outorigin) < even_length) {
        token = *in++;
          token = (token<<8) | (*in++);
          token = (token<<8) | (*in++);
          token = (token<<8) | (*in++);
        c = 1<<31;
        for(k = 0; k<32; k++) {
              if(c & token) {
                      jmatch = *in++;
                      word = que[jmatch];
                  /* Next, dynamically process the queue for match. */
jabove = (F1*jmatch) >> 4;
for(j = jmatch; j > jabove; j--) {
      que[j] = que[j-1];
}
que[jabove] = word;
}
else {
      /* Next, dynamically process the queue for unmatch. */
      word = *in++;
      word = (word << 8) | (*in++);
      for(j=QLEN-1; j > ABOVE; j--) {
              que[j] = que[j-1];
      }
      que[ABOVE] = word;
}
*out++ = (word >> 8) & 0xff;
*out++ = (word) & 0xff;
if((int)(out-outorigin) >= even_length) break;
c >>= 1;
}
}
if(even_length != length) *out++ = *in++;
return(length);
}

unsigned int
```

```
ex_compress(unsigned char *in, unsigned int inbytes,
            unsigned char *out)
/* Returns actual number of bytes emitted as compressed stream 'out.'
 */
{
unsigned int c, ct, j, jmatch, jabove, match;
unsigned int data[32], version;
unsigned int word, token, tokenct, total;
unsigned char *outorigin = out;

/* First, put version number into stream. */
*out++ = (METHOD_17_JUL_95>>24) & 0xff;
*out++ = (METHOD_17_JUL_95>>16) & 0xff;
*out++ = (METHOD_17_JUL_95>>8) & 0xff;
*out++ = (METHOD_17_JUL_95) & 0xff;
/* Next, put the initial size into stream. */
*out++ = (inbytes>>24) & 0xff;
*out++ = (inbytes>>16) & 0xff;
*out++ = (inbytes>>8) & 0xff;
*out++ = (inbytes) & 0xff;

for(ct=0; ct < QLEN; ct++) que[ct] = ct;
word = token = tokenct = 0;
for(ct = 0; ct < inbytes; ct++) {
/* Next, update bucket-brigade register. */
word = (word << 8) | (*in++);
if(ct % 2 == 1) {
word &= 0xffff;
match = 0;
for(j=0; j < QLEN; j++) {
     if(que[j] == word) {
           match = 1;
           jmatch = j;
           break;
     }
}
token = (token<<1) | match;
if(match) {/* 16-bit symbol is in queue. */
     c = que[jmatch];
     jabove = (F1 * jmatch) >> 4;
     for(j = jmatch; j > jabove; j--) {
           que[j] = que[j-1];
     }
     que[jabove] = c;
     data[tokenct++] = jmatch;
}
else {  /* 16-bit symbol is not in queue. */
     for(j=QLEN-1; j > ABOVE; j--) {
           que[j] = que[j-1];
     }
     que[ABOVE] = word;
```

```
          data[tokenct++] = word;
    }
    if(tokenct == 32) { /* Unload tokens and data. */
          *out++ = (token>>24) & 0xff;
          *out++ = (token>>16) & 0xff;
          *out++ = (token>>8) & 0xff;
          *out++ = (token) & 0xff;
          c = (1<<31);
          for(j = 0; j < tokenct; j++) {
                if(token & c) *out++ = data[j] & 0xff;
                else {
                        *out++ = (data[j] >> 8) & 0xff;
                        *out++ = (data[j]) & 0xff;
                }
                c >>= 1;
          }
          token = tokenct = 0;
    }
    }
    }
    if(tokenct > 0) {/* Flush final token and data. */
    token <<= (32-tokenct);
    *out++ = (token>>24) & 0xff;
    *out++ = (token>>16) & 0xff;
    *out++ = (token>>8) & 0xff;
    *out++ = (token) & 0xff;
    c = (1<<31);
    for(j = 0; j < tokenct; j++) {
    if(token & c) *out++ = data[j] & 0xff;
    else {
          *out++ = (data[j] >> 8) & 0xff;
          *out++ = (data[j]) & 0xff;
    }
    c >>= 1;
    }
    }
    if(ct % 2 == 1) *out++ = (word) & 0xff;
    return((int)(out-outorigin));
    }
```

bstw.c

```
/* Compressor for executables.

    % cc -O bstw.c bstwlib.c

    Usage:

    % a.out file > file.ex
    OR
```

```
        % a.out file file.ex

*/

#include  <stdio.h>

main(int argc, char *argv[])
{
    FILE *infile, *outfile;
    unsigned char *inbuffer, *outbuffer;
    unsigned int length, total;

    if(argc == 1) {
      fprintf(stderr, "Usage:\n> exc plainfile [compfile]\n");
      exit(0);
    }
    infile = fopen(argv[1], "r");
    if(argc == 2) outfile = stdout;
       else outfile = fopen(argv[2],"w");

    fseek(infile,0,2); length = ftell(infile); rewind(infile);
    inbuffer = (unsigned char *)malloc(length);
    fread(inbuffer, 1, length, infile);
    fclose(infile);
    outbuffer = (unsigned char *)malloc(length + (length + 15)/16);
    total = ex_compress(inbuffer, length, outbuffer);
    fwrite(outbuffer, 1, total, outfile);
    fprintf(stderr, "%d %d\nCompression ratio: %f\n", length, total,
            total/(1.0*length));
}
```

conlib.c

```
/* Nussbaumer convolution of base-p representations.
   This is a software design by J. Buhler, R. Crandall,
   and T. Donahue.  One feature of this design is that
   considerable memory is saved, relative to the memory
   requirements of a standard Nussbaumer implementation.
   Two memory improvements are: use of a discrete weighted
   transform (DWT) within the Nussbaumer algorithm, to
   obviate zero-padding; and second, use of an in-place
   transposition.  Yet more memory advantage is realized
   by calling cyc_dest(x, y, N) which is destructive
   on x (x is used for storage at a critical juncture).

   Usage:
   Compile this program (muldiv.h and rep.h must be
   present) and specify a signal length for
   cyclic convolution:
```

```
% a.out N
```

The cyclic convolution of length N is then performed
with every result modulo 700001.

To use as library, remove main() and call
cyc_dest(x, y, N), to get result in y with x destroyed
(the destruction saves memory).
 */

```c
#include <stdio.h>
#include <assert.h>
#include <math.h>
#include "muldiv.h"
#include "rep.h"

extern unsigned int p;
extern double recip;

rep dum0, *dum;

int
log_2(int n) {
      int c = 1, d = -1;
      while(c <= n) {
              c <<= 1;
              ++d;
      }
      return(d);
}

int power_up(int x,int n,int p)
{
  int y = 1;
  while( n > 0 ){
    while( (n&1) == 0 ){
      x = mul(x,x,p);
      n >>= 1;
    }
    y = mul(x,y,p);
    --n;
  }
  return y;
}

/* Should work on all ARCHs. */
int slowmul(unsigned int a,unsigned int b,unsigned int p)
{
      long long q = a;
      q *= b;
      q %= p;
```

```
        return((int) q);
}


/* Should work on all ARCHs. */
int slowquo(unsigned int a,unsigned int b,unsigned int p)
{
        long long q = a;
        q *= b;
        q /= p;
        return((int) q);
}

rep *
newa(int n) {
        rep *pp = (rep *)malloc(n*sizeof(rep));
        return(pp);
}

void
init_con() {
        dum = newa(MAX_DUMS);
}

void
freea(rep *p, int n) {
        free(p);
}

swapa(rep *a, rep *b, int n)
{
        int i,j;
        int *u = (int *) a;
        int *t = (int *) b;

        for(j=(n>>2); j != 0; --j) {
                i = *u;
                *u++ = *t;
                *t++ = i;
                i = *u;
                *u++ = *t;
                *t++ = i;
                i = *u;
                *u++ = *t;
                *t++ = i;
                i = *u;
                *u++ = *t;
                *t++ = i;
        }
        for(j=(n&3); j != 0; --j) {
                i = *u;
```

```
                    *u++ = *t;
                    *t++ = i;
            }
}

atoan(rep *a, rep *b, int n)
/* b := -a, for n elements. */
{
        int i,j;
        int *u = (int *) a;
        int *t = (int *) b;

        for(j=(n>>2); j != 0; --j) {
                if (i = *u++) *t++ = p - i;
                else *t++ = 0;
                if (i = *u++) *t++ = p - i;
                else *t++ = 0;
                if (i = *u++) *t++ = p - i;
                else *t++ = 0;
                if (i = *u++) *t++ = p - i;
                else *t++ = 0;
        }
        for(j=(n&3); j != 0; --j) {
                if (i = *u++) *t++ = p - i;
                else *t++ = 0;
        }
}

void
adda(rep *a, rep *b, int n)
/* b += a, for n elements. */
{
        int j,k;
        rep *u = a, *v = b;
        for(j=(n>>2); j != 0; --j) {
                k = *v + *u++;
                if (k >= p) k -= p;
                *v++ = k;
                k = *v + *u++;
                if (k >= p) k -= p;
                *v++ = k;
                k = *v + *u++;
                if (k >= p) k -= p;
                *v++ = k;
                k = *v + *u++;
                if (k >= p) k -= p;
                *v++ = k;
        }
        for(j=(n&3); j != 0; --j) {
                k = *v + *u++;
                if (k >= p) k -= p;
```

```
                 *v++ = k;
        }
}

void
suba(rep *a, rep *b, int n)
/* b -= a, for n elements. */
{
        int j,k;
        rep *u = a, *v = b;
        for(j=(n>>2); j != 0; --j) {
                k = *v - *u++;
                if (k < 0) k += p;
                *v++ = k;
                k = *v - *u++;
                if (k < 0) k += p;
                *v++ = k;
                k = *v - *u++;
                if (k < 0) k += p;
                *v++ = k;
                k = *v - *u++;
                if (k < 0) k += p;
                *v++ = k;
        }
        for(j=(n&3); j != 0; --j) {
                k = *v - *u++;
                if (k < 0) k += p;
                *v++ = k;
        }
}

void
cyclit(rep  *x, rep *y, int n)
/* Grammar-school cyclic. */
{
        int s, i, q;
        for(s = 0; s < n; s++) {
                dum[s] = 0;
                for(q = 0; q < n; q++) {
                        i = (s-q)%n;
                        if(i<0) i+= n;
                        RTOR(y[i], dum0);
                        MULR(x[q], dum0);
                        ADDR(dum0, dum[s]);
                }
        }
        atoa(dum, y, n);
}


static rep T[2*MAX], U[4*MAX], V[4*MAX];
```

```
void karatsuba(rep *x, rep *y, rep *z, int n)
/* z := x nega y, for n elements.  */
{
        rep a0, a1, a2, a3;
        rep b0, b1, b2, b3;
        rep s0,s1,t0,t1;
        rep m1,m2,m3;

        if(n==4) {
                a0 = *x++;
                a1 = *x++;
                a2 = *x++;
                a3 = *x;
                b0 = *y++;
                b1 = *y++;
                b2 = *y++;
                b3 = *y;
                RTOR(b0, m1); MULR(a0, m1); RTOR(b0, m2); ADDR(b1, m2);
                RTOR(a0, s0); ADDR(a1, s0); MULR(s0, m2); RTOR(b1, m3);
                MULR(a1, m3); RTOR(a0, s0); ADDR(a2, s0); RTOR(b0, t0);
                ADDR(b2, t0); RTOR(a1, s1); ADDR(a3, s1); RTOR(b1, t1);
                ADDR(b3, t1); RTOR(t0, b0); MULR(s0, b0); RTOR(t0, b1);
                ADDR(t1, b1); RTOR(s0, a0); ADDR(s1, a0); MULR(a0, b1);
                RTOR(t1, a0); MULR(s1, a0); RTOR(b2, a1); MULR(a2, a1);
                RTOR(a2, s0); ADDR(a3, s0); RTOR(b3, a2); ADDR(b2, a2);
                MULR(s0, a2); MULR(b3, a3); RTOR(m3, s0); SUBR(m2, s0);
                ADDR(m1, s0); RTOR(a3, t0); SUBR(a2, t0); ADDR(a1, t0);
                RTOR(m3, s1); SUBR(a1, s1);
                *z++ = m1;
                NEGR(s0);
                *z++ = s0;
                NEGR(m1); ADDR(b0, m1); ADDR(s1, m1);
                *z++ = m1;
                SUBR(s0, b1); SUBR(b0, b1); SUBR(a0, b1); ADDR(t0, b1);
                *z++ = b1;
                SUBR(s1, a0); SUBR(a3, a0);
                *z++ = a0;
                NEGR(t0);
                *z++ = t0;
                *z++ = a3;
                *z = 0;
        }
        else {
                int m = n>>1;
                rep *u = U + (n<<1), *v = V + (n<<1);

                karatsuba(x,y,z,m);
                karatsuba(x+m,y+m,z+n,m);

                atoa(x,u,m); adda(x+m,u,m);
                atoa(y,u+m,m); adda(y+m,u+m,m);
```

```
                karatsuba(u,u+m,v,m);
                suba(z,v,n-1);
                suba(z+n,v,n-1);
                adda(v,z+m,n-1);
        }
}


void
neglit(rep   *x, rep *y, int n)
{

        karatsuba(x, y, T, n);
        atoa(T, y, n);
        suba(T+n, y, n-1);


}


void
transa(int r, int m, rep *a, rep *b)
/* Array transpose. */
{
        int i,j;
        unsigned int *pa, *pb;

        for(i = 0; i< r; i++) {
                pa = (unsigned int *)&a[m*i];
                pb = (unsigned int *)&b[i];
                for(j=0; j<m; j++) {
                        *pb = *pa++;
                        pb += r;
                }
        }
}


selftransa(int r, int m, rep *a)
/* Array transpose IN PLACE (believe it or not!).
   This assumes (for performance reasons) that
   r and m are powers of 2.
*/
{
        int i, j, tmp, tmp2;
        unsigned int *pa, *pb;

        if (r == m) {
                for(i = 0; i < r-1; i++) {
                        pa = (unsigned int *)&a[i*m + i + 1];
                        pb = (unsigned int *)&a[i*m + i + m];
                        for(j = i+1; j < m; j++) {
                                tmp = *pb;
                                *pb = *pa;
                                *pa++ = tmp;
```

```
                              pb += r;
                      }
              }
      }
      else {
              int max = r*m-1;
              int cur = 1;
              int remains = (max-1)>>1;   /* Half due to symmetry */
              int rshift = log_2(r);
              int mshift = log_2(m);

              do {
              /* Move to the next non-transposed element */
                      while (a[cur] & 0x80000000)
                              a[cur++] &= 0x7fffffff;
                      tmp = a[cur];
                      tmp2 = a[max-cur];
                      i = cur;
                      do {
                              j = (i>>rshift) + ((i & (r-1))<<mshift);
                              if (j == cur) break;
                              a[i] = a[j] | 0x80000000;
                              a[max-i] = a[max-j] | 0x80000000;
                              i = j;
                              --remains;
                      }
                      while (1);
                      a[i] = tmp | 0x80000000;
                      a[max-i] = tmp2 | 0x80000000;
                      --remains;
              }
              while (remains > 0);
              while (cur <= max) a[cur++] &= 0x7fffffff;
      }
}

void
twista(rep *a, int r, int q)
{   /* Assumes r is power of 2 */
      int v;

      q &= 2*r-1;
      if (q == 0) return;
      if ( q < r ) {
              v = r-q;
              atoa(a, dum, v);
              atoan(a+v, a, q);
              atoa(dum, a+q, v);
      }
      else {
              q -= r;
```

```
            v = r-q;
            atoan(a, dum, v);
            atoa(a+v, a, q);
            atoa(dum, a+q, v);
      }
}

void
butter(rep *a, rep *b, int r) {
      int g, i,j,k,l,m,n;
      unsigned int *pa = (unsigned int *)a,
      *pb = (unsigned int *)b;
      for (g=(r>>2); g != 0; --g) {
            i = *pa;
            j = *pb;
            m = i+j;
            if (m >= p) m -= p;
            *pa++ = m;
            m = i-j;
            if (m < 0)   m += p;
            *pb++ = m;
            i = *pa;
            j = *pb;
            m = i+j;
            if (m >= p) m -= p;
            *pa++ = m;
            m = i-j;
            if (m < 0)   m += p;
            *pb++ = m;
            i = *pa;
            j = *pb;
            m = i+j;
            if (m >= p) m -= p;
            *pa++ = m;
            m = i-j;
            if (m < 0)   m += p;
            *pb++ = m;
            i = *pa;
            j = *pb;
            m = i+j;
            if (m >= p) m -= p;
            *pa++ = m;
            m = i-j;
            if (m < 0)   m += p;
            *pb++ = m;
      }
      for (g=(r&3); g != 0; --g) {
            i = *pa;
            j = *pb;
            m = i+j;
            if (m >= p) m -= p;
```

```
                *pa++ = m;
                m = i-j;
                if (m < 0)   m += p;
                *pb++ = m;
        }
}

fft_dif(rep *a, rep *b, int len, int root, int r) {
        int half = len/2, i, j, k, s, t, u, v, twok, twokr;

        for(k = half; k > 0; k >>= 1) {
                s = 0;
                t = k*r;
                twok = 2*k;
                twokr = 2*t;
                for(i = 0; i < len; i += twok) {
                        butter(a+s, a+t, r);
                        butter(b+s, b+t, r);
                        s += twokr;
                        t += twokr;
                }
                v = root*half/k;
                for(u=v, j=1; j<k; u += v, j++) {
                        s = j*r;
                        t = s + k*r;
                        for(i = j; i < len; i += twok) {
                                butter(a+s, a+t, r);
                                butter(b+s, b+t, r);
                                twista(a+t, r, u);
                                twista(b+t, r, u);
                                s += twokr;
                                t += twokr;
                        }
                }
        }
}

fft_dit(rep *b, int len, int root, int r) {
        int half = len/2, i, j, k, s, t, u, v, twok, twokr;
        for(k = 1; k < len; k += k) {
                s = 0;
                t = k*r;
                twok = 2*k;
                twokr = 2*t;
                for( i = 0; i < len; i += twok) {
                        butter(b+s, b+t, r);
                        s += twokr;
                        t += twokr;
                }
                v = -root*half/k;
                for(u = v, j = 1; j < k; u += v, j++) {
```

```
                    s = j*r;
                    t = s + k*r;
                    for( i = j; i < len; i += twok) {
                            /* Next, inverse butterfly action. */
                            twista(b+t, r, u);
                            butter(b+s, b+t, r);
                            s += twokr;
                            t += twokr;
                    }
            }
    }
}

void
rout(rep x) {
    printf("%d\n", x);
    fflush(stdout);
}

neg(rep *x, rep *y, rep *a, rep *b, int n)
/* Nussbaumer convolution; y:= x neg y.
 */
{
    int k, m, r, w, u, i, j, v, s, t, g, pow,
        twom, twok, twokr;
    int freeflag = 0;
    rep ay;

    if(n <= NEG_BREAK) {
            neglit(x, y, n);
            return;
    }
    if (!a) {a = newa(n); b = newa(n); freeflag = 1; }
    pow = log_2(n); m = 1<<(pow/2); r = n/m; w = r/m;

/* The idea is to find the acyclic convolution of a,b.  The classical
   Nussbaumer does the order-2m cyclic of
   {a,0,0,...}and {b,0,0,...}.
   Instead, we shall do the order-m cyclic of a,b;
   and the order-m negacyclic
   via a DWT.  Luckily an m-th root of (-1), namely w, is available
   for the DWT.
 */

/* Next, perform order-m cyclic. */
transa(r, m, x, a);
transa(r, m, y, b);
fft_dif(a, b, m, 2*w, r);
for(i = 0, k = -r;  i < m; i++) {
    k += r;
    neg(a+k, b+k, NULL, NULL, r);
```

```
}
fft_dit(b, m, 2*w, r);
/* Next, save cyclic by swapping it with y */
swapa(b,y,n);

/* Next, perform order-m negacyclic.  Start by weighting the a,b
signals. */
transa(r, m, x, a);
selftransa(r, m, b);
for(k=1, v = w, i = r; k < m; v += w, i += r, k++ ) {
     twista(a+i, r, v);
     twista(b+i, r, v);
}
fft_dif(a, b, m, 2*w, r);
for(i = 0, k = -r;  i < m; i++) {
     k += r;
     neg(a+k, b+k, NULL, NULL, r);
}
fft_dit(b, m, 2*w, r);
/* Next, unweight b. */
for(k = 1, i = r, v = -w; k < m; i += r, v -= w, k++ ) {
     twista(b+i, r, v);
}

/* Next, recover the acyclic as {b,y}:= {b+y, b-y}. */
atoan(b, a, n);
adda(y, a, n);
adda(b, y, n);
atoa(a,b,n);
/* The union {b,y}is now the desired acyclic convolution. */

for(k = 0; k < m-1; k++) {
     s = k*r;
     twista(b+s, r, 1);
     adda(b+s, y+s, r);
}
if (freeflag) {
     freea(a, n);
     freea(b, n);
}
selftransa(m, r, y);
/* Next, divide by normalizer. */
ay = power_up((p+1)/2, 1+pow/2, p);
for(j=0; j<n; j++) MULR(ay, y[j]);
}

void
cyc_dest(rep *x, rep *y, int n)
/* Cyclic convolution; y := x cyc y. */
{
rep *a, ay, t, u;
```

```
int j;

if(n <= CYC_BREAK) {
      cyclit(x, y, n);
      return;
}
n >>= 1;
a = newa(n);
atoa(y, a, n);
suba(y+n, a, n);
adda(y,y+n,n);
atoa(x, y, n);
adda(x+n, y, n);
cyc_dest(y, y+n, n);
atoa(x, y, n);
suba(x+n, y, n);
neg(y, a, x, x+n, n); /* Pass in x to use as a temporary */
atoa(y+n,y,n);
adda(a,y,n);
suba(a,y+n,n);

ay = (p+1)/2;
n <<= 1;
for(j=0; j<n; j++) {
      if((y[j] & 1) == 0) y[j] >>= 1;
      else {
              y[j] >>= 1;
              ADDR(ay, y[j]);
      }
}
freea(a, n);
}

#define GRAMMAR_LEN 8192
main(int argc, char **argv) {
int len = atoi(argv[1]);
int j;
rep  *x = newa(len), *y = newa(len), *z;

init_con();
p = 700001;

if(len <= GRAMMAR_LEN) z = newa(len);
for(j = 0; j < len; j++) {
      x[j] = j%p;
      y[j] = j%p;
      SLOW_MULR(j%p, y[j]);
      if(len <= GRAMMAR_LEN) z[j] = 0;
}

if (len <= GRAMMAR_LEN) {
```

```
        printf("Commencing literal cyclic...\n");
        fflush(stdout);
        atoa(y, z, len);
        cyclit(x, z, len);
}
printf("Commencing Nussbaumer cyclic\n");
fflush(stdout);
cyc_dest(x, y, len);

if(len > GRAMMAR_LEN) exit(0);

for(j=0; j<len; j++) {
        SUBR(z[j], y[j]);
        if(y[j]) {
                fprintf(stderr, "Convolution error.\n");
                exit(1);
        }
}
fprintf(stderr,"Convolution perfect.\n");
}
```

ConvolutionsRecursive.ma

```
(* New convolutions based upon recursive half-cyclic convolution. *)

cyclit[x_,y_] := Table[ (* Literal cyclic. *)
        Sum[x[[q+1]] y[[Mod[r-q, Length[x]]+1]],
                {q,0,Length[x]-1}],
                {r,0,Length[x]-1}];

neglit[x_,y_] := Table[ (* Literal negacyclic. *)
        Sum[x[[q+1]] y[[Mod[r-q, Length[x]]+1]] * If[q>r, -1,1],
                {q,0,Length[x]-1}],
                {r,0,Length[x]-1}];

bar[n_] := Round[N[2^Ceiling[Log[2,n]]]];   (* Least p.o.t. >=
argument. *)

pad[zz_] := Join[zz, Table[0,{bar[Length[zz]]-Length[zz]}]];

(* Next, the recursive half-cyclic convolution. *)
hcyc[x_, y_] := Module[{m = Length[x], n,u,v,c, k,z,s,t},
        If[m == 1, Print["cyc1"]; Return[{{x[[1]]*y[[1]]}}]];
        n = bar[m]/2;
        u = pad[x];
        v = pad[y];
        c = cyclit[u,v]; Print["cyc",Length[c]];
        If[m > 3n/2, (* Standard half-cyclic. *)
                d = neglit[u,v]; Print["neg",Length[d]];
                Return[Take[(c+d)/2, {1,m}]];
```

```
        ];
        k = 2m -2n -1;
        s = Take[x,{1,k}];
        t = Take[y,{1,k}];
        z = hcyc[s,t];
        Join[Take[z, {1,k}], Take[c, {k+1,m}]]
    ];

(* Next, the recursive acyclic convolution. *)
acyc[x_, y_] := Module[{m = Length[x], n, xe, xf, ye, yf, pd, c, d,
j, g, k},
        If[m == 1, Return[{x[[1]] y[[1]]}]];
        n = bar[m]/2;
        If[m > 3n/2, (* Standard acyclic. *)
            xp = pad[x]; yp = pad[y];
            c = cyclit[xp, yp]; Print["cyc",Length[c]];
            d = neglit[xp, yp]; Print["neg",Length[d]];
            j = Expand[Join[c+d, c-d]/2];
            Return[Take[j, {1,2m-1}]];
        ];
        xf = Take[x,{1,n}]; yf = Take[y,{1,n}];
        pd = Table[0,{2n-m}];
        xe = Join[Take[x,{n+1,m}], pd];
        ye = Join[Take[y,{n+1,m}], pd];
        c = cyclit[xf+xe, yf+ye]; Print["cyc",Length[c]];
        d = neglit[xf-xe, yf-ye]; Print["neg",Length[d]];
        j = Join[c+d, c-d]/2;
        k = 2m-2n-1;
        g = hcyc[Take[x, {1, k}], Take[y, {1, k}]];
        j = Join[j, Take[j, {1,k}]-g];
        j = Join[Take[j,{1,k}] - Take[j,{2n+1, 2n+k}],
                Take[j,{k+1,2m-1}]];
        j
    ];

(* Next, the recursive cyclic convolution. *)
fcyc[x_, y_] := Module[{m = Length[x], mbar, c, d, k, h, q},
            mbar = bar[m];
            c = cyclit[pad[x], pad[y]]; Print["cyc",Length[c]];
            If[m == mbar, Return[c]];
            k = 2m - mbar -1;
            h = hcyc[Take[x,{1,k}], Take[y,{1,k}]];
            d = Join[Take[c,{m+1, mbar}],
                Take[c,{1,k}] - h, {c[[m]]}];
            d += Join[Table[If[(q>k), c[[q]],
                h[[q]]],{q,1,m-1}], {0}];
            d
            ];

x = Array[a, 11, 0];
y = Array[b, 11, 0];
```

```
ac = Simplify[acyc[x,y]];
px = Sum[x[[q]] t^(q-1),{q,1,Length[x]}];
py = Sum[y[[q]] t^(q-1),{q,1,Length[y]}];
prod = Expand[px * py];
tab = Join[{prod /. t->0}, Table[Coefficient[prod,
t^q],{q,1,2*Length[x]-2}]];
Print[ac-tab];
Print[MatrixForm[ac]];
```

FastWavelet.ma

```
(* Fast wavelet transform, in place. *)

symbolic = False;

(* Daubechies (D4) wavelet choice. *)
hh[n_] := If[(n<0) || (n>=4), 0,
               If[symbolic, H[n],
                         N[Which[n==0,(1+Sqrt[3])/(4),
                     n==1,(3+Sqrt[3])/(4),
                     n==2,(3-Sqrt[3])/(4),
                     n==3,(1-Sqrt[3])/(4)]]
               ]
          ];

h[n_] := N[hh[n]/Sqrt[2]];
g[n_] := (-1)^n h[3-n]
p[i_] := Mod[i,2]
q[i_] := Floor[(i+1)/2]

m = 4;
n = 2^m;  (* Signal length. *)

(* First, create a signal. *)
Do[s[q] = N[Sin[q/3] * Exp[-3*q/n]], {q,0,n-1}]

Print["signal = ",Table[s[q],{q,0,n-1}]]
ListPlot[Table[s[q],{q,0,n-1}]];
(* Now do recursion, each time splitting the active array
into "s" and "d" parts. *)

For[r=0, r<m, r++,
    c = s[0]; d = s[2^r];
    For[k=0, k < n/2^(r+1)-1, k++,
        a = Sum[h[q] s[(q+2k) 2^r], {q,0,3}];
        b = Sum[g[q] s[(q+2k) 2^r], {q,0,3}];
        s[k 2^(r+1)] = a;
        s[k 2^(r+1) + 2^r] = b;
    ];
    k = n/2^(r+1)-1;
```

```
        a = Sum[h[q] s[(q+2k) 2^r], {q,0,1}] +
              h[2] c + h[3] d;
        b = Sum[g[q] s[(q+2k) 2^r], {q,0,1}] +
              g[2] c + g[3] d;
        s[k 2^(r+1)] = a;
        s[k 2^(r+1) + 2^r] = b;
]


Print["wtransform = ",Table[s[q],{q,0,n-1}]]
ListPlot[Table[s[q],{q,0,n-1}]];


(* Now perform the inverse FWT. *)
For[r=m, r>=1, r--,
    c = s[n-2^r]; d = s[n-2^r+2^(r-1)];
    For[k=n/2^r-1, k > 0, k--,
      a = Sum[h[2q] s[(k-q) 2^r] +
              g[2q] s[(k-q) 2^r + 2^(r-1)], {q,0,1}];
      b = Sum[h[2q+1] s[(k-q) 2^r] +
              g[2q+1] s[(k-q) 2^r + 2^(r-1)], {q,0,1}];
      s[k 2^r] = a;
      s[k 2^r + 2^(r-1)] = b;
    ];
    a = h[0] s[0] + h[2] c + g[0] s[2^(r-1)] + g[2] d;
    b = h[1] s[0] + h[3] c + g[1] s[2^(r-1)] + g[3] d;
    s[0] = a;
    s[2^(r-1)] = b;
]


Print["reconstruction = ",Table[s[q],{q,0,n-1}]]
ListPlot[Table[s[q],{q,0,n-1}]];
```

FFTs.ma

```
(* Gentleman-Sande, decimation in frequency radix-2 complex FFT.
   Scramble bits *after* this call. *)

fftfreq[x_] :=
    Module[{y,n,m,i,j,a,ii,im},
        y = x;
    n = Length[x];
        For[m = Floor[n/2] , m > 0 , m = Floor[m/2],
          For[j = 0, j<m, j++,
            For[ i = j, i < n, i += 2m,
              ii = i+1; im = i+m+1; (* List indices. *)
              a = Exp[-2 Pi I j/(2*m)];
              {y[[ii]],y[[im]]}=
                  {y[[ii]]+y[[im]], a*(y[[ii]]-y[[im]])};
            ];
```

```
                       ];
                    ];
                 y
             ];

(* Cooley-Tukey, decimation in time radix-2 complex FFT.
   Scramble bits *before* this call. *)

ffttime[x_] :=
     Module[{y, n,m,i,j,a,ii,im},
          y = x;
     n = Length[x];
          For[m = 1, m < n , m += m,
            For[j = 0, j<m, j++,
               For[ i = j, i < n, i += 2m,
                   ii = i+1; im = i+m+1; (* List indices. *)
                   a = Exp[-2 Pi I j/(2*m)];
                   {y[[ii]],y[[im]]}=
                       {y[[ii]]+a*y[[im]], y[[ii]]-a*y[[im]]};
               ];
             ];
           ];
          y
       ];

(* Next, bit scrambler intended to be used after a DIF FFT, but
before a DIT FFT. *)

scramble[x_] := Module[{y, i, j, k, tmp},
     y = x;
     n = Length[x];
     For[i=0;j=0,i<n-1,i++,
          If[i<j,
            tmp = y[[j+1]];
            y[[j+1]]=y[[i+1]];
            y[[i+1]]=tmp;
          ];
          k = Floor[n/2];
          While[k<=j,
               j -= k;
               k = Floor[k/2]
          ];
          j += k;
     ];
     y
]

z = {1,3,2,4,5,6,7,9};

xfreq = scramble[fftfreq[z]];
xtime = ffttime[scramble[z]];
```

```
xtest = Sqrt[Length[z]] InverseFourier[z];

Print[xfreq]
Print[xtime]
Print[N[xfreq-xtest]]
Print[N[xtime-xtest]]
```

ibstw.c

```
/* BSTW decompressor for executables.

   % cc -O ibstw.c bstwlib.c

   Usage:

   % a.out file.ex > file
   OR
   % a.out file.ex file

*/

#include  <stdio.h>

main(int argc, char *argv[])
{
    FILE *infile, *outfile;
    unsigned char *inbuffer, *outbuffer, c;
    unsigned int length, total;

    if(argc == 1) {
      fprintf(stderr, "Usage:\n> exc compfile [plainfile]\n");
      exit(0);
    }
    infile = fopen(argv[1], "r");
    if(argc == 2) outfile = stdout;
       else outfile = fopen(argv[2],"w");

    fseek(infile,0,2); length = ftell(infile); rewind(infile);
    inbuffer = (unsigned char *)malloc(length);
    fread(inbuffer, 1, length, infile);
    fclose(infile);

    inbuffer += 4;  /* Skip over version number, which is checked
                       later in ex_decompress(). */
/* Next, figure out malloc size using the next four bytes of the
   compressed stream.
 */
    length = *inbuffer++;
    length = (length<<8) | (*inbuffer++);
    length = (length<<8) | (*inbuffer++);
```

```
    length = (length<<8) | (*inbuffer++);
    inbuffer -= 8;
/* Now length is the exact byte count of the final, decompressed
stream. */

outbuffer = (unsigned char *)malloc(length);
total = ex_decompress(inbuffer, outbuffer);
fwrite(outbuffer, 1, length, outfile);
}
```

lzw.c

```
/* lzw.c: LZW variant skeleton.
   This code is intended as a playground for
   Lempel-Ziv, Lempel-Ziv-Welch experimentation.
 */

#include<stdio.h>
#include<math.h>

#define MAX_CHARS 8
#define MAX_STRS 1024
#define START_STRS 256

typedef struct {
    unsigned char str[MAX_CHARS];
    int len;
}lzstring;

int lzstrcount;
lzstring *lzstr;

int hist[MAX_STRS], count;

void
initentropy()
/* Experimentation can begin with a simple histogram. */
{
    int j;
    for(j=0; j< MAX_STRS; j++) hist[j] = 0;
}

void
reportentropy()
/* Report in Mathematica format. */
{
    int c;
    printf("{");
    for(c=0; c < MAX_STRS-1; c++) {
        printf("%d,",hist[c]);
```

```
                if(c%10 == 0) printf("\n");
        }
        printf("%d}\n",hist[MAX_STRS-1]);
}

void
initlzw()
/* Fill each starting string with a single char. */
{
        int j;

        lzstr = (lzstring *)malloc(MAX_STRS * sizeof(lzstring));
        for(j=0; j<START_STRS; j++) {
                lzstr[j].str[0] = j;
                lzstr[j].len = 1;
        }
        lzstrcount = START_STRS;
}

int
lzindex(unsigned char *s, int n)
/* Brute-force string match detector. */
{
        int j,k;

        for(j=0; j < lzstrcount; j++) {
                if(lzstr[j].len != n) continue;
                for(k=0; k < n; k++) {
                        if(lzstr[j].str[k] != s[k]) break;
                }
                if(k == n) return(j);
        }
        return(-1);
}

int
lzappend(unsigned char *s, int n)
{
        int j;

        if(lzstrcount == MAX_STRS-1) return(1);
        for(j=0; j<n; j++) lzstr[lzstrcount].str[j] = s[j];
        lzstr[lzstrcount++].len = n;
        return(0);
}

void
emanate(int root) {
        /* printf("%d\n", root); fflush(stdout); */
        ++hist[root];
}
```

```
main(int argc, char **argv) {
      int curlen, i, rooti, notok, c;
      unsigned char curstr[MAX_CHARS];
      FILE *fp = fopen(argv[1], "r");

      initlzw();
      curlen = 0;  /* Empty string. */
      rooti = -1;  /* Empty root. */
      while(1){
            while(1) {
                  if((c = fgetc(fp)) == EOF) break;
                  curstr[curlen++] = c;
                  i = lzindex(curstr, curlen);
                  if(i < 0) break;
                  rooti = i;  /* The most recent "found" string. */
                  if(curlen == MAX_CHARS) break;
            }
            if(c == EOF) {
                  emanate(rooti);
                  fclose(fp);
                  reportentropy();
                  exit(0);
            }
            if(i < 0) {
                  emanate(rooti);
                  if(notok = lzappend(curstr, curlen)) {
                        emanate(curstr[curlen-1]);
                        initlzw();
                        curlen = 0;
                        rooti = -1;
                        continue;
                  }
                  curstr[0] = curstr[curlen-1];
                  curlen = 1;
                  rooti = lzindex(curstr, curlen);
                  continue;
            }
            if(curlen == MAX_CHARS) {
                  emanate(rooti);
                  curlen = 0;
                  rooti = -1;
                  continue;
            }
      }
}
```

.

muldiv.h

```
/* Machine-specific routines for multiplication and
   division (mod p).  This definition file is used by
   the large-convolution library "conlib.c"

   mul(a,b,p)   returns (a*b) (mod p)
   quo(a,b,p)   returns (a*b) (div p)

   Note the floating-point default option is only good
   for arithmetic with p < 2^26.

   Note also that in "conlib.c" there are "long long"
   implementations (slowmul() and slowquo()) if full
   precision beyond the floating point default is desired.
 */

#import<math.h>
extern double recip;
#ifdef m68k
static inline int mul(unsigned int a,unsigned int b,unsigned int p)
{
    int r;

    asm("movel %2,d0;mulsl %1,%0:d0;divsl %3,%0:d0"
      : "=d"(r)
      : "dmsK"(a), "d"(b), "dmsK"(p)
      : "d0");
    return r;
}
#elif defined(i386)
static inline int mul(unsigned int a,unsigned int b,unsigned int p)
{
    int r;
    asm("
        imull %2
        idivl %3, %%eax
        movl %%edx, %%eax
        "
      : "=a" (r)
      : "a" (a), "r" (b), "r" (p)
      : "edx", "eax");
    return r;
}
#elif defined(hppa)
/* This next will only be good for arguments < 2^26. */
static int mul(unsigned int a,unsigned int b,unsigned int p)
{
    double c = a;
```

```
        c *= b;
        return(rint(c - ((double)p)*floor(c*recip)));
}
#else
/* This next will only be good for arguments < 2^26. */
static inline int mul(unsigned int a,unsigned int b,unsigned int p)
{
        double c = a;
        c *= b;
        return(rint(c - ((double)p)*floor(c*recip)));
}
#endif
#ifdef m68k
static inline int quo(unsigned int a,unsigned int b,unsigned int p)
{
    int r;


    asm("movel %2,%0;mulsl %1,d0:%0;divsl %3,d0:%0"
        : "=d"(r)
        : "dmsK"(a), "d"(b), "dmsK"(p)
        : "d0");
    return r;
}
#elif defined(i386)
static inline int quo(unsigned int a,unsigned int b,unsigned int p)
{
    int r;
    asm("
        imull %2
        idivl %3, %%eax
        "
        : "=a" (r)
        : "a" (a), "r" (b), "r" (p)
        : "eax", "edx");
    return r;
}
#elif defined(hppa)
static int quo(unsigned int a,unsigned int b,unsigned int p)
{       return(rint(floor(((double)a)*((double)b)*recip)));
}
#else
/* This next will only be good for arguments < 2^26. */

static inline int quo(unsigned int a,unsigned int b,unsigned int p)
{       return(rint(floor(((double)a)*((double)b)*recip)));
}
#endif
```

Nuss.ma

```
(* Nussbaumer convolution.
   Adapted from an implementation of [Buhler 1995].
   nega[x,y] returns the negacyclic convolution of Lists x,y.
 *)

neglit[x_, y_] := Table[
                    Sum[x[[i+1]] y[[Mod[m-i,Length[x]]+1]] *
                        If[m < i, -1,1]
                        ,{i,0,Length[x]-1}
                    ]
                    ,{m,0,Length[x]-1}
                 ];

cyclit[x_, y_] := Table[Sum[x[[i+1]] y[[Mod[m-i,Length[x]]+1]]
                    ,{i,0,Length[x]-1}]
                    ,{m,0,Length[x]-1}
                 ];

twist[a_, r_, u_, off_] := Module[{t,q},
                q = Mod[u, 2r];
                If[q < r,
                    t = Join[-Take[a,{r-q+off+1, r+off}],
                             Take[a,{off+1,r-q+off}]],
                    t = Join[Take[a,{2r-q+off+1, r+off}],
                             -Take[a,{off+1,2r-q+off}]]
                ];
                t
         ];

trans[r_, m_, a_] := Module[{b = a, i, j},
        Do[
          Do[
            b[[i+j*r+1]] = a[[m*i+j+1]],
          {j,0,m-1}],
          {i,0,r-1}
        ];
        b
    ];

(* Faster option, courtesy S. Wagon:
trans[r_, m_, a_] :=
    Join[Flatten[Transpose[Partition[Take[a, m r], m]]],
                Take[a, m r - Length[a]]]; *)

nega[x_, y_] := Module[{n = Length[x],a,b,c,k,m,r,u,v,i,j,g,s,t,w},
        If[n <= 16, Return[neglit[x,y]]];
        k = Floor[Log[2,n]];
    m = 2^Floor[k/2]; r = n/m; w = r/m;
```

```
(* Next, form polynomials and zero-pad. *)
a = trans[r, m, x]; b = trans[r, m, y];
a = Join[a, Table[0,{n}]]; b = Join[b, Table[0,{n}]];
(* Next, perform DIF FFT on a,b using root w. *)
For[k = m, k > 0, k = Floor[k/2],
        v = w*m/k;
        For[u = 0; j = 0, j < k, u += v; j++,
                For[i = j, i < 2m, i += 2k,
                (* Next, butterfly action. *)
                        s = i*r+1; t = (i+k)*r+1;
                        For[g = 0, g < r, g++,
                           {a[[s+g]], a[[t+g]]}=
                                {a[[s+g]] + a[[t+g]], a[[s+g]]-a[[t+g]]};
                           {b[[s+g]], b[[t+g]]}=
                                {b[[s+g]] + b[[t+g]], b[[s+g]]-b[[t+g]]};
                        ];
                        a = Join[Take[a,{1,t-1}], twist[a, r, u, t-1],
                                Take[a, {t+r, 2n}]];
                        b = Join[Take[b,{1,t-1}], twist[b, r, u, t-1],
                                Take[b, {t+r, 2n}]];
                ];
        ];
];
(* Next, form the dyadic product as a set of negacyclics. *)
For[i = 0; c = {},   i < 2 m, i++,
        c = Join[c,nega[Take[a,{i*r+1, (i+1)*r}],
                        Take[b,{i*r+1, (i+1)*r}]]];
];
(* Next, the DIT IFFT. *)
For[k = 1, k < 2m, k *= 2,
        v = -w*m/k;
        For[u = 0; j = 0, j < k, u += v; j++,
                For[i = j, i < 2m, i += 2k,
                (* Next, inverse butterfly action. *)
                        s = i*r+1; t = (i+k)*r+1;
                        c = Join[Take[c,{1,t-1}], twist[c, r, u, t-1],
                                Take[c, {t+r, 2n}]];
                        For[g = 0, g < r, g++,
                           {c[[s+g]], c[[t+g]]}=
                                {c[[s+g]] + c[[t+g]], c[[s+g]]-c[[t+g]]};
                        ];
                ];
        ];
];
For[k = 0, k < m-1, k++,
        t = (k+m)*r+1;
        c = Join[Take[c,{1,t-1}], twist[c, r, 1, t-1],
                Take[c, {t+r, 2n}]];
        c = Join[Take[c,{1,k*r}],
                Take[c,{k*r+1, k*r+r}]+Take[c,{t, t+r-1}],
                Take[c,{(k+1)*r+1,2n}]];
```

```
    ];
    Take[trans[m,r,c],{1,n}]/(2m)]
];

len = 64;
xx = Table[Random[Integer, 1000],{len}];
yy = Table[Random[Integer, 1000],{len}];
Timing[nuss = Expand[nega[xx,yy]]] [[1]]
Timing[lit = Expand[neglit[xx,yy]]] [[1]]
(nuss-lit) . (nuss-lit)
```

PSLQ.ma

```
(* PSLQ algorithm for integer relation detection.
   After [Bailey et. al. 1994]. The input vector x is checked
   exhaustively for relations a1 x1 + a2 x2 + ... + an xn = 0,
   up to reportable bounds on the ai.
 *)

prec = 14;
(* Next, to find a quintic polynomial having root:
   root = -1.277883036387392943188151033564172 54101817;
   x = Table[root^q,{q,0,5}];
 *)
(* Next, to find the coefficient in a modern Zeta[4] formula.
x = {Zeta[4], Sum[1/k^4 1/Binomial[2k,k], {k,1,30}]};
 *)

(* Next, find a zeta representation of a cotangent integral. *)
x = {NIntegrate[z^5 Cot[Pi z],{z,0,1/2}],
     Log[2]/Pi, Zeta[3]/Pi^3, Zeta[5]/Pi^5};
n = Length[x];
x = N[x, prec];
gam = Sqrt[4/3];
nint[t_] := If[t>0, Floor[t+1/2], Ceiling[t-1/2]];
a = b = IdentityMatrix[n];
s = Sqrt[Table[Sum[x[[q]]^2,{q,k,n}],{k,1,n}]];
y = x/s[[1]]; s = s/s[[1]];
h = Table[0,{i,1,n},{j,1,n-1}];
Do[
    Do[h[[i,j]] = 0, {j,i+1,n-1}];
    If[i <= n-1, h[[i,i]] = s[[i+1]]/s[[i]]];
    Do[h[[i,j]] = -y[[i]] y[[j]]/(s[[j]] s[[j+1]]),
        {j,1,i-1}],
    {i,1,n}
];
Do[
    Do[
        t = nint[h[[i,j]]/h[[j,j]]];
```

```
        y[[j]] += t y[[i]]; Do[ h[[i,k]] -= t h[[j,k]],{k,1,j}];
        a[[i]] -= t a[[j]]; Do[ b[[k,j]] += t b[[k,i]],{k,1,n}]
        ,{j,i-1,1,-1}
    ]
    ,{i,2,n}
];
While[True,
      max = N[gam Abs[h[[1,1]]], prec]; m = 1;
      Do[test = N[gam^i Abs[h[[i,i]]], prec];
         If[test > max, m = i; max = test]
         ,{i,2,n-1}
      ];
      Do[
        Do[
            t = nint[h[[i,j]]/h[[j,j]]];
          y[[j]] += t y[[i]];
          Do[ h[[i,k]] -= t h[[j,k]],{k,1,j}];
          a[[i]] -= t a[[j]];
          Do[ b[[k,j]] += t b[[k,i]],{k,1,n}]
            ,{j,Min[i-1, m+1],1,-1}
          ]
          ,{i,m+1,n}
      ];
      tmp = y[[m]]; y[[m]] = y[[m+1]]; y[[m+1]] = tmp;
      tmp = h[[m]]; h[[m]] = h[[m+1]]; h[[m+1]] = tmp;
      tmp = a[[m]]; a[[m]] = a[[m+1]]; a[[m+1]] = tmp;
      b = Transpose[b];
      tmp = b[[m]]; b[[m]] = b[[m+1]]; b[[m+1]] = tmp;
      b = Transpose[b];
      If[m < n-1,
            t0 = Sqrt[h[[m,m]]^2 + h[[m,m+1]]^2];
            t1 = h[[m,m]]/t0; t2 = h[[m,m+1]]/t0;
            Do[t3 = h[[i,m]]; t4 = h[[i,m+1]];
               h[[i,m]] = t1 t3 + t2 t4;
               h[[i,m+1]] = -t2 t3 + t1 t4
               ,{i,m,n}
               ]
      ];
      norms = Table[Sqrt[h[[j]] . h[[j]]], {j,1,n}];
      maxnorm = 1/Max[norms];
      Print["Norm bound: ",N[maxnorm, 14]];
      m = 1; min = Abs[y[[1]]];
      Do[test = N[Abs[y[[i]]], prec];
         If[test < min, m = i; min = test]
         ,{i,2,n}
      ];
      If[min < 10^(-prec+2),
            Print["Detection!"]; Print[Transpose[b][[m]]]; Break[]
      ];
      If[Max[Abs[a]] > 10^(prec-2),
            Print["Exhaustion!"]; Break[]
```

```
        ];
];
```

rep.h

```
/* Definitions for large-convolution library "conlib.c" */

typedef int rep;
#define RTOR(A, B) B = A
#define ADDR(A, B) B += A; if(B >= p) B -= p
#define SUBR(A, B) B -= A; if(B < 0) B += p
#define MULR(A, B) B = mul(A, B, p)
#define NEGR(B) B = p-B; if(B == p) B = 0
#define SLOW_MULR(A, B) B = slowmul(A, B, p)
unsigned int p;
#define MAX    1024
#define MAX_DUMS 8192
#define CYC_BREAK 32
#define NEG_BREAK 32
#define atoa(a,b,n) memcpy(b, a, n*sizeof(rep))
rep *newa(int n);
```

toomcook.c

```
/* Toom-Cook method for order-4 negacyclic convolution
   in 7 multiplies (disregarding absolute constant multiplies/
   divides).  The function nega4() is comprised of code generated
   automatically via a symbolic program.
 */

#include<stdio.h>
#include<math.h>

nega4(double *a, double *b, double *c) {

double r[64], s[64], t[64];

r[0] = a[0] - 3*a[1] + 9*a[2] - 27*a[3];
r[1] = a[0] - 2*a[1] + 4*a[2] - 8*a[3];
r[2] = a[0] - a[1] + a[2] - a[3];
r[3] = a[0];
r[4] = a[0] + a[1] + a[2] + a[3];
r[5] = a[0] + 2*a[1] + 4*a[2] + 8*a[3];
r[6] = a[0] + 3*a[1] + 9*a[2] + 27*a[3];
s[0] = b[0] - 3*b[1] + 9*b[2] - 27*b[3];
s[1] = b[0] - 2*b[1] + 4*b[2] - 8*b[3];
s[2] = b[0] - b[1] + b[2] - b[3];
s[3] = b[0];
s[4] = b[0] + b[1] + b[2] + b[3];
s[5] = b[0] + 2*b[1] + 4*b[2] + 8*b[3];
s[6] = b[0] + 3*b[1] + 9*b[2] + 27*b[3];
```

```
/* Here come the seven multiplies. */
t[0] = r[0] * s[0];
t[1] = r[1] * s[1];
t[2] = r[2] * s[2];
t[3] = r[3] * s[3];
t[4] = r[4] * s[4];
t[5] = r[5] * s[5];
t[6] = r[6] * s[6];
c[0] = t[0]/144 - t[1]/12 + (13*t[2])/48 + (11*t[3])/18 +
       (13*t[4])/48 - t[5]/12 + t[6]/144;
c[1] = -t[0]/80 + (2*t[1])/15 - (35*t[2])/48 + (35*t[4])/48 -
       (2*t[5])/15 + t[6]/80;
c[2] = t[0]/240 - t[1]/15 + (35*t[2])/48 - (4*t[3])/3 + (35*t[4])/48
       - t[5]/15 + t[6]/240;
c[3] = t[0]/48 - t[1]/6 + (13*t[2])/48 - (13*t[4])/48 + t[5]/6 -
       t[6]/48;
}

void
negagram(double  *x, double *y, double *z, int n)
/* Grammar-school negacyclic. */
{
      int p, i, q;
      double d;
      for(p = 0; p < n; p++) {
            z[p] = 0;
            for(q = 0; q < n; q++) {
                  i = (p-q)%n;
                  if(i<0) i+= n;
                  d = y[i] * x[q];
                  if(p >= q) z[p] += d;
                  else z[p] -= d;
            }
      }
}

main(int argc, char **argv) {
      double a[4], b[4], c[4], d[4];
      int j;
      for(j = 0; j < 4; j++) {
            a[j] = j;
            b[j] = j*j;
      }
      nega4(a,b,c);
      negagram(a,b,d,4);
      for(j = 0; j < 4; j++) {
            printf("%g %g\n", c[j], d[j]);
      }
}
```

References

Note to the reader

Throughout the text, the reference [*Projects* 1994] refers to the book to which the current work stands as a sequel. The full reference to the previous work is:

Crandall R E 1994, *Projects in Scientific Computation*, TELOS/
        Springer-Verlag.

Literature references

Abramowitz M and Stegun I 1965, *Handbook of Mathematical Functions (National Bureau of Standards Series 55)*, Wash. D.C., US Dept. Commerce

Abry P and Flandrin P 1994, *IEEE Signal proc. Lett.*, 1,2,32-34

Aho A, Hopcroft J, and Ullman J 1974, *The Design and Analysis of Computer Algorithms*, Addison Wesley Publishing Company

Andrews G E 1986, *Journal of Number Theory*, 3, 23, 285-293

Appel A 1985, *SIAM J. Sci. Statist. Comput.*, 6, 85-103

Apostol T 1976, *Introduction to Analytic Number Theory*, Springer-Verlag

Atkins *et. al.* 1995, *Advances in Cryptology - ASIACRYPT '94*, Lecture notes in Comp. Sci., Springer, to appear

Bailey D H 1988, *Math. Comp.*, 50, 181, 283-296

Bailey D H 1990, *J. Supercomputing*, 4, 357-371

Bailey D, Borwein J, and Crandall R 1995a, "On the Khintchine Constant,"
        manuscript.

Bailey D, Borwein P, and Plouffe S 1995b, "On the Rapid Computation of
        Various Polylogarithmic Constants," manuscript.

Bailey D, Borwein J, and Girgensohn R 1994, *Experimental Mathematics*,
        3, 17-30

Bailey D H and Swartztrauber P N 1991, *SIAM Rev.*, 33, 389-404

Bailey D H and Swartztrauber P N 1991, *SIAM J. Sci. Comput.*, 5, 15,
        1105-1110

Balmforth M J, Ierley G R, and Spiegel G A 1994, *SIAM J. Appl. Math.*,
        54, 5, 1291-1334

Banzhaf W 1989, *Phys. Lett. A*, 136, 1, 2, 45-51

Barnes J and Hut P 1986, *Nature*, 4, 324, 446-449

Barnsley M F 1988, *Fractals Everywhere*, Academic Press, New York

Bedau M 1995, *Three Illustrations of Artificial Life's Working Hypothesis*,
        in *Evolution and Biocomputation*, Banzhaf W and Eeckman F H
        eds., Springer-Verlag Berlin

Bell T C, Cleary J G, and Witten I H 1990, *Text Compression*, Prentice Hall,
        New Jersey

Berndt B, Evans R, and Williams K 1995, "Gauss and Jacobi Sums," Wiley Interscience, to appear

Bernstein D 1993, "Multidigit Multiplication, the FFT, and Nussbaumer's Algorithm," manuscript

Bernstein D 1995, "Multidigit Modular Multiplication with the Explicit Chinese Remainder Theorem," manuscript

Berry M V 1986, J. Phys. A. Math. Gen. 19, 2281-2296

Berry M V 1988, *Nonlinearity*, I, 399-407

Bobenko A, Kutz N, and Pinkall U 1993, *Phys. Lett. A*, 177, 399-404

Bogolmony E and Leboeuf P 1994, *Nonlinearity*, 7, 1155-1167

Borwein D, Borwein J M, and Girgensohn R 1994, "Explicit Evaluation of Euler Sums," manuscript.

Borwein J M and Borwein P B 1987, *Pi and the AGM*, John Wiley & Sons, Inc.

Borwein J M, Borwein P B, and Bailey D H 1989, *The American Mathematical monthly*, 3, 96, 201-219

Borwein P B 1995, "An Efficient Algorithm for the Riemann Zeta Function," manuscript

Brent R P 1976a, *J. ACM.*, 23, 242-251

Brent R P 1976b, "Multiple Precision Zero-Finding Methods and the Complexity of Elementary Function Evaluations," in *Analytic Computational Complexity*, Anderssen R S and Brent R P eds.,

Univ. of Queensland Press, Brisbane

Broadhurst D J 1992, *Zeitschrift furPhysik*, c54, 599- 604

Broadhurst D J and Kreimer D 1995, *Knots and Numbers in ϕ^4 Theory to 7 loops and Beyond*, manuscript, AI-HENP workshop, Pisa

Buhler J P 1995, private comm.

Buhler J P, Crandall R E, and Sompolski R W 1992, *Math. Comp.* 59, 200, 717-722

Buhler J, Crandall R, Ernvall R, and Metsankyla T 1993, *Math. Comp.*, 61, 201, 151-153

Chiarella C and Reichel A 1968, *Math. Comp.*, 22, 137-143

Chowla S, Dwork B, and Evans R 1986, *J. Number Theory*, 24, 188-196

Cohen H 1993, *A Course in Computational Algebraic Number Theory*, Springer-Verlag

Cooley J W and Tukey J W 1965, *Math. Comp.* 19, 297-301

Coppersmith D and Winograd S 1987, *Proc. of the 19th Ann. ACM Symp. Theor. Comp.*, 1-6

Coster M 1988, *J. Number Theory*, 29, 300-310

Crandall R 1991, *Mathematica for the Sciences*, Addison-Wesley Publishing Company, Inc.

Crandall R 1993, *J. Phys. A. Meth. Gen.*, 26, 3627-3648

Crandall R and Buhler J 1987, *J. Phys. A: Math. Gen*, 20, 5497-5510

Crandall R and Buhler J 1990, *J. Phys. A: Math. Gen*, 23, 2523-2528

Crandall R and Buhler J 1995, *Experimental Mathematics*, 3, 4, 275-285

Crandall R and Delord J 1987, *J. Phys. A:Math. Gen.*, 20, 2279-2292

Crandall R, Dilcher K, and Pomerance C 1995a, "A Search for Wieferich and Wilson Primes," (manuscript.)

Crandall R, Doenias J, Norrie C, Young J 1995b, *Math. Comp.*, 64, 210, April, 863-868

Crandall R and Fagin B 1994, *Math. Comp.*, 62, 205, 305-324

Crilly A J, Earnshaw R A, and Jones H 1991, *Fractals and Chaos*, Springer-Verlag, New York

Cuomo K M, Oppenheim A V, and Stroganz S H 1993, *IEEE Trans. Circ. Sys.II: Analog. and Dig. Proc.*, 10, 40, 626-633

Dettman C P and Frankel N E 1993, *J. Phys. A. : Math. Gen.*, 26, 1009-1022

Dobson I and Delchamps D F 1994, *J. Nonlinear*, 4, 315-328

Dubner H and Keller W 1993, "Factors of Generalized Fermat Numbers," manuscript

Engquist B, Osher S, and Zhong S 1994, *SIAM J. Sci. Comput.*, 4, 15, 755-775

Ferguson H R P and Bailey D H 1994, "A Polynomial Time, Numerically Stable Integer Reduction Algorithm," RNR Technical Report RNR-91-032, NASA Ames Research Center, MS T045-1, Moffett

Field, CA 94035-1000

Feuerverger A, Hall P, and Wood A T A 1992, *J. Time Series Analysis*, 6, 15, 586-606

Frey D R 1993, *IEEE Trans. Circ. Sys.II: Analog. and Dig. Proc.*, 10, 40, 660-666

Frigaard C, Gade J, Hemmingsen R R, and Sand T 1994, Network Communication, ref. e-mail: cfri91@mcenroe.control.auc.dk

Gerlach J 1994, *SIAM Review*, Vol. 36, 2, 272-276, June

Gersho A and Gray R M 1992, *Vector Quantization and Signal Compression*, Kluwer Academic Publishers

Glasser M L and Zucker I J 1980, "Lattice Sums," in *Theoretical Chemistry: Advances and Perspectives*, Academic Press, Inc., vol. 5, 67, 137

Goedecker S 1994, *SIAM J. Sci. Comput.*, 15, 5, 1059-1063

Graffagnino P 1995, private comm.

Granville A 1995, "Binomial coefficients modulo prime powers," manuscript

Guillemin V and Uribe A 1989, *Commun. Math. Phys.*, 122, 563-574

Guy R K 1981, *Unsolved Problems in Number Theory*, Springer-Verlag, New York

Hardy G H and Wright E M 1979, *An Introduction to the Theory of Numbers*, 5th Ed., Clarendon Press, Oxford

Hassard B, Zhang J, Hastings S P, and Troy W C 1994, *Appl. Math. Lett.*, 7, 1, 79-83

Heggie D C 1991, "Chaos in the N-body problem of Stellar Dynamics," *Predictability, Stability and Chaos in N-body Dynamical Systems*, Ed. Roy A E, Plenum Press, New York

Henrici P 1977, *Applied and Computational Complex Analysis, Vol. 2*, John Wiley & Sons, Inc.

Higham N J 1990, *AMS Trans. Math. Soft.*, 4, 16, 352-368

Hwang W-L and Mallat S 1994, *Applied and Computational Harmonic Analysis*, I, 316-328

Jaquin A E 1993, *Proc. IEEE*, vol. 81, 10, Oct., 1451-1465

Jessop C, Duncan M, and Chau W Y 1994, *J. Comput. Physics*, 115, 339-351

Johnson C R and Thorp J S 1994, *IEEE Sig. Proc. Lett.*, 1, 12, 194-195

Jones A and Mayer R 1995, private comm.

Jones P, Ma J, and Rokhlin V 1994, *J. Comput. Physics*, 113, 35-51

Junqua J-C, Mak B, and Reaves B, *IEEE Trans. Speech Audi Process.*, 2, 3, July, 406-412

Kanada Y 1995, private comm.

Karp A H and Markstein P 1994, "High Precision Division and Square Root," Report: Hewlett-Packard Laboratories, Dec.

Keiper J 1994, private comm.

Keller W and Morain F 1994, "The Complete Factorization of Some Large Mersenne Composites," manuscript

Keller W and Neibuhr W 1994, "Supplement to New Cullen Primes," manuscript

Khintchine A 1964, *Continued Fractions*,Chicago University Press, Chicago

Knuth D E 1973, 1981, *The Art of Computer Programming*, Vol. 2, Addison-Wesley Publishing Company, Inc., Phillipines

Koc C K and Gan S C 1992, *Computers Elect. Engng.*, 2, 18, 145-152

Kung 1974, *Numer. Math.*, 22, 341-348

Kuo Y-H, Kao, C-I, and Chen J-J, *IEEE Trans. Fuzzy Sys.*, 1, 3, 171-183

Lan B L and Fox R F 1991, *Phys. Rev. A*, 43, 2, 646-655

Lang M and Frenzel B-C 1994, *IEEE Signal Processing Letters*, 1, 10, 141-143

Lelewer D A and Hirschberg D S 1987, *ACM Computing Surveys*, 3, 19, Sept.

Lenstra A K and Lenstra H W Jr 1993, *The development of the Number Field Sieve*, Lecture Notes in Math. 1554, Springer

Montgomery P L 1987, *Math. Comp.*, 48, 177, 243-264

Montgomery P L 1992, "An FFT Extension of the Elliptic Curve Method of Factorization," Ph. D. Thesis, University of California, Los Angeles

McClellan J H and Rader C M 1979, *Number Theory in Digital Signal Processing*, Prentice-Hall, Englewood Cliffs, NJ

McIntosh R 1995, private comm.

Markett C 1994, *Journal of Number Theory*, 48, 113-132

Mitchell M 1992, *Genetic Algorithms*, in *Lectures in Complex Systems*,
Eds. Nadel L and Stein D, Santa Fe Institute studies in the
Sciences of Compexity, Lect. Vol. V, Addison-Wesley

Montgomery P 1992, *An FFT Extension of the Elliptic Curve Method of
Facorization*, Ph. D. Dissertation, University of California,
Los Angeles

Montgomery P and Silverman R 1990, *Math. Comp.*, 54, 839-854

Newland D D 1993, *An Introduction to Random Vibrations, Spectral and
Wavelet Analysis*, 3rd Ed., London Technical & Scientific, Essex,
England

Niederreiter H 1992, *Random Number Generation and Quasi-Monte-Carlo
Methods*, S.I.A.M. 1992

Nussbaumer H J 1981, *Fast Fourier Transform and Convolution Algorithms*,
Springer-Verlag

Odegard J E, Gopinath R A, and Burrus C S 1994, "Design of Linear Phase
Cosine Modulated Filter Banks for Sibband Image Compression,"
manuscript, Rice University, subm. ICIP Austin, Texas

Odlyzko A M 1995a, "Analytic Computations in Number Theory,"
Proceedings of Symposia in Applied Mathematics,
to appear

Odlyzko A M 1995b, "The future of integer factorization and discrete
logarithms," manuscript

Odlyzko A M and te Riele H J J 1985, *J. reine angew. Math.*, 357, 138-160

Paneras D, Mani R, and Nawab H 1994, *IEEE Sig. proc. Lett.*, 1, 4, 61-63

Plouffe S 1995, private comm.

Pomerance C 1990, *Cryptology and Computational Number Theory*, Amer. Math. Soc.

Press W H *et. al.* 1988, *Numerical Recipes in C*, Cambridge University Press

Press W H and Teukolsky 1989, *Computers in Physics*, Jan/Feb, 91-94

Pritchard P A, Moran A, and Thyssen A 1995, *Math. Comp.*, 64, 211, 1337-1339

Rabinowitz S and Wagon S 1995, *The American mathematical Monthly*, 3, 102,195-203

Ribenboim P 1988, *The Book of Prime Number Records*, Springer-Verlag New York

Salamin E 1976, *Math. Comp.* , 30, 565-570

Schonhage A, Grotefeld A F W, and Vetter E 1994, *Fast Algorithms: A Multitape Turing Machine Implementation*, Bibliographisches Institut & F A Brockhaus AG, Mannheim

Schonhage A and Strassen V 1971, *Computing*, 7, 282-292

Shanks D and Wrench 1959, *The American Mathematical Monthly*, 4, 6, 276-279.

Shokrollahi A 1994, private comm.

Siegel C L 1949, *Transcendental Numbers*, Princeton University Press

Sieveking 1972, *Computing*, 10, 153-156

Singh J P 1993, "Parallel Hierarchical N-body Methods and Their
     Implications for Microprocessors," Thesis, Stanford University,

Smith D 1994, "A Multiple-Precision Division Algorithm," manuscript,
     Loyola Marymount University, Los Angeles, CA

Spouge J L 1994, *Siam J. Numer. Anal.*, 3, 31, 931-944

Sun Z-H and Sun Z-W 1992, *Acta Arithmetica*, 60, 371-388

Taswell C and McGill K C 1994, *ACM Trans. Math. Soft.*, 3, 20, 398-412

Titchmarsh E C 1967, *The Theory of the Riemann Zeta-Function*,
     University Press, Oxford

Trevisan V and Carvalho J B 1994, "The Compositness of the Twenty-second
     Fermat Number," manuscript

Unser M 1994, *IEEE Sig. Proc. Lett.*, 1, 4, 76-79

Van Loan C 1992, *Computational Frameworks for the Fast Fourier
     Transform*, S. I. A. M., Philadelphia

Vardi I 1991, *Computational Recreations in Mathematica*, Addison-Wesley

Veljan D 1994, *Information Processing Letters*, 49, 33-37

Voros A 1980, *Nuclear Physics*, B165, 209-236

Wang J, Yu X, Loh N K, Qin Z, and Miller W C 1994, *IEEE Signal Processing Letters*, 1, 3, 58-60

Wang Z, Jullien A, and Miller W C 1994, *IEEE Signal Processing Letters*, 1, 7, 101-102

Washington L 1982, *Introduction to Cyclotomic Fields*, Springer-Verlag, New York

Wendemuth A 1995, *J. Phys. A: Math. Gen.*, 28, 5423-5436

Wheeler N A 1995, private comm.

Wieting T. 1995, private comm.

Wolf A 1959, *A History of Science, Technology and Philosophy in the 16th and 17th Centuries*, Vol II, Harper Torchbooks USA

Wolpert D H and Macready W G 1995, "No Free Lunch Theorems for Search," manuscript, Santa Fe Institute, 12 July

Wong S S M 1992, *Computational Methods in Physics & Engineering*, Prentice-Hall, London

Wu G, Wang J, and Hootman J 1994, *Math. Comput. Modelling*, 1, 20, 13-21

Yagle A E 1994, *IEEE Sig. Proc. Lett.*, 1, 9, 134-135

Zagier D 1994, "Values of Zeta Functions and their Applications," manuscript.

Zhu X, Cheng B and Titterington D M 1994, *IEEE Proc.-Vis. Image Signal Process.*, Vol. 141, No. 5, October, 318-324

Index

TOPICS IN ADVANCED SCIENTIFIC COMPUTATION

REGISTRATION CARD

Since this field is fast-moving, we expect updates and changes to occur that might necessitate sending you the most current pertinent information by paper, electronic media, or both, regarding *Topics in Advanced Scientific Computation*. Therefore, in order to not miss out on receiving your important update information, please fill out this card and return it to us promptly. Thank you.

Name: _____

Title: _____

Company: _____

Address: _____

City: _____ State: _____ Zip: _____

Country: _____ Phone: _____

E-mail: _____

Areas of Interest / Technical Expertise: _____

Comments on this Publication: _____

_____

_____

_____

□ Please check this box to indicate that we may use your comments in our promotion and advertising for this publication.

Purchased from: _____

Date of Purchase: _____

□ Please add me to your mailing list to receive updated information on *Topics in Advanced Scientific Computation* and other TELOS publications.

□ I have a   □ IBM compatible   □ Macintosh   □ UNIX   □ other

Designate specific model _____

TELOS

THE ELECTRONIC LIBRARY OF SCIENCE

Return your postage-paid registration card today!

BUSINESS REPLY MAIL

FIRST CLASS MAIL PERMIT NO. 1314 SANTA CLARA, CA

POSTAGE WILL BE PAID BY ADDRESSEE

THE
ELECTRONIC
LIBRARY
OF
SCIENCE

**3600 PRUNERIDGE AVE STE 200
SANTA CLARA CA 95051-9835**